THE TRIUMPH OF POLITICS

The Return of the Left in Venezuela, Bolivia and Ecuador

D1504429

GEORGE PHILIP AND FRANCISCO PANIZZA

polity

First published in 2011 by Polity Press

Polity Press
65 Bridge Street
Cambridge CB2 1UR, UK

Polity Press
350 Main Street
Malden, MA 02148, USA

ISBN-13: 978-0-7456-4748-7
ISBN-13: 978-0-7456-4749-4(pb)

A catalogue record for this book is available from the British Library.

Typeset in 10.5 on 12 pt Sabon
by Toppan Best-set Premedia Limited
Printed and bound in Great Britain by MPG Books Group Limited, Bodmin, Cornwall

The publisher has used its best endeavours to ensure that the URLs for external websites referred to in this book are correct and active at the time of going to press. However, the publisher has no responsibility for the websites and can make no guarantee that a site will remain live or that the content is or will remain appropriate.

Every effort has been made to trace all copyright holders, but if any have been inadvertently overlooked the publisher will be pleased to include any necessary credits in any subsequent reprint or edition.

For further information on Polity, visit our website: www.politybooks.com

THE TRIUMPH OF POLITICS

CONTENTS

Acknowledgements   vi
List of Abbreviations   vii

**Introduction: The Triumph of Politics in Venezuela,
Bolivia and Ecuador**   1

1   **The Military and the Rise of the Left**   13
2   **The Politics of Mass Protests**   41
3   **Populism and the Return of the Political**   68
4   **Personalism, Plebiscites and Institutions**   102
5   **The Politics of Oil and Gas: Twenty-First Century
    Socialism in Practice**   123
6   **The Fault Lines of Latin American Integration**   149

Conclusion   174
Notes   185
References   194
Index   215

ACKNOWLEDGEMENTS

The authors are grateful to Guy Burton and Ursula Durand for their help in reading the complete draft of the work and for their many helpful suggestions, both editorial and substantive. Thanks are also due to John Hughes for comments on chapter 1, to Gustavo Bonifaz, Carlos de la Torre and Sven Harten for their insights on chapters 2 and 3, to Vesselin Dimitrov for his comments on chapter 4, to Dudley Ankerson for his comments on chapter 5 and to Dexter Boniface for his discussant role when an earlier version of chapter 1 was presented at the Ibero Americana in Mexico City.

LIST OF ABBREVIATIONS

AD Accion Democratica

ALBA Alianza Bolivariana para los Pueblos de Nuestra América

COB Central Obrera Boliviana

CONAIE Confederación de Nacionalidades Indígenas del Ecuador

CONDEPA Conciencia de Patria

CODENPE Consejo de Desarrollo de las Nacionales y Pueblos del Ecuador

COPEI Comité de Organización Política Electoral Independiente

CPESC Confederaciones de las Personas Etnicas de Santa Cruz

CSO civil society organization

CSUTCB Confederación Sindical Única de Trabajadores Campesinos de Bolivia

CTV Confederación de Trabajadores de Venezuela

FCO Foreign and Commonwealth Office

FEDECÁMERAS Federación Venezolana de Cameras y Asociaciones de Comercio y Producción

FETCTC Federación Especial de Trabajadores Campesinos del Trópico de Cochabamba

FTAA Free Trade Area of the Americas

IDB Inter-American Development Bank

IEA International Energy Agency

IMF International Monetary Fund

ISI Import Substituting Industrialization

MAS Movimiento al Socialismo

MERCOSUR Mercado Común del Sur

MIP Movimiento Indígena Pachakuti

MIR Movimiento de Izquierda Revolucionaria

MNR Movimiento Nacionalista Revolucionario

MRTK Movimiento Revolucionario Túpac Katari

MST Movimento dos Trabalhadores Rurais Sem Terra

NAFTA North American Free Trade Agreement

NGO Non-Governmental Organization

OAS Organization of American States

OPEC Organization of Petroleum Exporting Countries

PdVSA Petróleos de Venezuela

PETROSUR Petróleos del Sur

PODEMOS Poder Democrático y Social

PSUV Partido Socialista Unificado de Venezuela

UNASUR Unión de Naciones Suramericanas

UCS Unidad Cívica Solidaridad

WHO World Health Organization

INTRODUCTION: THE TRIUMPH OF POLITICS IN VENEZUELA, BOLIVIA AND ECUADOR

During the 1990s, there was a broad consensus across most of Latin America on the desirability of free trade, market reform, representative democracy and 'good governance' – a concept that included the strengthening of autonomous institutions in areas such as law enforcement. This can be called the 'Miami Consensus' after the heads of government meeting in that city in 1994. It was compatible with but broader than the so-called Washington Consensus, which focused mostly on specifically economic issues (Williamson 1990).

This is not to say that the entire region adopted 'Miami Consensus' principles in practice, or even in aspiration. There are some cases where this clearly did not happen. For example, Cuba's version of communism survived the collapse of the Soviet Union, and Fujimori's Peru was much closer to being a personalist autocracy than a representative democracy. There were also many examples of 'bad governance' in almost every country and a significant degree of political turbulence in many.

The claim being made here is more about internationally accepted normative ideas. The decade from 1982–91 saw some dramatic events impact on the region, the vast majority of which worked to discredit ideas of economic nationalism, authoritarianism and left-wing political radicalism – all of which were at certain periods in the past very influential in Latin America. As well as the ending of the Cold War and the collapse of Soviet communism, there were also regionally significant events. These included the debt crisis that hit Latin America in 1982 and lasted in many countries for the rest of the decade, the military defeat of the Argentine junta in the South Atlantic in the same year, the experience of hyperinflation in several countries, and the US-sponsored Brady Plan which offered some debt forgiveness in return for economic reforms. In this new context, the majority of Latin American governments pushed ahead enthusiastically with both market and governance reform and were often rewarded with re-election. This trend was widely noted. For example, the Inter-American Development Bank's (IDB) Annual Report for 1997 started with the claim that 'Over the past ten years, the countries of Latin America have come into their own as democratic societies and market economies' (Inter-American Development Bank 1997). In retrospect, this claim proved premature, but it seemed plausible to many people at the time.

Today, however, fundamental ideological debate has returned to much of the region. A key step in this transformation was the election of Hugo Chávez to the presidency of Venezuela in December 1998. Whatever his faults, Chávez has never lacked ambition or leadership skills and he soon made it clear that he saw himself as a challenger to almost the whole set of 'Miami Consensus' ideas. He is not the only such challenger, but he is one of the most determined and personally effective ones.

Chávez has now enjoyed more than a decade of power in Venezuela. His election was followed more recently by the first electoral victories of his political allies Evo Morales in Bolivia (in 2005) and Rafael Correa in Ecuador (in 2006). These three clearly represent a radical brand of left-wing politics – this book will adopt their self-identification as 'twenty-first century socialists' – that distinguishes them in significant ways from the rest of Latin America. There are however some ways in which all three – in breaking radically from the 'Miami Consensus' – have brought back some traditional Latin American ideas to do with political organization, political rhetoric and economic policy. At least some of the notions which seemed hopelessly discredited at the time of the Miami Consensus have been resuscitated by the three, alongside some genuinely new ideas and political tactics. This book departs from the argument that the political strategies, ideas and claims made by the three need to be taken seriously although not necessarily at face value. It claims that the combination of novelty and Old Left values that all three embody represents something important and distinctive in the politics of the region as a whole. Their willingness to use both electoral and extra-constitutional tactics against democratically elected governments and legislatures, their radical populist rhetoric, their use of plebiscites to strengthen the presidency, their economic nationalism and strong anti-US stance together form a distinctive political brew.

Twenty-first century socialists in regional context

Chávez, Morales and Correa are not complete outliers in every respect. Indeed, left-of-centre presidential candidates have achieved considerable electoral success in quite a number of Latin American countries during the past decade. However, we are dealing here with a particular kind of left. Where it has achieved electoral success elsewhere in the region, the left has often been far less personalist and far more institutionalist than Chávez, Morales and Correa have. This contrast is commonly drawn in the literature (Castañeda 2006; Panizza 2009; Reid 2007) and both sides generally recognize it, despite describing it in somewhat different ways. Indeed, there have been times when Chávez and Lula, the president of Brazil during 2002–10, have been seen as rivals for the intellectual leadership of South America. Even though it may be true that Lula – like Chávez, Morales and Correa – entered politics as an outsider and largely built up his own political party, there are more differences between them than similarities.

Of all the major countries in Latin America, Argentina is probably the least dissimilar in terms of governance to our three cases. Carlos Menem, president throughout the 1990s, pursued essentially a 'Miami Consensus' agenda – though his critics saw his presidency as somewhat autocratic (O'Donnell 1994). Argentina's radical free market economic policies ended in severe crisis in 2001–3, for which they were largely blamed. Argentina then moved to the left as a reaction.

In the respect that Argentina moved to the left in reaction to the perception that market economics had failed, there is an evident similarity in political trajectory with Venezuela, Bolivia and Ecuador. Other points of similarity include the fact that, at the deepest point of its economic crisis, Argentina experienced intense street protests that temporarily destabilized the entire political system. Moreover, though winning elections after the worst of the economic crisis had passed, both Néstor and Cristina Kirchner (presidents 2003–7 and since 2007 respectively) sought to centralize power in the presidency and repeatedly used (and possibly exceeded) their constitutional powers to legislate by presidential decree. There has also been a degree of political friendship between Argentina under Néstor and Cristina Kirchner and Venezuela under Chávez.

However, in the end, the focus of this book is mainly on areas in which the differences between Argentina and our three cases outweigh their similarities. Most important is the fact that neither member of the Kirchner family successfully changed the bases of Argentina's political system, either when seeking power or maintaining it. Instead, they have operated within Argentina's admittedly rather flexible institutions. Néstor Kirchner was very much an insider, though by no means a national leader, when he first became president in 2003. Although the Kirchners have sought to acquire a political base of their own since 2003, they remain Peronists and their leadership of Peronism is far from undisputed. Some observers have commented on similarities between Chávez in particular and the original Peronist movement of the 1940s (there are differences as well), but this only serves to highlight some of the differences between Chavismo and Peronismo today. The Kirchners inherited part of the Peronist legacy rather than building up a movement of their own. By way of contrast, Chávez, Morales and Correa started as political outsiders before building up their own political movements.

Given these contrasts, the view that Chávez, Morales and Correa belong in a class of their own is the one adopted here. This may not have been the case if politics in several other countries had turned out differently. There was significant potential affinity between the three and Peru's Ollanta Humala and (to a lesser degree) Mexico's Lopez Obrador who both narrowly failed to be elected to the presidency in their respective countries in 2006. Nevertheless, Chávez, Morales and Correa, and what they represent, have influenced politics outside their borders. They have certainly influenced politics in Paraguay, Honduras and Nicaragua, but the fundamental criterion dividing them from the rest of the region is that our three cases have re-founded politics in their respective countries while the others have not – at least not yet – done so.

Other common factors: High politics and socio-economic issues

What unites the various themes explored in this book is 'high politics'. In other words, we are mainly concerned with the choices made by political actors and their motivations and consequences. The book does not deal very much with the infinitely disputable issue of the inherent merits of socialism, neoliberalism or social democracy. Rather, we see Chávez, Morales and Correa primarily as (thus far) successful politicians and are interested in what made them so and what they have done with power. This discussion therefore focuses on their political tactics and strategy, political rhetoric, relationship with social movements, economic nationalism and regional economic diplomacy. This is quite a long list; inevitably, for reasons of space, there are also some things that it is impossible to cover.

It is high politics, more than anything else, which unites the experiences of Venezuela, Bolivia and Ecuador. While common economic, institutional and demographic considerations in the three countries almost certainly do have explanatory power, there are countries in the region whose similar structural features have not – at least not thus far – produced similar political outcomes. The case of Peru is particularly apposite here. Peru has a number of features in common with Ecuador and Bolivia (fewer with Venezuela) but quite a different recent history of politics and government. It would be possible to write about comparative Andean politics (see, for example, Drake and Hershberg 2006; Mainwaring, Bejarano, Leongómez 2006) but that would be a different book.

It is also important not to stretch the extent to which Venezuela, Bolivia and Ecuador themselves share common characteristics. The governing philosophies of Chávez, Morales and Correa may be very similar but the countries over which they preside are in many ways quite different. Venezuela has less ethnically in common with Ecuador and Bolivia than the latter two countries have with each other and it is economically much more dependent on resource rents from oil. Nevertheless, a brief mention of some relevant structural factors may be useful to some extent. We can then focus better on what we need high politics to explain and what we do not.

One common factor that unites the three (but also Peru) is economic decline over quite a long period of time. Between 1980 and 2000, they seem to have had untypically unsuccessful economic records in the Latin American context. Statistics provided by Sheahan (in Drake and Hershberg 2006: 102), make the point clearly. Most of Latin America did not enjoy good economic times during 1980–2000 but the vast majority of countries did achieve some per capita economic growth. This was in the order of 9% in the region as a whole (Sheahan 2006: 102). However, real per capita income in Venezuela, Bolivia and Ecuador actually fell – by a significant 6% in Bolivia, 8% in Ecuador and a dramatic 17% in the case of Venezuela.

Economic decline also occurred in Peru by 8% over the corresponding period. While the Peruvian case argues against any general claim that economic decline in Latin American democracies necessarily moves voters towards the left, it may well be the case that we can see some kind of causal mechanism in which sustained economic decline tends to weaken institutions. The Peruvian electorate – like those of Venezuela, Ecuador and Bolivia – comprehensively rejected the established political democratic parties at times of crisis. Peru elected an outsider to the presidency in 1990. Peruvian public opinion then actively supported the forcible closure of Congress in 1992 and voted for Alberto Fujimori, the president responsible for the closing of Congress, in presidential elections of 1995 and (though more ambiguously) of 2000. In Peru, though, this crisis of institutions mostly benefited the political right.

Nevertheless, at a general level, it makes sense to suppose that negative sum politics can be difficult for any democratic institutions to handle if it persists for long enough. In our three countries, it is not hard to see why some kind of politics of protest should have attracted support. In all of them, economic decline tended to interact with institutional decline. For many years, living standards failed to rise, governments became out of touch and unrepresentative and income distribution worsened. (For country studies of Venezuela, Bolivia and Ecuador, see Alberts 2008; Buxton 2005; Salman 2006.) Governments were unable to deliver serious reform even as electorates grew impatient, and changes of government did not lead to visible improvements in the lives of majorities.

Moving forward to the current millennium, Chávez and to some extent Morales and Correa later benefited as incumbents from rising commodity prices. Morales also enjoyed the benefits of sharply rising natural gas production, which was actually a result of the policies of his predecessors. Relatively favourable conditions for commodity exporters – particularly oil exporters – have had an effect on politics in our three countries, all of which are exporters of either oil or natural gas (Dunning 2008).

It does therefore seem likely that the economic conditions – decline in the 1980s and 1990s followed by a recovery after around 2000 – probably played some part in the politics of our three countries. However, once we turn to specifics, then the distinctiveness of national factors becomes evident once more. For example, oil-related issues are evidently central to politics in Venezuela, to a much greater extent than in Ecuador and Bolivia, even though the latter two are also exporters of hydrocarbons (Dunning 2008; Karl 1997). The oil-related issues that are most important in Venezuela include (but are not limited to) the political effect of the so-called resource curse and the acute disappointment of expectations following a period of economic overconfidence during the 1970s. Venezuela experienced high rates of economic growth over quite a long previous period (roughly 1925–1980) and Venezuelans during this time were repeatedly told by their leaders and others that Venezuela was a rich country because it had oil. This message was generally believed (Romero 1997) and it made the subsequent sense of disappointment especially bitter.

Conversely, the Bolivian political environment was decisively shaped by the politics of coca, the full economic importance of which is difficult to capture in official figures because of its illegality. However, whereas the problem with oil is that resource rents are paid directly to the government – with the potential risk of mismanagement and frustrated popular expectations – the coca economy is decisively shaped by its illegality. What made this issue decisive was that in the late 1990s the US government pressured successive Bolivian governments to pursue domestically unpopular policies geared towards coca eradication. As a result of US inducements on the one side and the domestic militancy of the coca growers on the other, successive Bolivian governments found themselves between a rock and a hard place. Subsequently, pressures for eradication significantly created a 'cocalero' identity in the most affected areas of Bolivia that in turn played a part in creating common political ground among otherwise disparate groups. This common ground provided a basis for internal unity and collective action on the part of radical opponents of the system (Durand 2010). In keeping with the idea of national distinctiveness, there is also a direct historical link between the radical militancy of Bolivia's tin miners and the current militancy of the cocaleros. Even here, though, we need to be careful about assuming that similar material conditions will produce similar patterns of politics. Indeed, the politics of coca production in Bolivia has so far played out quite differently from coca related issues in Peru (Durand 2008). On this issue, too, we have to deal mainly with separate national stories.

Another important international issue, more relevant to Ecuador and Bolivia than to Venezuela, has been the growing political involvement of indigenous people and their role in radical social movements. This is certainly an important aspect of democratization on which there is much more to be said (Van Cott 2003, 2005, 2008; Yashar 2006). However, the basic demographics of South America put Bolivia and Ecuador alongside Peru in a category quite different to the rest of the region. Van Cott (in Diamond 2008: 34) quotes an estimate that indigenous people make up 71% of the population of Bolivia, 47% of Peru and 43% of Ecuador. No other South American country is more than 8% indigenous. Here as well, then, we have a potential category that includes Peru but not Venezuela.

Indigenous politics also has to be seen in context. In both Ecuador and Bolivia, class inequalities were for many years reinforced by a system of social stratification based on ethnicity and a variable but keenly felt degree of racial discrimination. Even when dictatorship gave way to democracy in Bolivia and Ecuador, the electoral politics that resulted coexisted with informal systems of social exclusion and state bias which indigenous groups resented and, increasingly, found the means to combat.

Notwithstanding the different demographics in Venezuela, it has been claimed that ethnic issues played a significant part in the politics of Chavismo (Herrera Salas 2007). This is a bold claim, which is hard to evaluate fully on the basis of available evidence. It is certainly true that racial thinking exists to some extent in Venezuela (as in other parts of the world) and Chávez's physical appearance surely plays some part in the way he is viewed across all levels of Venezuelan society. However, the kind of ethnic self-identification that has featured prominently in the construction of social movements in Bolivia and Ecuador clearly does not operate in Venezuela.

Taking these various factors together, there seems to be no completely convincing way of relating the emergence of 'twenty-first century socialism' to any set of factors that fit Venezuela, Bolivia and Ecuador and nowhere else. Yet the purpose of this work is to look at key issues in which Chávez, Morales and Correa have adopted ideas and strategies – and achieved successful outcomes – that are similar to each other and different from the rest of the region. While structural factors will be brought into the discussion where appropriate, the best way of approaching the key question informing this work is to focus on high politics issues which essentially relate to the acquisition of political power and the uses to which it has been and can be put.

This 'high politics' focus is however designed to do more than fill the gaps left by weaknesses in other kinds of explanation. The book makes the much stronger claim that the tactical, rhetorical, organizational and institutional aspects of politics not only matter to the general study of politics but are of particular significance in our three cases. It is also claimed that policy successes (to the extent to which these have been achieved) have so far been less important to the continued political strength of our three presidents than policy failure was to the weakening of their predecessors.

The logic of the book

The book starts from the premise that, despite the significant amount of literature that already exists, there is more that can be learned about the viewpoints and strategies adopted by Chávez, Morales and Correa. However, the claims made by the three should not be regarded uncritically. There are both economic and political perils involved in what they have been trying to do, and, despite a clear measure of good fortune, there are aspects of vulnerability and failure in their policy performances. Nevertheless, we cannot discount the fact that these three have come to enjoy significant political triumphs based on sustained majoritarian support. This support is evidently real, and it has made a more autonomous pattern of political leadership more feasible than it otherwise might have been. The reality of this support should not obscure the element of state bias and manipulation that is there as well. The fundamental question for the future of majoritarian democracy in these cases is how far autonomous public opinion can maintain some kind of control over the ambitions of powerful and charismatic political leaders and the scarcely less powerful force of political contestation.

The book is organized around three themes, each of which takes up two chapters. It starts by seeking to explain key factors behind the rise of Chávez, Morales and Correa. How did they achieve national power and why was their mixture of constitutional and extra-constitutional tactics as successful as it turned out to be? In an earlier generation, left-of-centre governments in South America – except for the most anodyne and moderate kinds – were once routinely overthrown or vetoed by the military, and this came close to happening again when Chávez was nearly overthrown by a coup in 2002.

Electoral victory and the absence of a military veto are necessary parts of the explanation for this outcome but not sufficient ones. Confrontational political tactics played a role as well. If Chávez had not launched a failed coup attempt in 1992, he would almost certainly not have been elected president in 1998. If Morales had not (with his allies) used radical tactics of civil disobedience to polarize the political situation and isolate an unpopular but constitutionally elected president, he would probably not have reached the presidency either.

The second chapter looks at similar issues but this time from the perspective of the protest movements. These have proved powerful engines of popular mobilization and encouraged political participation among previously excluded groups, but they have also enabled the emergence of populist leaders with little respect for institutional principles or procedures. The chapter considers whether the mobilizing potential of protest politics is ultimately supportive of democratic values or whether it may lead to the further weakening of already weak pluralist democratic institutions that the cause of democracy would have been better served by strengthening. Given the ambiguities of public opinion, conflicting normative principles are involved in these new kinds of politics and the resulting issues are finely balanced.

The middle section of the book looks at some of the means by which Chávez, Morales and Correa have maintained themselves in power. The discussion adopts the idea of radical populism, both in its ideological aspects and in its organizational ones. The chapter claims that, when appropriately defined, this notion of radical populism does enable us to locate some significant aspects of politics in all three cases. However, we need to bear in mind certain caveats. The populist label needs to be applied carefully. It is not an all-embracing explanation or characterization of everything. It is important to emphasize as well that the radical populist label is not intended to be either belittling or dismissive.

Populism, following Laclau (2006) is defined here as a political strategy based on the discourse of popular unity and the stigmatization of unpopular elites. Populism may correlate with other things, such as economic policies, but these are not part of any definition as such. It should be emphasized too that this is not a work about 'economic populism' which is something altogether different. Readers looking to this book for systematic discussion of the economic performance of these governments will be disappointed. Any relationship between populism as understood here and policy is an empirical matter, even perhaps a contingent one. Notoriously, some populist leaders are serious about social reform whereas others are mandate-breakers exhibiting various degrees of cynicism (Stokes 2001).

Following on from a discussion of populism, the book then looks at the institutional means by which the three leaders consolidated their power. This was essentially through the use of constitutional reform via plebiscite. The ultimate objective was to strengthen the presidency and enhance the centralization of effective power (notwithstanding some aspects of greater political devolution). The political contribution of this institutional engineering was to convert potentially transient popularity into a potentially lasting source of power. The chosen formula – calling for a plebiscite for a Constituent

10

Assembly, drawing up a new constitution that strengthened central power, holding a plebiscite to approve the new constitution, and closing the whole issue by means of fresh elections – was largely developed by Chávez. Morales and Correa, both elected several years later, largely followed the pattern. One of the ironies of the process is that plebiscitary tactics were prior to Chávez much more common on the political right than the left.

However, these plebiscitary tactics, though effective, were only possible because the three leaders were popular enough to win plebiscites. Not every president in the region was in so happy a position. It is therefore insufficient to attribute the popularity of these leaders to their radical populism or to their political tactics. This popularity is an empirical fact and not a definitional property of populism itself or a matter of plebiscitary sleight of hand. It is instead something that has to be explained. There is a very old joke about an apocryphal 'people's popular party' whose leaders constantly risk being pelted with tomatoes by a hostile public. It is true to say that populists seek popularity but so, in a democratic context, do non-populists. They simply do so by different rhetorical means.

The final part of the book moves the discussion to broader economic and international policy issues. One chapter has to do with the politics of oil and gas. What this chapter seeks to do is to discuss the policy consequences within a key economic area of some of the political themes discussed in the book as a whole. These include a radical populist tendency to look for 'others' to denounce – nothing offers a better target for this than a foreign owned oil or gas company although (as Chávez showed) a technocratically run state oil company can come a close second. Oil and gas policy in both Venezuela and Bolivia also reflects the presidentialization of economic policy making, not so much as any particular ultimate objective as in a political need to be seen to be in control. This chapter looks at key decisions made mainly in Venezuela and also in Bolivia. However, when looking at policy consequences, Venezuelan oil and gas policy matters more and it has taken on a clearer shape than in Bolivia and, still more, Ecuador. Not only has Chávez been in power for much longer, but the Venezuelan oil industry is globally significant (unlike those of Ecuador and Bolivia) and Venezuela is also much more dependent on oil and gas than the other two.

The final chapter deals with a key aspect of regional diplomacy, and at the role played by Chávez in particular in blocking the US-led Free Trade of the Americas initiative, which played such a key role in the Miami Consensus of the 1990s. It also considers the changing

11

balance of diplomatic power within South America in a more general way. Both chapters consider mainly a style of policy making which is confrontational and drama-seeking rather than considered and bureaucratic, and therefore fully in keeping with Chávez's domestic political style. In some respects, particularly Venezuela's inability to avoid a decline in its oil production, this has proved costly. However, Chávez's ability to internationalize effectively – notably his role in the reinvigoration of OPEC and Venezuela's much higher diplomatic profile within Latin America – has to some extent to be set against policy failures at home, though the resulting balance looks fragile.

Looking ahead, there must be real uncertainties about the future trajectory of politics in all three cases. All three countries remain democracies of a kind but, since the fundamental basis on which these presidents rest is their domestic popularity, they may find themselves very exposed if things start to go wrong. In such an eventuality, they would almost certainly become either more openly authoritarian or weaker or both. Indeed, even as it is, it is not clear that politics in any of the three countries can now be re-institutionalized in an unambiguously democratic setting without some further process of political upheaval. This is something discussed again in the conclusions.

— 1 —

THE MILITARY AND THE RISE
OF THE LEFT

Chávez, Morales and Correa all reached the presidency through democratic election but did so in far from normal circumstances. Chávez first came to prominence as a coup leader when, as a lieutenant colonel, he led a dramatic but unsuccessful attempt to seize power in February 1992. Although unsuccessful, the coup provided a major shock to the system and played a part in inducing the Venezuelan Congress to impeach the incumbent president Pérez in 1993. There was a further coup attempt – not led by Chávez – in November 1992 and yet another potential coup attempt in 1993. There followed a further period of institutional decline, this time affecting Venezuela's once-strong party system, before Chávez won the presidential election in December 1998. Chávez himself was then at the receiving end of a coup attempt in 2002 that he only narrowly survived. In Venezuela, therefore, the key crisis events concerned coup attempts, even though none of them actually succeeded.

Morales was and is a civilian. His background is indigenous and he was a coca producer. In 1998, he formed and led a political party, the Movimiento al Socialismo, which opposed the market oriented policies of Bolivia's elected governments. Morales became one of the main leaders, and the main political beneficiary, of a highly effective campaign of civil disobedience which started to take on momentum in 2000 and led to the downfall of constitutional governments in 2003 and 2005. Morales emerged from this process as a credible presidential candidate and was elected in December 2005. By winning with an outright majority, Morales broke a long historical sequence in which presidents were chosen by Congress after winning only a plurality of the popular vote. Morales has continued to serve as democratically elected president, despite some periods of high

13

political tension, including in August 2008 when the military ignored calls made by some of the right-wing opposition for a coup. In Bolivia, then, we are dealing mainly with military non-support of the civil power at decisive moments. The military in 2003 and 2005 ultimately stood back and let civil disobedience take its course, though in 2008 it did support an embattled constitutional government when some right-wing politicians were calling for a coup. It is also interesting that General Hugo Banzer, who governed Bolivia as a right-wing dictator between 1971 and 1978, later converted himself into a conservative but democratic politician and won national elections in 1997. It was under the former general that Bolivia's civil disobedience campaign first took off to a significant degree.

Correa is a civilian and a technocrat with a doctorate in economics from the University of Illinois. His first major political experience was in alliance with the anti-Gutiérrez movement that led to the removal of an unpopular president in 2005. Correa served briefly as economics minister in the subsequent caretaker government and used this position to raise his profile somewhat as a presidential candidate in 2006. Even so, he received no more than 22.8% of the vote on the first round (Conaghan 2008) but he was able to mobilize a range of anti-status quo forces to win the second round run-off against the better-known favourite. Correa can best be seen as the main beneficiary of a series of crisis events that involved him only tangentially. These crisis events did however involve the military and included a semi-failed coup attempt in 2000.

All three, then, rose to power from different backgrounds. The events that led to their rise were nationally specific. However, the three political careers do have quite a number of things in common. All were elected in the context of very turbulent political situations – indeed after prolonged political crisis. All three were either rebels or (in the case of Correa) largely unknown figures before they came to power. They are all self-proclaimed socialists, and they radicalized rather than moderated when in power. This was a combination whose emergence was not seriously anticipated by the Miami Consensus of the 1990s.

This chapter looks mainly at the role of the military in shaping these events. A pessimistic set of observers might have expected that the kinds of crisis that led to the rise of Chávez, Morales and Correa would instead lead to full scale democratic breakdown – or indeed that it might yet do so. Yet Venezuela, Bolivia and Ecuador have so far all consistently met the minimum Schumpeterian criterion for democracy, namely competitive and honestly counted elections

(Schumpeter 1950). Even so, the military, and popular attitudes towards the military, also played a significant role in determining political outcomes.

Crises and democratic near-breakdown: A comparative perspective

Before discussing our three cases in detail, it will be helpful to look first at how they fit the broader regional context. In fact, they are not really typical. Most Latin American countries have not seen significant military involvement in politics since the development of 'third wave' democracy. The purpose of this chapter is only tangentially concerned with why this should be so. We are concerned more with what happened when the military did intervene, whether directly or indirectly.

It would, though, not be true either to say that our three cases are complete outliers. Within the region as a whole, there is a significant number of countries – essentially Peru, Paraguay, Honduras, and for a time Argentina, together with Venezuela, Bolivia and Ecuador – in which the military has become involved directly in 'third wave' democratic politics. All of these need at least a brief discussion. The cases of Paraguay, Honduras and Argentina are mentioned below while Peru – which is a more apposite comparator for our three countries in many ways – is discussed in some detail later in the chapter.

For several years, essentially between 1996 and 2003, Paraguay went through a period in which elections, civil disobedience and coup attempts continued and interacted. There were elections in 1998 (and then 2003), coup attempts in 1996 and 2000, and the impeachment and criminal prosecution of a president in 1999, following some kind of civil uprising. These events clearly show some kind of (in this case highly conflictive) interactive process at work between personalist military officers, coup attempts and the holding of elections. There were coup attempts but no actual return to dictatorship.

In Honduras in 2009, the military physically overthrew incumbent president Zelaya at the request of the Supreme Court backed by the National Congress. What led this overthrow to be described (by opponents of the process) as a coup was the fact that the military arrested and then exiled Zelaya, while Congress installed a new interim president. The use of the word 'coup' therefore relates to the violation of constitutional legalities, including Zelaya's right to defend himself in court, and not to any suggestion that the military was the prime mover in Zelaya's overthrow. (As we shall see in chapter 4, there have been a considerable number of examples in Latin America of presidential removal by a hostile congressional majority, sometimes via questionable constitutional means.) The Honduran case fits a broader argument about the military, namely that it may feel a need to intervene when it cannot avoid involvement in constitutional crises but that it then shows a marked reluctance to try to rule as a dictatorship. In Honduras, the overthrow of Zelaya did not prevent pre-planned national elections going ahead on schedule later in 2009. Again, we see a pattern in which military intervention and the electoral process somehow interacted.

In Argentina, the military was restive in the late 1980s (Norden 1996) but has become much more docile since. Some medium-rank army officers, radicalized by their experience of military defeat in the South Atlantic in 1982, rebelled against elected president Alfonsín on several occasions during 1987–9, by which time economic problems were making the Alfonsín government increasingly unpopular. Here, too, military-political activity did not suppress the electoral process but did influence it, in Argentina's case helping to bring about the ending of Alfonsín's presidential term a few months before the constitutional term limit in 1989. The military was effectively pacified after Carlos Menem, who was throughout his term a relatively popular president, suppressed a military rebellion in 1990. It has since stayed out of politics, notably remaining on the sidelines during Argentina's very deep political and economic crisis of 2001–3 (Levitsky 2003). In the Argentine case, military rebels were prepared to put pressure on an unpopular president, but popular presidents were able to control the military. In 2001, the military stayed out of politics and allowed the semi-constitutional removal of an unpopular president by a much more popular Peronist party.

We see some kind of pattern here which will be elaborated further when we look at a further set of comparisons later in the chapter. However, we need first to try to make sense of what we have seen so far, and look at the way that the nature of military intervention in politics has changed since the onset of 'third wave' democratization.

Changed patterns of military-political behaviour

Studies of military-political behaviour that were conducted before the arrival of 'third wave' democratization mostly concluded that there

16

were multiple paths via which military officers could be drawn into politics (Fitch 1978; Lowenthal 1976; Needler 1964; Nun 1976; Philip 1985; Stepan 1971; Villanueva 1972). Some of these were quite opportunistic. There certainly were politically ambitious officers who welcomed the chance to play an interventionist role, and these included both left- and right-wingers. A lot of the time, in fact, active politics within the military involved competition between highly politicized military minorities. However, less politically minded officers sometimes supported intervention if they saw this as necessary to protect military institutionality (i.e., internal military order and discipline rather than political institutionality) if they saw this as coming under threat. Because the military is inevitably based on notions of hierarchy and obedience, there was also a link in the minds of many officers between intensive social mobilization, 'subversion' and military insubordination. Fear of this combination of factors could certainly trigger a coup and what might be called hierarchism explains a lot of right-wing bias in military-political behaviour.

Civilians, too, sometimes invited participation by the military. Intervention could be triggered either by direct invitation (famously called 'knocking on the doors of the barracks' (Imaz 1964), or via acts of civil unrest designed to pressure the military to define its position. Anti-government demonstrators in Chile in 1973 notoriously banged empty saucepans. Moreover, once some officers came to believe that others were preparing to intervene in the political process, the logic of pre-emption came into play. For these reasons, while most military interventions in Latin America between 1948 and 1982 were right of centre and authoritarian, there was inevitably a degree of unpredictability in any specific case and some outcomes were surprising.

Today, it seems that top army officers generally avoid trying to impose dictatorship even if they find it necessary to arbitrate institutional conflicts at times of crisis. This reluctance to try to take power outright seems to be less in evidence in the case of middle-ranking officers and officers from the navy and air force. In these latter cases, a coup attempt may be as much a rebellion against the military establishment as against the elected government. It is noteworthy that, of the five coup attempts in our three countries, two were led by middle-ranking officers (Chávez and Gutiérrez) and one was led by a naval officer with air force support (Gruber, in Venezuela, in November 1992). Of the others, the coup attempt in Venezuela in 2002 was the result of a deliberate attempt by the right-wing civilian opposition to provoke a crisis so as to create the conditions that might appear to justify military intervention. Not much is known about the potential coup leadership in Venezuela 1993 but in the event no coup took place.

Coup attempts led either by middle-ranking army officers or by senior officers from the navy or air force, though potentially more radical (because less hierarchical), are less likely to succeed militarily than those led by the army high command because they are more likely to encounter opposition from within the military itself. The military superiors of middle-ranking golpista officers will have institutional and personal motives for remaining loyal to the government. If they are overthrown by their juniors, their military careers are likely to end. Very senior officers have a better chance of purely military success when attempting coups because they should be able to command obedience even in the absence of enthusiastic support. However, under conditions of 'third wave' democracy, very senior officers have seemed happier to avoid overt dictatorship, even in cases where they have effectively usurped power – as in Honduras in 2009 and (as we shall see) Peru in 1992.

It should be noted that the discussion so far relates to the military as an organization. Ex-military officers in civilian clothes can sometimes achieve electoral success as individuals. Both Chávez and Gutiérrez were elected to the presidency after having been jailed for leading failed coup attempts. Although they did not meet with as much electoral success as Chávez did, a number of other Venezuelan officers involved in both of the 1992 coup attempts made some kind of transition to electoral politics thereafter (Norden 2003). Outside Venezuela, it may still be relatively unusual in Latin America for former military officers to become credible civilian candidates in elections but it is by no means unheard of. Bolivia's Hugo Banzer was elected to the presidency in 1997, Ollanta Humala narrowly failed to be elected in Peru in 2006 and even Pinochet retained a significant vote in the Chilean plebiscite in 1988. Prior to the 'third wave' of democratization, it was still more common for former military officers to convert themselves into successful politicians than it is today. Examples include Argentina's Perón, Chile's Ibáñez and Peru's Odría. Similarly, Brazil's Vargas, though a civilian, presided over an authoritarian regime for fifteen years before being overthrown in 1945 and coming back to win the presidential election in 1950.

Explaining military intervention without dictatorship

When trying to explain why the top military leadership is generally reluctant to impose dictatorship, region-wide factors are probably

18

key. It certainly makes more sense to refer to the changed international climate in general rather than just to the role of the US government. The US government vacillated in its response to the Venezuelan coup attempt of 2002, as indeed it has vacillated in its response to other coup attempts in the region (such as Ecuador in 2000). The international community reacted negatively to the Peruvian *auto-golpe* in 1992 but gradually allowed itself to be won over when Fujimori 're-constitutionalized' his regime (Costa 1993). However, while the US has sometimes indicated that it would accept conveniently patched-up deals that violated the national constitution, it could not support the open abandonment of democracy as such. Perhaps as important as the government in Washington, and certainly more consistent, has been the role of various regional and international organizations in discouraging outright military dictatorships (Santa Cruz 2005).

One new concern is that the military and – still more so – pro-government civilians are today much more likely to be subject to reprisals if they threaten or try to use excessive force. Prior to the 1980s, judicial measures against coup leaders or despots were virtually unknown in South America, except to the extent that junior officers and NCOs could face harsh discipline from their seniors for military insubordination. The development of legal accountability for military or political figures directly involved in repression started in Argentina after 1983, proceeded slowly and uncertainly for a time but developed increased momentum during the 1990s (McAdams 1997). The arrest of Pinochet in London in 1998 was an important further step in the development of this process. Today, the military and their civilian allies face real risks of international criminal proceedings, and this can be a real deterrent. The effect of such a change can be to create dilemmas since there are legal risks involved both in overthrowing a government and in using excessive force to support one.

To sum up the argument so far, there seem to be three binding constraints on military political behaviour in Latin America. One is the outright overthrow of democracy and imposition of dictatorship. Since the early 1980s, this has not happened anywhere in the region. The second is that the military will dislike getting on the 'wrong side' of public opinion. The third, connected to the second, is that the military dislikes having to use massive force to defend an incumbent government. These constraints do not rule out all forms of military-political activity. They do help us understand what the military is likely to do when it does intervene. Forms of military-political activity that do not violate these constraints, including the transformation of military officers into civilian politicians, remain feasible and can influence the political process.

A Peruvian comparison

We can learn more about this and a semi-military kind or semi-electoral kind of politics by looking at Peru, which in the 1990s was the only major country in Latin America in which there was a full-scale military coup. In fact, Peru between 1992 and 2000 is the nearest that any Latin American country has come to a genuine democratic breakdown under 'third wave' conditions.

The Peruvian crisis went through a series of stages. Coming into politics as a complete unknown at a time of hyperinflation and serious insurgency, Alberto Fujimori won presidential elections in 1990 when Peru's party system – which was never very strong – effectively collapsed. However, Fujimori was elected without a congressional majority and his relations with Congress soon deteriorated (Cotler 1995). Facing an unpromising economic and security situation and fearing possible impeachment, Fujimori with the help of his security chief Montesinos organized a military *autogolpe* in 1992 that kept him in the presidency while the military closed the National Congress (Kenney 2004). The military had been restive for some time previously and there had been some plotting even before the election of Fujimori (Rospigliosi 2000). In 1992, a decisive weight of senior military officers was persuaded to participate in a kind of political marriage of convenience in which Fujimori's popularity and standing as legally elected president was combined with the military's command of force. There was some military opposition to the *autogolpe* but this did not prove effective.

The *autogolpe* turned out to be popular in the short run (Carrion 1996). Some significant policy successes subsequently helped Fujimori maintain his popularity. As a result, he was able to re-legitimate himself to some extent as a democrat – organizing a series of national votes in which a new Constituent Assembly was elected and a new constitution then approved by plebiscite. Fujimori then won presidential re-election in 1995. This continued process of post-coup voting eventually brought around most of the international community, whose first response to the *autogolpe* had been hostile, to a reluctant acquiescence (Costa 1993).

After being re-elected in 1995, Fujimori used his legislative majority to change the constitution in order to allow him to stand for
another term of office in 2000. When the Supreme Court ruled this
new measure unconstitutional, the legislature impeached and replaced
the judges who had held out against it. Fujimori ran for election again
in 2000 but by this time his popularity was on the decline. Rather
than give way gracefully, Fujimori used all the forces of the state,
including the military, in support of his candidacy and was declared
the winner in the second round of presidential elections after his main
opponent withdrew at the end of the first round, alleging fraud.
(First-round voting put Fujimori's vote at just below 50 per cent, so
making the second round essentially a formality.) What seems to have
happened was not so much fraud per se, though international observers did note some actual irregularities (Santa Cruz 2005), but a
broader issue of 'state bias' in which the incumbent used superior
access to state funding, selective intimidation and non-impartial law
enforcement to overpower the opposition. As we shall see below, this
is not an unfamiliar story.

Even with the advantage of incumbency, Fujimori's party did not
win congressional elections and, when one of his aides was 'caught
on camera' bribing a legislator to change sides and support the government, the ensuing scandal essentially finished his government.
After a series of almost farcical events that highlighted growing opposition to a further term of office for Fujimori, he sent in a fax containing his resignation when out of the country on a state visit to
Asia. Congress did not accept this resignation and impeached him
instead. Either way, Fujimori's government was at an end.

The reasons for the fall of Fujimori are ambiguous and different
scholars interpret them differently. Some authors (for example,
Tanaka in Hagopian and Mainwaring 2005) have claimed that
Fujimori's government had sufficient access to coercion to have over-
powered the opposition and that it essentially collapsed from within.
According to Tanaka, the decisive political event was the breach
between Fujimori and Montesinos, by then Peru's intelligence chief,
which made it possible for military dissent to find expression.
Conaghan (2005) suggests that a contingent event – the filming of an
act of corruption – provided a decisive tipping point that united the
opposition, divided the government and shifted the political agenda.
It was a close-run thing but, in the end, the military proved willing
to support a form of popular semi-authoritarianism but unwilling to
follow it to the ultimate point of supporting an outright dictatorship.

By one means or another, the Fujimori government had overreached itself and lost decisive support.

Crises and the rise of the left in Venezuela, Ecuador and Bolivia

We now turn to a more detailed study of the political role of the military in our three countries. The cases to be considered include four actual or potential coup attempts in Venezuela (February 1992, November 1992, 1993 and 2002), plus one in Ecuador (in 2000). There was an earlier event in Caracas in 1989 in which the military was called in to put down rioting, and the Bolivian military also came to the aid of the elected civil power in a potential crisis situation in 1985. There were two cases in which the military essentially arbitrated civilian conflicts (Ecuador 1998 and 2005). Finally, there were three cases in which the military eventually withdrew support from an elected but embattled government, thereby allowing its downfall (Ecuador 1997, Bolivia 2003 and 2005).

Venezuela in 1989

Venezuela, particularly in Caracas, experienced severe urban riots in February 1989. These took place a few months after Pérez was convincingly re-elected to the presidency (his first period in office was 1974–9). Pérez had clearly over-promised in his successful presidential campaign and what triggered the riots was his imposition of austerity measures, including increases in petrol prices and bus fares, in the first few weeks of the new presidency. These were insensitively imposed but both Pérez and most observers were surprised by the rapidity of the change in popular mood and by the extent of public anger.

Initially, the government's response to the rioting was confused and uncertain (Ellner 2008). The military was eventually called in to suppress the riots, and did so, using considerable force in the process. Public opinion was broadly supportive of the military's actions (Trinkunas 2005) but very much less supportive of the civilian government and party system, which were blamed for both the repression and the economic austerity measures that triggered the riots in the first place. Some efforts were later made to examine the military's subsequent use of force from the viewpoint of human rights violations, but these did not immediately prosper. Notwithstanding, in July 2009 Italo del Valle, a civilian who was Pérez's defence minister in 1989, was charged with human rights violations by a Venezuelan court in connection with the suppression of the riots.

One factor that played an important part in influencing the military's reluctant decision to support the civilian authorities in 1989 was the weakness of the anti-system political leadership at that time, and the uncontrolled nature of the rioting itself. While the repression of the rioting did much to create an atmosphere in which anti-system politics grew in importance, anti-government forces were not in 1989 sufficiently well organized to form a viable alternative to the existing order. What happened was a riot and not a politically led act of revolt.

In the medium term, though, the Pérez government paid a high political price for the violence of 1989. While this was not the whole reason for the 1992 coup attempts, it was a contributing factor. The experience changed some attitudes within the military. A sense that Perez had abused the role of the military by involving it in suppressing internal disorders certainly persuaded some officers, who might not otherwise have done so, to support the 1992 coup.

Subsequent military unrest was not actually caused by the suppression of the 1989 riots. Chávez and his allies were already plotting. One consequence, though, was that the popularity of the government collapsed after the riots and did not revive. There were also broader issues of democratic legitimation. After February 1989, it became much harder for Pérez to make a credible claim that his policies represented the democratic will (Burggraaff and Millet 1995) and the argument against using force to overthrow a legitimately elected government became less compelling as a result.

Subsequently, President Caldera (1994–9) believed that he could not necessarily rely on the military if he ever had to face a further outbreak of social disorder (private information). This mattered in policy terms. When Caldera had to cope with a collapse in the Venezuelan banking system in 1994, he sought to manoeuvre within political as well as economic constraints. One of his advisers (in private conversation) referred to the administration's fear of what he called an 'Albanian situation', alluding to an incident in the latter country in which a bank collapse triggered a collapse in the process of government itself.

Venezuela in February 1992

In February 1992, Hugo Chávez attempted a coup against the Pérez government. We do not know exactly how many officers took part

23

in the attempt, but numbers certainly amounted to hundreds. Coup leadership came from the middle ranks of the army and it also attracted support from junior officers. There were also some civilian politicians who were aware of the coup and who had promised to support it. According to Buxton (2001: 162), Pablo Medina, a leader of the Causa R, met Chávez in January 1992 to discuss who might be in a post-coup cabinet. Some of the potential supporters of the coup failed to show themselves in the event, though they might well have come forward to offer support later had the military aspect of the coup succeeded. The coup narrowly failed in military terms. Chávez surrendered and was jailed.

Chávez was from his youth an ideological opponent of the whole Venezuelan party system, which had been designed to stabilize the democratic system by coalitional politics excluding the Marxist left and the authoritarian right. Chávez was influenced by the Peruvian military government of General Velasco (1968–75) which involved a (more or less happy) combination of left-wing military leaders, less politically motivated army officers, and small left-wing civilian parties, including the Peruvian Communist Party. Some other Venezuelan officers were also interested in trying to replicate this kind of alliance and some initial contacts were made in the early 1980s between a group of young officers who would eventually emerge as coup leaders (Blanco Muñoz 1998; Garrido 2000; Gott 2000; Zago 1998).

It is important to note that Chávez did not particularly represent the Venezuelan military in any broad sense, at least at the beginning of his military-political career. There is no reason to suppose that more than a small minority of Venezuelan officers were left-wing ideologues in the 1980s. A series of additional factors were needed to turn the activities of a relatively small number of radicals into a popular majoritarian government fifteen years later. These included purely professional discontents with a clientelistically controlled military in a context of national economic decline and budgetary shortages. After 1989, they also included the extreme unpopularity of the Pérez government and its political insensitivity. Perhaps more than anything there was the general out-of-touchness of Venezuela's democratic but corrupt political establishment. What more than anything else transformed Chavismo into a political movement was the popularity of the Chávez coup attempt itself.

Contemporary observers, including the British Embassy (according to papers revealed under the Freedom of Information Act), are largely united in their view that the coup attempt was popular, and the sub-

24

sequent electoral success of politicians associated with the coup attempt rather vindicates this initial judgement. During 1992, some polls were picking up in the region of 25 per cent support for military rule in principle (quoted in Philip 1992). This was not by any means a majority, but it was a lot better than the single-digit support for incumbent Pérez and has to be interpreted against the fact that open advocacy of a coup was illegal. A poll in 1993 put retrospective support for the February 1992 coup attempt as high as 59 per cent (Myers and O'Connor 1998). Given the choice between supporting a flawed but undoubtedly institutional democratic system and a personalist military challenge to it, many Venezuelans preferred the latter. Of those who were actual or potential supporters of a coup, many people had the self-image of democrats, merely expressing distaste for the corrupted status quo (Myers and O'Connor 1998).

Though a military failure, therefore, the coup was a considerable political success. It won national attention, and Chávez became a household name in its aftermath. Pérez, despite surviving the coup, soon found his position untenable. Although it was not foreseeable in 1992 that Chávez would be elected to the presidency less than seven years after the coup attempt, it was clear immediately that something decisive had happened to Venezuelan politics.

A key factor in Chávez's successful relaunch as a politician was the willingness of Rafael Caldera – an ex-president of Venezuela, a respected elder statesman and an independent candidate for the presidency in 1993 – publicly to support the aims, though not the methods, of the coup leaders. Caldera's speech in moral support of the coup leaders caused a sensation and allowed him to rise to first place in the opinion polls ahead of the 1993 presidential elections – elections that he subsequently won. While Caldera's election promise to amnesty the coup leaders harks back in some ways to an earlier period of military immunity, it was also made in the expectation that it would help Caldera electorally – as indeed it did. The election of Caldera in 1993 was a direct result of the Chávez coup attempt and Caldera's amnesty enabled Chávez to avoid the full criminal penalty for military rebellion and, later, to emerge as a credible candidate for the presidency.

The outcome of the February 1992 coup attempt – a military failure but a political success – had much to do with contingent factors. Military intelligence under Pérez had performed badly, partly because some of its members were at that time caught up in a corruption scandal. Nevertheless, if Pérez had listened more to the intelligence that he actually received, the coup attempt might have failed quickly and ignominiously (Trinkunas 2005). If Chávez had not been allowed to broadcast to the nation as a condition of his surrender, he would not have been able to make the dramatic statement that – in effect – launched his presidential candidacy for 1998 (Gott 2000). By the same token, the military failure of the coup attempt – which had much to do with an absence of support from the most senior officers – meant that Chávez did not have to form a government, or try to do so. While we will never know for certain, it seems highly probable that a Chávez-led military government in 1992 would have failed and discredited its own cause – much as would happen with Carmona in 2002.

Venezuela in 1992 and 1993

It is worth briefly mentioning a second coup attempt, which took place in November, and a third that was in the process of being planned in the following year. These coup attempts were much less significant in the long run than the February attempt, but they show up the broadly based loss of credibility of the constitutional order in Venezuela. Already, on 23 September 1992, the British Embassy in Caracas reported to the FCO that 'rumours of another coup attempt have become almost daily affairs' (FCO). On 27 November 1992, there was indeed another coup attempt, this time a more conservatively led one based more on military grievances and less on any political philosophy. Although this failed, military unrest continued. The British Embassy on 2 December 1992 reported on 'suggestions, which have come principally from the US, that a third military coup is now imminent'.

There were fresh coup rumours in Venezuela in 1993, believed among others by the interim president, Ramón J. Velásquez, who confided his fears to the British ambassador (private information). There is in fact some evidence that the Banco Latino (which eventually failed in 1994) was involved in trying to finance a military coup as part of a desperate attempt to ward off its own impending bankruptcy (Buxton 2001). However, the Clinton administration made it clear that no such coup would be accepted (confidential interview with a British diplomat). By this time, too, the impeachment of Pérez had taken some of the heat out of popular anger. Presidential elections were scheduled for December 1993. When serious election campaigning began, it seemed at the time as though the political situation was in the process of returning to normal. Yet again, we see a process by which elections and military political behaviour can inter-act. However, while Chávez disappeared below the political perimeter for some years, he had acquired the name recognition and was in a position to start to accumulate the political capital that would turn him into a serious presidential candidate in 1998.

Venezuela's 2002 coup attempt

In 2002, there was another coup attempt in Venezuela, this time directed against President Chávez. Chávez had been elected to the presidency in December 1998 with an impressive 56 per cent of the vote. Chávez's policy orientation was initially rather cautious (Ellner 2008). The first thirty months or so of his presidency were largely taken up with plebiscitary and constitutional issues (discussed in a later chapter). However, in late 2001 he made his left-wing orienta-tion clearer. This contributed to political polarization in which Chávez and his supporters faced opposition from the old politicians, the Church, conservative Venezuelans and from the US government. A significant step in the direction of polarization occurred in November 2001 when the National Assembly allowed Chávez to enact a series of laws with a serious socialist content, encompassing agrarian reform, the partial renationalization of oil (discussed in a later chapter) and support for worker co-operatives. This set of laws led to the mobilization of the opposition, and to the formation of an anti-*Chavista* bloc entitled the 'Coordinadora Democrática' (Ellner 2008). The purpose of the Coordinadora was Chávez's downfall.

In early 2002, Chávez's popularity was in decline, but it did not fall to the very low levels that would have indicated serious vulner-ability. Datanalisis (quoted in Leon 2002: 150) put Chávez's approval rating at 34.4 per cent just before the coup – not wonderful but by no means disastrous. Datanalisis polls are by no means gospel but the general picture, in which support for Chávez was falling back somewhat from a high level, is probably accurate. Of more signifi-cance in the event was a poll finding (Datanalisis, quoted in Leon 2002: 151) in February 2002 in which 81 per cent of respondents declared themselves against or strongly against a military coup. When the coup attempt was over, Chávez's popularity rose noticeably.

Although the precise pattern of events of April 2002 remains highly contested, the balance of the evidence suggests that there was indeed a premeditated conspiracy and not the spontaneous social reflex that the coup leaders pretended was happening in order to cover up the issue of premeditation (Cannon 2004). While claims of US authorship of the coup seem implausible, the CIA did report several times – on 11 March, 1 April and then 6 April – that a coup attempt was being organized (Jones 2008: 314). There is indeed overwhelming evidence that something of the kind was going on.

Before any military action took place, the opposition ratcheted up the political tension. A strike began in Petroleos de Venezuela (PdVSA: see chapter 5) on 5 April, followed by a general strike a few days later in which the union confederation, the Confederación de Trabajadores de Venezuela (CTV), and the employers' organization Fedecameras jointly participated. On 11 April, demonstrations and counter-demonstrations, supportive and hostile to the administration, clashed in Caracas. The result was confrontation and a number of people were killed. Some senior military officers, immediately blaming Chávez for the violence, called on him to step down and so triggered the coup. In the course of subsequent events, Chávez was physically captured by pro-coup officers. A statement was then put out in his name, saying that he had resigned – something later denied. The coup leaders then declared Pedro Carmona – a leading Venezuelan businessman – interim president. Carmona immediately made it clear that he intended a radical break with the past, announcing the suspension of the National Assembly and the dismissal of the president of the Supreme Court. This announcement was enormously, perhaps fatally, damaging to the coup leaders. Carmona's initial announcements made it clear that he intended to conduct a comprehensive purge of the state. Any doubt about the intentions of at least some of the coup leaders was thereby quickly dispelled.

In political terms, the coup was a failure. Those who supported or participated in the coup lost, rather than gained, political credibility as a result. There was no sense of the military defeat but political victory that Chávez had encountered in February 1992. The interesting question is why this outcome should have been so unequivocal. Disunity within the military was a partial explanation (Norden 2003). Some loyal *Chavista* officers were caught by surprise when the coup happened and rallied in support as soon as they were able. Others simply vacillated and waited to see who would come out on top. The need to avoid conflict within the military itself would have played a part in the thinking of some officers. However, in purely military terms, the key point is that the coup briefly succeeded. The key point is that the coup leaders did achieve their most important military objective, which was the capture of Chávez himself. It is self-evident that they had the purely physical means of putting an end to the Chávez presidency.

The central question, therefore, is why they did not do so. The answer seems to be that they had neither sufficient guns nor sufficient social support to impose an open dictatorship and had no credible plan to do anything else. Any attempt to impose a Pinochet-style regime would certainly have isolated the coup leaders and probably have divided them to a fatal degree. However, a strategy of removing Chávez while maintaining a veneer of constitutionality (something similar was successfully attempted in Ecuador in 2000) would only have been plausible if Chávez had been completely discredited with the broader public, which was not the case. Instead, the streets were soon occupied by Chávez supporters demanding the reinstatement of the president.

When we consider the coup leaders' options, there is an instructive contrast to be drawn between the failed 2002 coup attempt in Venezuela and the successful overthrow of Chile's Salvador Allende in 1973. The general Latin American political situation was supportive of dictatorships in 1973 but not in 2002. The most important difference between the two cases was the fact that the Chilean coup leaders could 'win' by imposing a dictatorship whereas the Venezuelan coup leaders had to have an effective strategy for post-coup politics, something that in the end proved beyond them. The task facing the Chilean coup leaders was much simpler. Admittedly, they did benefit from some earlier political destabilization of the Allende government but on the day of the coup they needed only to run an effective military operation.

Once in power, the Chilean coup leaders could expect recognition from most South American governments, many of which were themselves dictatorships, and of course from the US. They could afford to postpone serious thinking about how to govern until they had used sufficient force to destroy the overthrown government beyond the possibility of its return. To do this, they could coerce and if necessary murder their political opponents without the expectation of later personal accountability, and this allowed them to be much more ruthless than their Venezuelan counterparts could afford to be. The use of state repression in the early days of the Chilean military dictatorship was massive and unconstrained. It is inconceivable that Allende could have fallen physically into the hands of the Chilean coup leaders in 1973, remained prisoner for a few days and then returned to his position as head of government.

In Venezuela in 2002, temporary control over Chávez himself was not enough to assure the success of the coup, due to what turned out to be insuperable problems of post-coup legitimation. International factors did play some part in this. The Bush administration initially seemed to welcome the fall of Chávez, but strenuous opposition from other Latin American governments and from within the US itself left it in two minds. While the Bush administration would have been happy enough to see Chávez removed, an unconcealed dictatorship in Venezuela would have made an overt mockery of stated US foreign policy objectives to support democracy.

Probably more important than these international aspects were domestic political considerations. Here, the coup leaders faced a set of unattractive options. While a lot of complex factors were involved, the key point being made here is that any strategic plan that the coup leaders could have adopted – whether trying to impose dictatorship or to establish some kind of democracy without Chávez – would probably have failed. For a decisive part of both military and civilian opinion, the imposition of an open and repressive right-wing dictatorship, perhaps over a long period, would have been even less acceptable than allowing Chávez to continue in office. Even for officers prepared to consider an authoritarian option, the prospect of being governed by Carmona – a businessman with extreme views and little popular appeal – was not reassuring.

The softer-line alternative, of somehow keeping a democratic process going while either sidelining or removing Chávez, would only have been possible if Chávez had been terminally discredited. Even if Chávez was deemed to have resigned, something that the opposition did attempt to claim, there remained a *Chavista* majority in the National Assembly, which had been elected in 2000. This could not constitutionally be dismissed. If Chávez had been radically unpopular, the coup leaders might nevertheless have tried to proceed on the basis that the *Chavista* constitution was illegitimate. However, such a claim would almost certainly not have passed any electoral test, with the coup leaders being manifestly less popular than the government that they were attempting to overthrow. Any idea that a soft-line strategy might have been feasible was stopped by the mobilization of Chávez's supporters on the streets.

Ecuador in 1997

Until 1979, when military rule gave way to democracy, Ecuador's political system could be described as civil–military with many coups, many elections, parties based on individual personalities and little constitutional continuity in government. Velasco Ibarra won five presidential elections and did not successfully complete a single term. It may be significant for more recent politics that the military regime in power from1972–9 defined itself as progressive and, while not very seriously reformist, was certainly not as repressive as the dictatorships of the Southern Cone.

The Ecuadorian military retained some considerable political capital subsequent to democratization. This respect for the military was enhanced after 1995 when the Ecuadorian army acquitted itself reasonably well in a border conflict with Peru. Even after Ecuador's return to democratic government, the military played a behind-the-scenes political role. According to Fitch (1998: 152), among other things it indicated its opposition to the privatization of state assets during the 1990s.

There were isolated cases of military unrest during the 1980s, but Ecuador for a time settled down into a fairly conservative democracy. Its weak multi-party system and a powerful Congress made it easy for veto groups to block unpopular presidential initiatives. As in Bolivia, indigenous organizations emerged during the democratic period and soon posed a significant challenge to the status quo. Though not the only indigenous organization, CONAIE (the Confederación de Nacionalidades Indígenas del Ecuador) – which was founded in 1986 – was by the 1990s the most important. It led a number of campaigns of civil disobedience during the 1990s (Van Cott 2005) to which the authorities responded with offers to negotiate rather than with repression. The effect was to embolden CONAIE, which on several occasions in the late 1990s called for major popular protests against the (rather feeble) market-oriented direction of economic policy.

Political instability intensified with the election of Abdalá Bucaram in 1996. Bucaram was a highly personalist figure who had adopted a classic 'bait and switch' tactic of making lavish promises to get elected and adopting economically orthodox policies thereafter. He clearly disappointed his own original supporters by doing this. Bucaram adopted politically polarizing tactics around his own personality (Lechner 2006), doing little to dispel stories of large-scale corruption which were especially damaging because they emerged when he was already becoming unpopular. Bucaram also responded to the failure of an ambitious tax reform in Congress by increasing a number of politically sensitive administered prices that the government did control (Lechner 2006). These price increases provided a focal point for civil protest and led to civil disorder, in which CONAIE took an active part. In an atmosphere of growing crisis, the Ecuadorian

31

Congress voted to remove Bucaram from office on the ground of mental instability.

The protests against Bucaram brought the military into politics because they involved the threat of civil disorder. Congress adopted an approach of doubtful constitutionality in its treatment of Bucaram. Not only was a vote to declare Bucaram mentally unstable somewhat questionable empirically, but the correct constitutional provisions governing this procedure were not followed (Gerlach 2003). What in effect occurred was a congressional vote of no confidence against a constitutionally elected but unpopular head of government. The military had no choice but to define its position in such a situation, and in the event acquiesced in the outcome. It did so by prioritizing public order and 'will of the people' arguments over institutional procedures. One leading military figure, General Moncayo, was quoted as saying of Bucaram, 'For God's sake, make him understand that he has to leave because the people are in the streets and do not want him to continue as president' (Gerlach 2003: 102).

The removal of Bucaram led to a subsequent dispute between the supporters of Vice-President Rosalía Arteaga, who had the better constitutional right to succeed, and Fabián Alarcón, who had the necessary congressional and national political support. The military helped broker a constitutional fix, by which Arteaga formally took over but resigned almost immediately in favour of Alarcón. Elections were meanwhile brought forward to 1998. A plebiscite was held to approve this new arrangement, and this approved the plan for transition.

Up to this point, the Ecuadorian military played a political role that corresponded to what in South America was once called a 'moderator'. It essentially arbitrated the demands of the various political actors, not 'neutrally' (Arteaga was not alone in suspecting an anti-female bias in its attitudes) but in what it no doubt genuinely saw as the best interest of the country. It did not seek political power but did its best to manage a situation that it did not welcome. The key points from the military perspective were to avoid internal military disunity at all costs, and also to make political decisions (when these became unavoidable) in line with popular opinion so as to avoid having to adopt high-profile repressive measures. Formal institutionalities were essentially secondary considerations, though it is fair to point out that the institutions that the military only tepidly defended did not have much legitimacy among the broader Ecuadorian public either.

Ecuador in 2000: The Gutiérrez coup

In the very short term, Bucaram's overthrow was followed by a degree of constitutional normality. A market-reforming candidate, Jamil Mahuad, was elected to the presidency in 1998. Faced with a sharp deterioration in the economic situation, including a fall in the international oil price and a collapse in the banking system, Mahuad adopted some highly unpopular austerity measures, including a freeze on bank deposits. These led to militant public opposition in which CONAIE once more played an active part. CONAIE twice called major demonstrations in 1999. Mahuad survived these thanks in part to the loyalty of the military, but his popularity with the general public remained low.

On 15 January 2000, a further set of popular protests began with a march on the Ecuadorian Congress. This, once more, put the military on the spot and – when the key troop commander Colonel Brito told a reporter that the military believed that it had a duty to negotiate rather than repress – Mahuad's position became untenable. Brito and some other senior officers believed that they were adopting a policy of crisis management in which the military would continue to play an arbitrating role. However, on 21 January, Colonel Lucio Gutiérrez launched what clearly amounted to a coup attempt.

There is some suggestion that the leadership of the coup was inspired by the Chávez example in Venezuela. Although prompted by acts of civil disobedience, it seems to have been a premeditated attempt to seize power. It has been reported (Nebbia and Vann 2000; Gerlach 2003) that junior officers had been meeting in the month before the coup to protest about cuts in the military budget. They were also concerned about what they saw as the over-generous terms offered to Peru when a peace settlement was finally reached in 1998. Gutiérrez was then approached by this group and agreed to provide leadership, making contact with CONAIE to discuss joint tactics. It may be that the street protests of early 2000 were intended as cover.

As with the 2002 coup attempt in Venezuela, the coup leaders (albeit of a different political persuasion) achieved an initial military success but were unable to consolidate this into the formation of a new government. Ecuador's most senior officers opposed the coup leaders, as was always likely given the anti-hierarchic nature of a junior officers' coup, and Gutiérrez was also strongly opposed by

Washington and the Organization of American States. Meanwhile, the civilian political establishment rallied behind the vice-president, Gustavo Noboa. In the end, Gutiérrez was persuaded that his objective of heading a military government was unachievable, due to excessive political opposition, and the coup attempt was gradually defused and demobilized. Mahuad was, however, removed from power and replaced by Noboa.

Ecuador in 2005

Gutiérrez was briefly jailed but thereafter was allowed to participate fully in the political process. Fresh elections were held in 2002 and Gutiérrez was elected to the presidency with the support of CONAIE. Once more, there are parallels with the Chávez case, in that both had led coup attempts, failed in military terms, been jailed and then been elected president. However, that is where the comparison ends. Gutiérrez tried to govern from the right, using clientelist methods in a successful strategy of weakening CONAIE (Wolff 2009). Gutiérrez, like Bucaram but unlike Chávez, also adopted 'bait and switch' tactics, allying himself with conservative parties, seeking support from the US government and adopting market-oriented policies. The left-wing parties that were originally willing to support him withdrew their support when his policy orientation changed.

Gutiérrez then abandoned his own supporters and looked for deals with Ecuador's traditional politicians. Matters culminated in late 2004 when he attempted to purge the Supreme Court in what was believed to be part of a deal with Abdalá Bucaram (Alberts 2008: 856; Conaghan 2008). Politics once more moved to the streets and there were strong popular demonstrations against Gutiérrez. Public opinion polls showed that the majority took the side of the Supreme Court rather than Gutiérrez, whose popularity fell decisively as the crisis developed (*Latin American Weekly Report*, 19 April 2005). As the crisis continued, Gutiérrez faced a further depletion in congressional support as defections occurred from among his supporters.

In the end, Gutiérrez was removed from office on the grounds that he had vacated his position by virtue of neglecting his constitutional duties. This was an absurd charge, but it was an effective way of resolving the power struggle. The military did not intervene, though some officers did consider doing so. There is a suggestion that the military may have looked at the idea of taking over the government before finally drawing back but no coup attempt actually took place (Levitt

2007: 233). It appears that the US again made it clear that it would not support a military seizure of power. As a result of this military decision to look the other way, Vice-President Alfredo Palacio replaced Gutiérrez until fresh elections were held in 2006. Gutiérrez's party contested these but performed relatively poorly. The winner of those was Rafael Correa, who had served in the Palacio government but was essentially a little-known political outsider when he ran as an anti-system candidate and emerged to win the presidency on the second round.

Bolivia in the 1980s

Bolivia is an interesting case for several reasons. Bolivia is one of the few countries in South America to experience what seemed at the time like a genuine revolution in 1952 when the military, rather unusually for South America, split in the face of a popular rising. Bolivia was then governed for over a decade by a broadly nationalist party, the Movimiento Nacionalista Revolucionario (MNR), whose own split in 1964 brought back the military. The military then governed Bolivia until 1982. These military regimes were of several orientations, but right-wing governance predominated. In 1980, a particularly harsh, quasi-criminal, military regime held power for a short time before giving way under significant international pressure.

Military unrest did not end immediately after the return to barracks. There were several potential military conspiracies which reached various stages of development before fizzling out, and there was even an incident in June 1984 during which the president was kidnapped and briefly held hostage. Meanwhile, Bolivia's trade unions – who had a long history of radicalism and defiance of the state (Dunkerley 1984) – re-emerged in militant mood when democracy returned. This militancy both resulted from and contributed to rising rates of inflation which by 1984 had reached hyperinflationary levels.

President Siles Zuazo (1982–5), who had previously been in office in the 1950s, was a moderate figure who presided over a weak government. He had neither the desire nor the political base necessary to cope decisively with severe economic problems and responded to popular demands mainly by making concessions (Ibáñez Rojo 2000). Hyperinflation consequently developed and destroyed what remained of the popularity of the government. Siles therefore agreed in 1985 to step down early from his term of office and call new elections. These were won by Paz Estensoro, who was also a former president from the MNR but a more conservative one. He almost immediately imposed orthodox and drastic neoliberal austerity measures. These amounted to a real economic shock and the trade union confederation called a series of general strikes in protest. These were broken by the police and military under a state of siege. On this occasion, therefore, the military effectively supported the civil power.

Bolivia in 2003: The government collapses

Paz's austerity measures opened the way for around fifteen years of elected, broadly conservative government, which came to be viewed as progressive by a number of observers. The re-emergence of widespread popular discontent within Bolivia at the turn of the millennium is, however, unambiguous. It started with protests against an increase in water charges in Cochabamba in April 2000 (Lazar 2006; McNeish 2007). These protests included road blockades, which in Bolivia were a time-honoured means of protest. In September of that year, there were further protests, this time against the government's coca eradication policies. There followed a whole series of further protests that continued until the Sánchez de Lozada government finally resigned in October 2003.

At one level, this popular frustration is not hard to understand. Bolivia is a country in which abundant raw materials have not produced generally successful development. It is also a country with a strong historical tradition of radical popular mobilization. Even so, Bolivia in the 1990s looked to some like a successful case of democracy and market reform. In some ways there was real progress – export growth was substantial – but there was a failure to make ordinary Bolivians feel better off. Moreover, market reform did nothing to reduce the Bolivian economy's vulnerability to external shocks and the economic crisis that started in Asia in 1997 soon reached Bolivia and forced its economy into renewed decline. Harsher coca eradication policies, adopted by the Banzer government at the end of the 1990s under pressure from the United States, were also unpopular and gave the left-wing opposition a broader focal point around which they could rally. The dramatic re-emergence of populist and polarizing politics after 2000 was not widely expected during the 1990s but in hindsight many of the social and historical preconditions generally regarded as conducive to radical popular mobilization were in place.

A new political party, the left-wing MAS, was formed in 1998 under the leadership of Evo Morales and was initially supported largely by coca growers in the Chapare region. Gradually the MAS broadened its base to include some of the traditional Marxist left, and some indigenous organizations, and started to pose a national challenge. After some years of being on the political margins, the MAS achieved just over 20 per cent of the vote in the 2002 elections. Other indigenous-based parties, though polling less well, garnered enough votes to indicate that radical opposition to the system was on the rise. There was still a narrow majority for traditional politicians, but the radical opposition for the first time had real electoral weight.

The rise of militant politics also became more evident on the streets. This street-based militancy came to be combined after 2002 with a more institutionalist basis of opposition led by left-wing parties in the legislature. There was also a catalysing event that sparked off the final crisis. The key event itself was a protest against the proposed export of Bolivian natural gas to the United States via Chile, which soon became the focus, allowing some rather disparate opponents of the system to come together.

The question that needs to be addressed, however, is why the Bolivian military was ultimately unable or unwilling to repress the popular rising, despite its initial support for the government at the outset of popular disturbances. The authorities had already resorted to military force in the face of disturbances several times previously, including sending military and police units into El Alto (a poor district of La Paz) in February 2003 to confront a protest against tax increases. There were a number of deaths on that occasion. Sánchez de Lozada had employed a notoriously harsh defence minister, Sánchez Barzain, who had already served as interior minister during Sánchez de Lozada's first presidential term. He was as committed as the president himself to a policy of imposing order. It is not clear either that a repressive response to the civil disturbances that began in September 2003 would have lacked international support. The US government also verbally and unequivocally supported the government, which had after all been constitutionally elected. A matter of days before Sánchez de Lozada's resignation, his government also received verbal support from the OAS (Council on Hemispheric Affairs 2003). In fact, the government's initial response to the street protests was to use force. However government support in the legislature essentially collapsed, leaving the military with nothing to defend.

When trying to explain this collapse, we are drawn back to issues of popularity and political organization. Polls conducted during his last months in office showed Sánchez de Lozada to be highly unpopular with support in single digits (Council for Hemispheric Affairs 2003). This lack of popularity meant that the government confronted a vicious circle. The consistent need to repress made it increasingly unpopular and its unpopularity made it more repressive. Confrontational tactics by the leaders of the protest were therefore likely to succeed if they could keep going. The logic was the same as that in some of the other cases considered in this chapter. Absent an option to impose a full-scale dictatorship, the military had much more to lose than to gain from trying to keep an unpopular elected government in power via repression.

The government was meanwhile faced by opposition that partly took the form of civil unrest but also had a significant basis in the Bolivian Congress, which was the result of the electoral support that the radical left parties had won in the 2002 elections. This meant that defectors from the ruling coalition did have somewhere to go. The possibility of defection existed because the government coalition included soft-liners who did not support repression and hoped for a negotiated way out of what for them was a desperately difficult situation. They seem to have played the 'swing' role in bringing the government down. It was in fact the soft-line Vice-President Carlos Mesa's resignation on 13 October in protest against the repression that proved to be the decisive step in the fall of the government. When the small but pivotally placed Nueva Fuerza Republicana party withdrew support from the government as well, the government lost control over Congress. By this point, there were signs that the military itself was no longer taking a united position against the protesters. When the security forces allowed popular demonstrations to take place in the capital, the government quickly collapsed.

Another government collapse: Bolivia in 2005

Carlos Mesa succeeded Sánchez de Lozada and remained in office for just 21 months. He ended his period of government as he had begun it, as a benign but weak figure who was unable to deal with the political forces that had been roused during 2000–3. A consistent policy of conciliation – on gas issues and on regional autonomy issues – did not successfully defuse the potential for militancy that had already been built up. Faced with renewed popular unrest, Mesa resigned in June 2005 and was replaced by Eduardo Rodríguez, who was seen by all as an interim president. Fresh elections were promised later in that year and were won by Evo Morales (Salman 2006).

Faced with renewed mobilization, Mesa clearly had no stomach for repression. If the line could not be held against popular protests in 2003, then one could almost certainly not have been held in 2005, and Mesa was surely wise not to attempt such a strategy. The MAS was already on a rising political trend in 2002, and its progress from just over 20 per cent of the vote in 2002 to 53 per cent of the vote in 2005 is clear evidence that Morales's involvement in extra-constitutional politics did not damage his popular appeal and may have enhanced it.

Conclusions

Some questions to do with military intervention are probably best answered at national level. These include, for example, why poor policy performance has generated crisis in some countries but not in others and why crises have involved the military in some countries but not in others. The broader regional point is that, despite a considerable amount of military involvement in politics in our three countries and some others, no open dictatorship has been imposed by the military anywhere in the region since the 1980s. It is likely that there are region-wide factors involved here and that these represent essentially binding constraints.

However, it is also clear that the absence of dictatorship does not invariably reflect the strengthening, or 'consolidation', of institutions. Democracy may be held in place by quite other factors than the legitimacy of its political institutions. The result of a situation in which democracy is held in place by constraints on non-democracy rather than institutional legitimation has been that elections and extra-constitutional forms of politics (military unrest, civil disobedience, etc.) have interacted with each other – both influencing political outcomes.

In all our three cases, elections remained by far the most important means of selecting presidents. In general, too, votes have for the most part been honestly counted. However, presidential removal could be brought about on the streets via the barracks or via adverse votes in Congress – or by some combination of the three. (This is something discussed again in chapter 4.) With the road to dictatorship closed and human rights issues more salient than they once were, protesters have had less to fear from repression. This has given them a real chance of persuading defenders of an unpopular status quo that abandonment was a better option than holding out to the end.

Moreover, once the political environment has become sufficiently turbulent to bring people out onto the streets or the military out of the barracks, the resulting political process may well shape future electoral outcomes. For example, Chávez and Gutiérrez exploited their roles in failed coup attempts to reinvent themselves as democratic politicians. With political institutions discredited, many voters may prefer a popular rebel against an unpopular status quo to an ineffectual or unpopular incumbent. If this is so, then those involved in violating the national constitution are as likely to be electorally rewarded as punished. It has indeed been possible for former coup leaders or leaders of civil disobedience movements to contest and indeed win elections. Under conditions of extreme Schumpeterian democracy – in which elections involve competition for the popular vote but impose few other restraints on politics – an ex-coup leader, a coca-growers' union leader, or a little-known left-of-centre technocrat running as a political outsider had every chance of reaching the presidency.

— 2 —

THE POLITICS OF MASS PROTESTS

We explored in chapter 1 the political role of the military when called to arbitrate civil disorders that challenged lawfully elected but unpopular governments. This chapter addresses the politics of mass protests that have led to the fall of constitutionally elected presidents. While the circumstances that led to the presidents' ousting varied considerably throughout the region and so did the legal (or quasi-legal) procedures used to appoint their successors, street politics, or mass praetorianism, as Samuel Huntington (2006) labelled them, have been in most cases a decisive factor in the unfolding of the crises. The claim does not amount to ignoring the importance of military action (or inaction) at times of crises, as discussed in the previous chapter, or that in most cases Congress has played a decisive role in determining their outcome, sanctioning the removal of incumbents and legitimizing the appointment of their successors. Rather, it is to argue that in times of institutional crises the political decisions of both the military and Congress have been strongly influenced by the size and strength of mass protests and particularly by considerations about which course of action would be more in line with the run of popular feelings as expressed by the protests.

Arguably, as the political influence of the military has waned, the importance of mass protests in shaping the outcome of institutional crises has made mobilized civil society the new *moderating power* of Latin American politics. Kathryn Hochstetler's (2008) study of challenges to presidential authority in 40 Latin American presidencies between 1978 and 2003 shows that the presence or absence of street protests was crucial for the outcome of the challenges. While both political elites and organized civil society have sought the early removal of presidents, all successful challenges included civil society actors mobilized in the streets. Street politics have also led to inter-civil society conflicts leading to further institutional crises. In the context of extreme polarization, rival groups have battled in the streets in favour and against incumbents, justifying their actions by claiming to represent the popular will. The role of mass protests in institutional crises raises a number of empirical and normative questions concerning what is a common theme across this book, namely the relation between politics, institutions and democracy. Among the empirical ones is how and why do civil society organizations (CSOs) become involved in mass protests that challenge constitutional orders and what explains the increasing salience of mass mobilizations in institutional crises. Among the normative ones is the relation between CSOs and democracy: is civil society's role in the removal of a constitutionally elected president part of the democratic process or is it rather a coup by other name? And, what are the implications for democracy when politicized social movements battle for supremacy in the streets rather than channelling their disputes through political institutions? This chapter considers these various issues with special reference to Bolivia and Ecuador. The two countries have experienced both intense popular mobilizations and repeated institutional crises in recent times. In Bolivia, mass popular protests led to the forced resignation of two presidents, Gonzalo Sánchez de Lozada in 2003 and Carlos Mesa in 2005, while in Ecuador three presidents – Abdalá Bucaram in 1997, Jamil Mahuad in 2000 and Lucio Gutiérrez in 2005 – were unable to finish their constitutional mandates through a combination of street protests, military interventions and congressional manoeuvres. Moreover, in both countries mass mobilizations did not just topple constitutionally elected presidents but radically changed their political landscapes with the election of advocates of 'twenty-first century socialism' in Evo Morales and Rafael Correa respectively. We leave out the case of Venezuela on the grounds that, while it experienced several coup attempts in the 1990s and 2000s, it did not experience a successful 'civil society coup', although it did experience a failed one in 2002.[1] Altogether, the recent history of the two countries provides a wealth of examples of the politics of mass protest that allows us to explore their origins, nature and relations with democracy.

The return of mass praetorianism?

The contemporary literature on democratization that emphasizes the democratic role of civil society (Burnell and Calvert 2004; Gill 2000;

42

THE POLITICS OF MASS PROTESTS

Grugel 1999; Linz and Stepan 1996) has overshadowed the argument that a highly mobilized civil society can undermine a political order, whether democratic or not. This argument was forcefully presented in accounts of political instability in developing societies by Samuel P. Huntington (2006) in his classical work, *Political Order in Changing Societies*. Originally published in 1968, Huntington's work challenged modernization theory's optimistic assumption that economic development goes hand in hand with democratization in a virtuous circle of economic and political modernization. He argued that premature increases in political participation – including events like early elections – could destabilize fragile political systems. If social mobilization outpaces the development of political institutions, there is a risk of political instability, as new social actors find that they are unable to participate in the political system and political demands overflow institutional channels and state capabilities. He noted that, in developing societies, political decay is at least as likely as political development, and that the actual experience of newly independent countries was one of increasing social and political disorder. Among the political destabilizing factors highlighted by Huntington is economic growth followed by sudden reversals, a situation familiar to Latin America in the 1980s and 1990s. The result is a condition he called *mass praetorianism*, which he regarded as the leading cause of insurgencies, military coups and weak or disorganized governments (Huntington 2006). Huntington's argument has authoritarian connotations. The notion that political order comes first and economic development and democracy follows was used to give intellectual legitimacy to authoritarian regimes in Latin America and elsewhere in the 1970s, whereby dictatorships were meant to provide political order as a condition for successful economic development. Stripped of its conservative political connotations, mass praetorianism became integral to Guillermo O'Donnell's (1973) classical analysis of the Latin American military dictatorships of the late 1960s and 1970s, the so-called Bureaucratic Authoritarian States.

For most of the 1980s and 1990s Huntington's views appeared to have lost their relevance. With perhaps the partial exception of Chile, the Latin American military dictatorships of the 1970s largely failed in their modernizing projects. CSO mobilization, both in the streets of Latin American cities and in lobbying western governments and international organizations against the military regimes, played an important role in undermining military rulers. Social movements' activism lost its destabilizing potential, first because of the self-restraint shown by CSOs in the initial phases of democratic transition and later through the weakening of the trade unions and other social movements as a result of the socio-economic transformations of the early 1990s. In a twist on modernization theory that maintained the theory's optimistic assumptions, democracy was regarded not as an obstacle but as a condition for economic development, which was now to be driven by free markets rather than by authoritarian states. A depoliticized civil society conceived more as a conglomerate of non-governmental organizations (NGOs) than old fashioned social movements became an integral part of the neo-modernizers' project (Miorelli 2009). The new role of CSOs was to become agents of socio-economic development in lieu of the state and promoters of transparency in the non-market allocation of economic resources. Civil society was also meant to advance good governance and democracy by limiting the encroachment of the state on civic life and by voicing the needs of the poor more transparently than political parties and traditional corporatist actors (World Bank 2000, 2006). While social movements were regarded in the 1960s as dangerously hyper-politicized actors that threatened the political order, civil society was now conceived as a trust-building arena essential for acquiring the social capital and civic virtues without which democratic institutions or market economy could not properly function (Edwards, Foley and Diani 2001; Hooghe and Stolle 2003; Prakash and Selle 2004; Putnam 2000). Civil society still retained an open political role. But when CSOs challenged the political order, as they did in Latin America in the 1970s and under the 'coloured revolutions' of Central and Eastern Europe in the 1980s and 1990s, it was done in the name of liberal democracy and against authoritarian regimes (Beissinger 2007; McFaul 2005).

It soon became apparent that the neo-modernizers' benign view of civil society as binding together liberal democracy and free market reforms in a harmonious relation was as simplistic as modernization theory's original assumption about the benign linear relation between economic development and democracy. The traditional disclaimer about inappropriate generalizations regarding Latin America applies, as countries such as Brazil, Chile and Uruguay have turned into largely consolidated democracies with strong and active civil societies. But elsewhere in Latin America, particularly in the Andean region, the implosion of party systems, the rise of autocratic insiders and populist outsiders and the predominance of political mobilizations over constitutional rules in determining the survival of presidents have brought into question if not necessarily the survival then certainly the quality of democracy in the region (Drake and Hershberg

2006; Mainwaring, Bejarano and Pizarro Leongómez 2006). Arguments about the flawed nature of democracy in the region are reflected in Fareed Zakaria's (2003) claim that democracy works better in societies where it is preceded by constitutional liberalism and that countries which simply hold elections without a strong institutional order end up becoming what he called illiberal democracies, i.e., democracies where elections coexist with majoritarian politics, the un-rule of law and weak political institutions in an unstable relationship.

Behind Zakaria's liberal argument lurk the views of his mentor, Huntington, on political order: that in weakly institutionalized democracies mass political participation risks destabilizing the political order.[2] But, while 1970s mass praetorianism ended in the restoration of order by military dictatorships, in the changing political landscape of the late 1990s and early 2000s, social mobilization has outpaced political institutionalization while coexisting with institutionally fragile and unstable but still democratic political orders. A reference to Huntington is explicit in Omar Encarnación's (2002: 38–9) analysis of the April 2002 mobilizations and counter-mobilizations that led to Hugo Chávez's brief removal and return to the Venezuelan presidency. Encarnación notes that civil society can only serve as an effective foundation for democracy where there are credible functioning state institutions and strong political parties with deep roots in civil society. In its absence, a mobilized and energized civil society in the midst of failing political institutions can become a source of instability, disorder and even violence, a social framework conducive to the so-called 'civil society coups', a term used to characterize the deposition of democratically elected rulers by extra-constitutional means such as riots, mass protests, roads blockages and other forms of direct political action.

Encarnación's warning about the potential dangers for democratic stability of a mobilized civil society contrasts with views of civil society as a school of *civicness* that installs in its members the values and dispositions needed for democratic governance. As Michael Foley and Bob Edwards (1996: 39) note, behind the contrasting images of civil society as an essential component of a democratic order and as a potentially destabilizing force lie two contrasting versions of the civil society argument. The first one originates in Alexis de Tocqueville's *Democracy in America* and emphasizes the ability of associational life in general and the habits of association in particular to foster trust and reciprocity in the interactions of citizens, which is a necessary condition for a healthy democracy. Foley and Edwards called this family of arguments 'Civil Society I'. The benign view of civil society has been given added political weight by Robert Putnam's (2000) arguments about civil society organizations as generators of social capital and by advocates of participatory democracy in which civil society organizations either complement or supplant political parties in public life.[3]

The second version, rooted in Latin America's history of resistance to military dictatorships and mirrored in the civic challenges to the Soviet-controlled regimes of Eastern Europe, is what Foley and Edwards call 'Civil Society II'. This view portrays civil society as a sphere of action that is independent of the state and capable – precisely for this reason – of energizing resistance to an authoritarian regime. A further distinction about the role of civil society can be added to Foley and Edwards's classification which makes its political implications even more complex. This is the case when CSOs challenge not authoritarian regimes but democratically elected ones, as exemplified by the cases explored in this chapter.[4] The distinction between Civil Society I and Civil Society II is particularly relevant for our enquiry. As discussed in more detail below, similar underlying mechanisms of socialization and activation can generate both types of civil society actions (McAdam, Tarrow and Tilly 2001) with contrasting effects on the political order, particularly when political conflict cuts across civil society, as has been, for instance, the case in Bolivia, and Ecuador in recent years.

Mass protests in comparative perspective

As noted in the introduction to this book, while the two countries' political processes share some distinctive features in common, such as the crucial role of street politics alongside electoral politics, they are not complete outliers. We examine these cases of Bolivia and Ecuador below but, before we present our case studies, it is necessary to briefly look at some other cases in which popular protests brought down constitutionally elected presidents in contemporary Latin America to better appreciate their commonalities and differences with our case studies.

One of the earlier examples of mass protests contributing to the ousting of a constitutionally elected president was the civil society mobilizations that led to the resignation of President Fernando Collor de Mello in Brazil on 29 December 1992 when he was on the verge of being impeached. Significantly, Collor gained power as a political outsider (or rather a pseudo outsider) with an anti-establishment message, in which he sided himself with the social and politically excluded against a corrupt political and economic establishment. Yet, the anti-establishment message that was key to his electoral triumph did not become the foundation of a new political and economic order: Collor neither sought to organize and mobilize his supporters, nor, once in office, did he attempt to restructure his country's economy and political institutions, as was the case with Chávez, Correa and Morales. While his stabilization plans gave him strong popular support, he never truly addressed demands for social justice and economic redistribution that are usually at the heart of popular mobilizations by economically excluded sectors. Thus, when, weakened by allegations of corruption and undermined by the failure of his stabilization plan, he appealed to the people to come to the streets in his support, instead of the *descamisados* (the shirtless) of classical populism, he faced students demanding his resignation in the name of democracy. His impeachment showed the considerable power of mobilized civil society to influence Congress's decision to impeach him (Panizza 2000). But crucially the people in the streets were shouting 'Collor out' rather than 'all politicians out'. It was a demand addressed to the Brazilian Congress rather than to the military or to some political outsider. Ultimately, it was the very same political establishment against which Collor had campaigned that turned against him and threw him out of office by using the constitutional process of impeachment in a case in which there was strong prima facie evidence that Collor had been engaged in serious matters of corruption.

The contrast between Collor's impeachment and the events that led to the forced resignation of President Fernando de la Rúa in Argentina in December 2001 is illustrative of broader themes that are part of this chapter. In 2001, after years of being lauded as a model of successful economic reform and democratic institutionalization, Argentina saw its incumbent president resign in the midst of massive protests against not just the government but, more generally, against the political order. Between November 2001 and February 2002, a combination of organized social movements and spontaneous protesters took to the streets of Buenos Aires and other Argentinian cities. Protesters ranged from shanty town-dwellers cutting roads (the so-called *piqueteros*) to middle-class housewives banging pots on the balconies of their flats. In common, they expressed the anger of vast sectors of the population against the political establishment encapsulated in the slogan '*que se vayan todos*' ('all politicians out'). Mass mobilizations exposed the underlying institutional weakness of the country's democratic order, masked by the years of stability that followed the resignation of President Raúl Alfonsín in 1989 (Levitsky and Murillo 2005).

The protests that forced the resignation of De la Rua and of three provisional presidents in quick succession threatened the collapse of the country's political order. As Grugel and Riggirozzi (2009: 94) put it, '*Que se vayan todos* was a measure of the enormous distance that had opened between government and society. It represented a frontal rejection of what was now perceived as a self-serving and corrupt governing class and a loss of faith in neoliberalism, which was blamed for having brought Argentina once more to the brink of chaos.' But while protesters showed a considerable capacity to disrupt the institutional order, they lacked the capacity to organize themselves as political actors able to present an alternative to discredited political parties, as would be the case of the MAS party in Bolivia in 2005. Instead, the Peronist (Justicialista) party played a significant role in both promoting the protest against President de la Rua and in shaping institutional solutions to the protests. First under the presidency of Eduardo Duhalde (2002–3) and later under that of Néstor Kirchner (2003–7), the two Peronist presidents managed to restore political and economic stability. To achieve this, they drew on the national popular legacy of Peronismo to promote a political break with the economic and political legacy of neoliberalism, which they associated with the administrations of presidents Menem and De la Rua. But both operated from within the system rather than from outside it. They secured congressional majorities and used the presidential power to issue law-like decrees to pass economic reforms. They used federal funds to reward loyal state governors. Traditional links with the unions were reinforced to secure social governability and generous social programmes damped the militancy of the *piqueteros*. Thus, the Peronist party, which has historically been regarded as an obstacle to the consolidation of liberal democratic institutions in Argentina, played a crucial role in preventing its collapse.

The role of mass popular protests in the removal of constitutionally elected presidents is always indicative of a crisis of representation but, as the cases of Brazil in 1992 and Argentina in 2001–2 show, the scope and nature of the crises may be very different. As shown below, the crises of representation in Ecuador and Bolivia were closer to that of Argentina than to the one in Brazil. But while the political crisis in Argentina brought significant changes to the country's party system, its political order maintained a much higher level of institutional continuity than those of the Andean countries. The outcome of a crisis of representation depends on a number of factors, including the residual legitimacy of political institutions to reconstruct channels of representation, a role played by Congress in Brazil and by the Peronist (Justicialista) party in Argentina. The nature of the street protests also plays an important role in explaining different outcomes. Street protest can be spontaneous explosions of anger by disorganized citizens or the result of the mobilization of well-organized popular movements. Protests in Buenos Aires in 2001–2 combined both organized groups, such as the *piqueteros*, and disorganized ones, such as the middle-class housewives. The case of the 1989 *Caracazo* in Venezuela is illustrative of how mass grievances can flare up in street riots but, as noted in chapter 1, the protesters lacked unity and political organization to constitute a viable alternative to the existing order. Crucial for the outcome of a crisis is the capacity of the protest movement to sustain itself over time and to make the transition from social to political actors, a relatively rare event in the history of street protests. As will be shown below, this transition was accomplished more successfully in Bolivia than in Ecuador but in common with popular protests in both countries, it was part of a resurgent wave of popular mobilizations in the region.

The claim that an all-powerful neoliberal offensive and a too-weak democratic order emasculated civil society (Adrianzén and Ballón 1992; Brysk 1994; Levitsky 2003; Portes and Hoffman 2003; Ranis 1995; Roberts 1997, 2002) makes it difficult to account for the resurgence of powerful social movements that engaged in mass popular protests in the late 1990s and early 2000s. While there was no general backlash against the free market reforms or common pattern of opposition to them, the mixture of economic reform, democratization and globalization characteristic of the 1990s produced deep social dislocations that created political opportunities for popular mobilization (Arce and Rice 2009). In seeking to radically change socio-economic structures, free market reforms provided an accumulation of grievances to all those affected by change. In an argument that draws comparisons with Karl Polanyi's (1957) classical study of the social and political upheavals that took place in England during the rise of the market economy, Eduardo Silva (2007: 5) claims that the encroachment of market relations on social life creates social tensions that inevitably lead individuals and society to seek protection from the market's impersonal, unpredictable, ever-changing and frequently destructive powers. Protests were not limited to economic matters. Democracy contributed to the emergence of a new politics of rights and undermined traditional forms of the state and economic elites' control over people and organizations. In addition, it limited the state's ability to use force to repress popular protest. Globalization allowed the development of new forms of communication that facilitated the establishment of horizontal networks between social movements at local, national and international levels and made state action against mass protests more visible to international public opinion (De Sousa Santos 2008; Hammond 2005).

In the late 1990s, social movements regained political centrality through their ability to engage in political contestation in a number of countries of the region, particularly in Argentina, Bolivia, Ecuador and Venezuela. Underlying socio-economic factors and political opportunities are important but insufficient factors in explaining the resurgence of movements of mass protest. The social movements' new role cannot be properly understood without taking into consideration the collective action strategies, institutional environment and framing processes that made it possible for localized social movements to expand their political reach and to challenge the political order (Benford and Snow 2000; Harten 2008). Social movements in Latin America generally respond to multiple grievances, have overlapping identities and are characterized by expanding goals (Muse Sinek 2006). As seen in the case of the Movimento dos Trabalhadores Rurais Sem Terra (MST) in Brazil, social movements use both transgressive and institutional mobilizing strategies and mix specific demands with broader political goals (Branford and Rocha 2002). In analysing their actions, the distinction between political and economic grievances becomes blurred, as does the distinction between identity-based movements and interest-based ones and that between social and political movements. In many cases, the fight against neoliberalism provided a master frame (Durand 2010) for the joint mobilization of a variety of movements that cut across social cleavages. But attacks on neoliberalism were as much about politics as they were about the economic model. Mass protests against free market reforms were usually articulated with attacks against unpopular presidents and discredited political parties and demands were wrapped in the political discourse of nationalism and the new language of collective cultural and social rights, as well as in appeals for the preservation of the environment and the equitable distribution of rents from natural resources. The indigenous movements that were at the vanguard of mass protests in Ecuador and Bolivia (Van Cott 2005; Yashar 2006) are good examples of the new politics of mass protests in late twentieth century and early twenty-first century Latin America.

Indigenous movements and the politics of mass protests in Ecuador

Ecuador and Bolivia are home to the most successful indigenous movements in contemporary Latin America. Indigenous organizations are not the only politically relevant social movements in the two countries but in the 1990s they became an important catalyst for wider social movement activity, often unifying a range of organizations around common goals (Mattiace 2005: 237). The strength of indigenous organizations in Bolivia may be explained by their proportion of the population, constituting around 71 per cent of Bolivian nationals (Van Cott 2008: 34).[5] But the ethnic make-up of the population is insufficient to explain the growing political relevance of indigenous organizations in the late 1990s and early 2000s since the country's ethnic composition has changed little over past decades. Moreover, indigenous self-identification appears to be the result rather than the cause of social mobilization, as the number of people that identified themselves as members of one of the country's indigenous groups grew substantially after indigenous movements gained political prominence (Dunkerley 2007).

Indigenous people constitute a relatively smaller proportion of Ecuador's population. In the 2001 census, only 6.6 per cent of all Ecuadorians identified themselves as Indians, rising to 14.3 per cent when including those who declared that they or their parents spoke indigenous languages (Zamosc 2007: 8). Other sources, however, put the proportion of Indians at around 25 per cent of the population (CIA World Factbook 2009). Irrespective of the figures, indigenous organizations have played a major role in the politics of mass protest in the country. As Amalia Pallares (2002) points out, there was nothing predetermined about the emergence of a national Indian movement in Ecuador. Indigenous identity in Ecuador has always been highly fragmented and heterogeneous. Particularly important are regional divisions between those living in the Andean highlands and the inhabitants of the Amazonian lowlands, as well as ethnic divisions between different indigenous communities. Indigenous citizens engage both as communities and as individuals in a wide variety of economic activities, particularly as independent *minifundistas* (*campesinos* – peasants), farm workers, self-employed urban informal workers and small entrepreneurs which places them at different locations in the country's class structure. There is also an urban indigenous intelligentsia (Wolff 2007).

The modern origins of Ecuador's Indian movement can be traced to the campaigns of local and regional organizations in the 1970s and 1980s around traditional *campesino* demands for land, credit and access to markets. To these was added a resurgent indigenous agenda for the recognition of the pluri-cultural nature of the Ecuadorian state and the fight against racial discrimination. Demands for cultural rights became an early unifying frame for otherwise disparate regional identities and economic interests. The process of democratization that began with a new constitution and the election of Jaime Roldós as president in 1979 provided the political framework for the further advancement of the indigenous cause.[6] As Jonas Wolff (2007) put it, democratization not only opened and guaranteed spaces and venues for contentious mobilization but also entailed expectations of political incorporation and socio-economic progress. Elite-controlled democratic institutions and free market reforms largely failed to fulfil the promises of political and economic incorporation that they produced. These dislocations became conditions of possibility for the politics of mass protests.

A number of politically active indigenous regional organizations came together in 1986 to form the Confederación de Nacionalidades Indígenas del Ecuador (CONAIE, the Confederation of Indigenous Nationalities in Ecuador) (Becker 2008a; Zamosc 2007) which gave indigenous communities a unified voice at national level, centred on the common demands for land reform and bilingual education.[7] CONAIE and its allied indigenous organizations raised a macro-political agenda that denounced neoliberalism and the political establishment and a sector-specific one that demanded the redefinition of Ecuador as a pluri-national state, including territorial autonomy for indigenous communities and indigenous representation in state institutions. Macro-political demands were combined with micro-specific ones, such as credits for rural development, land tenure regularization and local public works, which were connected to the territorial settings from which the mobilization process originated. Raising local grievances, which required negotiations with the state, was crucial for developing the indigenous organizations' social capital and grassroots political support and thus for building up and sustaining their mobilizing capacities in the wider political scene (Wolff 2007: 14).

At national level, indigenous organizations engaged in both extra-institutional contentious collective action and institutional politics. CONAIE's first show of political strength at national level was the June 1990 *levantamiento* (uprising), in which indigenous people blocked roads throughout the country when demanding bilingual education, agrarian reform and the recognition of the pluri-national nature of Ecuador. The protesters effectively cut off food supplies to the cities and shut down the country for a week. The strength of the mobilization, the largest ever by indigenous groups in Ecuador's modern history, forced the government to negotiate with CONAIE. It placed the indigenous movement in the leadership of a wider protest movement and came to be seen as a model of how civil society should campaign to fight for its rights (Becker 2008a: 167; Zamosc 2007). Throughout the 1990s, CONAIE maintained a high level of political mobilization, staging mass protests with nationwide repercussions in April 1992, June 1994, January and February 1997, January 2000 and January 2001 (de la Torre 2006). Indigenous organizations also became part of broader alliances of social movements. In 1995, CONAIE participated in the setting up of the Coordinadora de Movimientos Sociales, an umbrella organization that included trade unions, neighbourhood associations, peasant groups and human rights associations (Tamayo 1996). CONAIE's mobilizations played an important role in the 1997 protests that resulted in the deposition of President Abdalá Bucaram by Congress on the dubious ground of insanity. The organization's mobilizing power reached its peak in 2000 when CONAIE and other indigenous groups called for the removal of President Jamil Mahuad and joined a group of lower ranking military officers in the January military/ indigenous coup against the democratically elected president. The then president of CONAIE, Antonio Vargas, participated in the 'Triumvirate of National Salvation' that took power for a few hours. But, as noted in chapter 1, while Mahuad was forced to resign, the coup collapsed when the military withdrew support for the new leaders and Congress appointed Vice-President Gustavo Noboa as Mahuad's successor.

In parallel to staging mass protests, CONAIE made the transition from a social movement to a political party by setting up a mainly indigenous party, the Movimiento de Unidad Plurinacional Pachakutik – Nuevo País, in December 1995.[8] The party, which identified itself as part of a new Latin American left, represented the culmination of CONAIE's drive to promote indigenous self-representation in the political arena (Becker 2008a). More broadly, it opposed the government's neoliberal economic policies and favoured forms of participatory democracy. Pachakutik came fourth in the 1996 congressional elections and elected mayors in several municipalities throughout the country. The party gained around 10 per cent of the seats in the

1997 elections for a Constituent Assembly that defined Ecuador as a multicultural state and recognized social, cultural and political rights for indigenous people (Andolina 2003; Zamosc 2007). CONAIE, together with other indigenous organizations, also gained control of the Council for the Development of the Nationalities and Peoples of Ecuador (CODENPE), a state development agency set up in 1998 which allocated funds for economic and social development in indigenous communities and became an important source of local funding and political patronage.[9] Pachakutik reached the peak of its political influence when the party backed the presidential candidacy of Colonel Lucio Gutiérrez in 2002. The party's support was crucial for Gutiérrez's victory, as he qualified for the second-round run by a margin of less than 5 per cent of the vote. Following Gutiérrez's victory, Pachakutik leaders were appointed to positions in his cabinet but, as noted in chapter 1, the alliance was short-lived. Gutiérrez's shift to the right and the promotion of free market economic policies contributed to the alliance's collapse in August 2003 when Gutiérrez dismissed its ministers and Pachakutik joined the opposition (Zamosc 2007).

Since then, both CONAIE and Pachakutik have been in political decline. Indigenous organizations played no significant role in the mass protests that brought down President Lucio Gutiérrez in 2005 and were sidelined by Rafael Correa in his successful presidential campaigns of 2006 and 2009. The indigenous movement has become divided along regional, political and religious lines. Pachakutik has been weakened by sectarian infighting and its previously close alliance with CONAIE has come under strain (Stahler-Sholk, Vanden and Kuecker 2007; Van Cott 2005). Pachakutik did poorly in the 2006 elections that chose Rafael Correa as the new president of Ecuador and, in the September 2007 elections for the Constituent Assembly promoted by Correa, the party won just a couple of seats. While the new constitution has incorporated key demands of the indigenous communities that reflect the real gains of over two decades of Indian activism, President Correa has not made formal alliances with indigenous organizations. As he made clear, his politics of anti-politics is 'a citizens' revolution', not a social movement-based one (Becker 2011). Correa's distance from the once mighty indigenous movement became apparent in January 2009 when he closed down CODENPE, accusing the organization's indigenous executive secretary, Lourdes Tibán, of diverting funds to her home province of Cotopaxi. Relations between Correa and the indigenous movement became further strained in October the same year when indigenous organizations, some linked to Pachakutik, launched what they called a 'national uprising' against a bill governing the use of water, which the indigenous groups said amounted to privatization through the back door. President Correa called the mobilizations 'a total failure' and dismissed their organizers as 'golden ponchos' flush with state funds for community development (*The Economist*, 2009).

The political rise and subsequent decline of CONAIE and of its political arm, Pachakutik, illustrates the strengths and limitations of the politics of mass protest in Ecuador. CONAIE achieved significant success in unifying fragmented indigenous communities and diverse local interests into a new nationwide social movement. It also succeeded in transforming a historically excluded social group into one of the most powerful political actors in contemporary Ecuadorian politics. It played a leading role in the broader movement of opposition to neoliberal reforms in Ecuador and in the street protests that toppled two presidents. It won legal and political recognition for Indian rights and the constitutional recognition of Ecuador as a pluri-national state. It achieved these goals by combining the roles of Civil Society I and Civil Society II. As a Civil Society I-type organization, it fostered associational links between indigenous communities at grassroots level, developed the indigenous communities' social capital and engaged successive governments to negotiate the successful recognition of cultural rights and social assistance. As a Civil Society II-type organization, it used street power to (largely peacefully) back up its demands with mass protests, which contributed to the de-legitimization of the country's corrupt and self-serving political parties. But the Civil Society I/ Civil Society II distinction fails to capture four crucial aspects of CONAIE's political journey.

Firstly, mass protests can bring together diverse social movements in antagonism to the political system but, lacking a politico-institutional foundation, unity was precarious and difficult to preserve beyond the level of street politics. Second, CONAIE's campaigns, including mass protests, were an integral part of the process of incorporation of previously excluded social sectors to Ecuador's political system but the movement's strategy raises questions about its commitment to liberal democracy. Particularly hard to justify is the alliance between CONAIE and the military officers that deposed President Mahuad in 2000. As Deborah Yashar (2005: 151) put it, it was a social movement organization that had entered but not made peace with electoral politics. Third, CONAIE's mass protests were more effective in undermining the political order than in shaping the new one. In the events that followed Mahuad's resignation, Congress and the military, rather than CONAIE, played a decisive role, and in the aftermath of Gutiérrez's resignation, a political outsider (Rafael Correa) was the main architect of the new political order. Finally, the setting up of Pachakutik as a party aimed at representing indigenous people suggests that the Civil Society I/Civil Society II dichotomy fails to take into account the implications of making the transition from social to political actor without setting a clear dividing line between the social and political arenas. As a political party, Pachakutik entered into political alliances and political games that did not necessarily correspond to CONAIE's extra-parliamentary strategy, creating tensions between the party and the social movement. Lacking enough representation to have a powerful influence in a highly fragmented Congress, Pachakutik needed to forge alliances to increase its political presence but coalition politics diffused its original appeal as a party untainted by the political ills of the country's *partidocracia*. As a result, many Ecuadorians came to see Pachakutik as just another party more interested in patronage and parliamentary politics than in social justice. Pachakutik's political decline was also partly attributable to the party's shift from its previous broad popular appeal that transcended its ethnic origins and established close ties with various mestizo-dominated organizations into a more ethno-nationalist direction. Many of the mestizo-dominated unions and organizations that had supported Pachakutik in past elections abandoned it in 2006, partly because of concerns about the growing dominance of the *indigenista* faction within the party (Madrid 2008: 507). In contrast, as will be noted in chapter 3, studies show that the MAS electoral performance in Bolivia improved considerably over time as it became more inclusive, attracting the support of a broad variety of voters with indigenous backgrounds as well as of politically disenchanted voters and of voters with leftist and nationalist views (ibid.). This has clear implications for political representation and highlights the difficulty of putting into practice the notion that representatives should be drawn from the same sociocultural groups as the represented. While there is a long history of social movements setting up political parties, including social democratic movements in Europe and the Workers' Party (PT) in Brazil, the success of the social movements' political enterprise appears at least partly to depend on the ability of these parties to transcend their social roots in order to reach a broader social constituency, particularly in highly fragmented societies.

Indigenous politics and political power in Bolivia

The case of Bolivia shows a different outcome from the politics of mass protest. In contrast to CONAIE in Ecuador, the social movements that engaged in mass protests between 2000 and 2005 have remained highly influential in the country's new political order. MAS, the party set up by the rural *sindicatos* (unions) of the coca growers, has became the largest party in the country and its leader, Evo Morales, Bolivia's first indigenous president. We deal in considerable detail with Bolivia's political process, including the setting up of the MAS party and the election of Evo Morales as president of Bolivia, in chapter 3. In this section, we limit our analysis to the role of CSOs, particularly the cocalero movement, in the politics of mass protest that led to the fall of Presidents Sánchez de Lozada and Mesa.

Bolivia has a lengthy tradition of social protest and direct political action, frequently at the margins of the political system (Crabtree 2005). The strength of social mobilizations has created two parallel political arenas in an almost permanent cycle of conflict and negotiation. As Laurence Whitehead (2001: 10) put it, on the one hand, Bolivia has a long tradition of legal formalism reflected in a quite sophisticated system of constitutional rules and precedents. On the other hand, it boasts an equally strong tradition of direct political participation that breaks in upon elite games and defies their constraints in the name of an excluded populace. Political contestation is rooted in the leading role of the miners in the 1952 revolution that marked the first wave of incorporation of the popular sectors into the country's political system. In the following years, the mining unions, organized in the powerful Central Obrera Boliviana (COB), played a central role in Bolivia's political life in an unstable mixture of confrontations, pacts and negotiations with the Movimiento Nacionalista Revolucionario (MNR)-dominated civilian administrations of the 1950s and early 1960s. Trade unions were repressed by the military governments that largely controlled Bolivian politics between 1964 and 1982. They returned to the politics of contention in their opposition to the economic policies of the democratic administration of President Hernán Siles Suazo (1982–5). But while the unions effectively blocked government policies, they were perceived by important sectors of the population as co-responsible for the crisis of governability and the economic chaos that characterized the Siles Suazo government. Moreover, they were unable to resist the free market economic reforms imposed by Siles Suazo's successor, Víctor Paz Estenssoro (Ibañez Rojo 2000; Sanabria 1999).

Peasants (overwhelmingly Indians) were also part of the 1952 revolutionary movement. The MNR governments distributed land to the peasants and established *sindicatos campesinos* (peasant unions) in almost every village (particularly in the Andean highlands) both to control and mobilize the rural population (Harten 2008; Vanden 2008). Indians were also able to exercise their voting rights by the granting of universal suffrage. But indigenous communities remained heavily dependent on state patronage and the rural unions lacked the political centrality and mobilizing capacity of the miners and remained subordinated to the industrial unions within the COB (Durand 2010). Following the 1964 military coup that ended the MNR's political dominance, the military governments continued the tradition of subordinated incorporation of the Indians by establishing the so-called Peasant–Military Pact (Healy 1988).

Since the country's return to democracy in 1982, a number of economic and political developments have led to the decline of the industrial unions and to the rise in the mobilizing capacity of the rural unions, particularly of the coca growers of the Chapare region. The main reason for the weakening of the industrial unions was the collapse of the state-owned mining sector that followed the introduction of free market reforms in 1985 (Arce and Rice 2009; Whitehead 2001). The decline in the mining industry produced two developments that contributed to a shift in the internal balance of forces of the trade union movement in favour of the rural unions: firstly, the fall in output of one of the country's main sources of foreign exchange (tin) increased the economic importance of the coca economy as a source of both foreign exchange and of livelihood for thousands of peasants. Second, many of the highly politicized miners that lost their jobs migrated to the Chapare region to cultivate coca, contributing to strengthening the coca growers' political militancy and social organization (Durand 2010). Democratization, globalization and social change also facilitated the growth of Indian nationalism and the emergence of a new wave of social organizations in urban areas with close links to the rural ones.

The strength of the rural unions has been grounded in the *sindicatos*' control of social life at grassroots level in the coca-growing communities. The *sindicato* exercises a more central role in communities than a traditional union. In the absence or weak presence of the state at local level, the *sindicatos*, grouped in the Federación Especial de Trabajadores Campesinos del Trópico de Cochabamba (FETCTC), effectively structure social life in the Trópico de Cochabamba. They provide security and some forms of justice and self-defence, regulate land tenure, manage coca markets, build schools, organize leisure time (particularly football competitions) and raise funds for public works (Durand 2010; Harten 2008). Decisions about community affairs are taken by consensus in meetings that may last several hours and in which all members of the union have the right to speak. Unpaid leaders are elected, also by consensus in the annual Congress, for a two-year period and cannot usually be re-elected (Harten 2008). We should not idealize the democratic elements of the coca grower unions' authority over the local population. The centrality of the *sindicatos* in their communities' social and economic life makes it very difficult for anybody to live and work in the area without belonging to the union. Expression of dissent in such close-knit communities can be socially costly (de la Torre 2009). It is clear, however, that at the grassroots level the rural *sindicatos* perform Civil Society I-type functions of promoting community links, building social capital and developing relations of trust among its members. In parallel, because they organize and represent peasants engaged in the cultivation of a forbidden plant, coca, the *sindicatos* also exercise Civil Society II-type activities of resisting (sometimes violently) state power. The confrontational aspect of the *sindicatos* activities was exacerbated by the criminalization in 1988 of all coca production except for 12,000 hectares in the Yungas and particularly by President Hugo Bánzer's (1997–2000) forced coca eradication policy, undertaken under heavy influence from the US, the so-called 'Plan Dignidad'.

While the coca growers remained isolated in a narrow, rural, geographical location, the frequently violent conflict between the *sindicatos* and the government did not threaten the political order. Two developments allowed the rural *sindicatos* to transcend their geographical and political boundaries and become part of a wider mass movement that challenged the country's political order. The first was the rise of an independent Aymara intellectual and political movement in Bolivia's highlands. The Indian movement was led by a new generation of educated, urbanized Aymaras who maintained ties to rural communities (Ticona 2000; Van Cott 2003). An alternative current of Aymara nationalism emerged among the peasantry of the *altiplano* led by former guerrilla leader Felipe Quispe Huanca (known as El Mallku, or 'the leader'). It demanded separate nationhood and land for the Aymara nation and pursued confrontation rather than accommodation with non-indigenous forces. In 2000, Quispe founded the Pachakuti Indigenous Movement (MIP, Movimiento Indígena

Pachakuti) that obtained 2.2 per cent of the popular vote in the 2002 legislative elections. In spite of the failure to fully translate ethnic politicization into electoral support, indigenous nationalism had a significant influence in the emergence of a new generation of politically active grassroots leaders. In 1979, the union-oriented Tupac Katari Revolutionary Movement (Movimiento Revolucionario Túpac Katari – MRTK) formed Bolivia's first autonomous peasant organization, the Confederación Sindical Única de Trabajadores Campesinos de Bolivia (CSUTCB), of which Quispe was the general secretary. The organization became the power base of the coca growers' unions, which exercised an increasing influence within the CSUTCB throughout the 1980s and 1990s, eventually becoming its most powerful affiliated organization. The MAS party, although not explicitly an indigenous party, adopted many elements of the Katarista discourse and of the Aymara movement's Indian nationalist agenda, as did some non-indigenous parties. The party, however, transcended its indigenous social roots and identity to become more the political representative of the *excluded*, as it adopted a number of peasant and urban demands and gathered support from grassroots movements such as those in the El Alto township (Durand 2010; Madrid 2008; Ticona 2000; Van Cott 2003; Whitehead 2001).

The other development was the explosion of mass protests between 2000 and 2005, centred on the so-called water and gas wars of 2000 and 2003 respectively. The mobilizations brought together indigenous and non-indigenous protesters, as well as rural and urban social movements, that converged against the political establishment. Of these, the gas war was the defining struggle that led to the radical overhaul of the country's political system. The gas war was a national, and nationalist, uprising, initially involving the central site of El Alto and the rural *altiplano* that spread out across much of the country (Perreault 2006: 165). For some, it represented the culmination of a rising indigenous radicalism and the ultimate exposure of the racist cleavage that cuts across Bolivia's history and society. For others, it signified a convergence between the old national-popular traditions of the miners and the nationalist left and the new ethno-nationalism of highly politicized indigenous sectors. Finally, some saw as its cause the social failure of the neoliberal model. The confrontation crystallized the political antagonism that defined the frontiers of Bolivia's fractured political order along two opposite camps and made possible the coming together of different popular actors. As Spronk and Webber put it:

The 'us' included the urban popular classes and indigenous peoples demanding national control of natural resources, the redistribution of oil rents and the re-foundation of the Bolivian nation on different political, ethnic and socio-economic principles. The 'them' included the traditional parties, transnational gas corporations, the neoliberal model personified in the presidency of Sánchez de Lozada, and US imperialism writ large. The pathways of change involved the ousting of the neoliberal president, the nationalization of gas and the convocation of a Constituent Assembly. (Spronk and Webber 2008: 82–3)

Mass popular protests in Bolivia used a mixture of different forms of direct action, such as marches, roadblocks and the seizure of public buildings, which straddled the boundary between legality and illegality. Violent confrontations between protesters and the security forces (mostly the army) between 2000 and 2005 resulted in dozens of deaths and raised questions about the democratic limits of both direct action and of state repression and how state reactions to mass protests shape conflicts. Government responses to protesters' direct action oscillated between weakness and the disproportionate use of force, often within the same conflict. The 2000–5 wave of mass protests registered several episodes of this type. In the so-called water war in Cochabamba, protests became increasingly violent, with the Bolivian government despatching riot police to control the movement. A bullet from a sniper claimed the life of a young man, which radicalized the protests and brought 100,000 people into the streets (Spronk and Webber 2008). The direct action in Cochabamba was quickly followed by mass protests in the traditionally conflictive *altiplano* peasant settlement of Achacachi. On 9 April 2000, large numbers of peasants took to the roads to block traffic, leaving the security forces with the dilemma of whether to repress them or to capitulate. Following the intervention of the Catholic Church, the government chose to withdraw its forces and negotiate – from a position of political weakness. For Laurence Whitehead (2001: 12–13), 'Whatever its official line, the government could no longer exercise its full authority. Bolivians have abundant experience with this kind of situation, and thus they prepared themselves for a second round of challenges and demands, which duly arrived six months later.' In what came to be known as 'Black September', protesters blocked the country's main roads for almost a month. The greater number of participants in the September 2000 mobilizations introduced a new dimension to traditional roadblocks through the physical occupation of large sections of the country's roads that made removing them by the military difficult. The protests concluded with the signing of a lengthy accord between the government and the protest organizers. According to Bolivia's Permanent Assembly on Human Rights, 15 civilians and five soldiers lost their lives in confrontations (Arce and Rice 2009: 92; Whitehead 2001).

The dialectics of direct action and state repression was also crucial in the unfolding of the 2003 gas war. As David Pion-Berlin (2007) recalls, initially the government's response to the protesters' actions was desultory, allowing protesters to continue so long as they remained non-violent and did not infringe the rights of citizens. Then, on 20 September the government ordered military and police units in a resort near Lake Titicaca to 'rescue' tourists trapped by the road barricades imposed by indigenous protesters. There are conflicting versions about what triggered the violent military and police reaction but the end result was the killing of five civilians and the wounding of another seventeen. In the following weeks, roadblocks spread throughout the country, blocking international routes and access to the capital, La Paz. The worst confrontations took place the follow-ing month in the protesters' stronghold of El Alto that surrounds La Paz. In the incidents that followed, clashes between the security forces and protesters left a balance of several deaths among the pro-testers (Pion-Berlin 2007). With the mounting number of civilian deaths affecting the reputation of the army, military chiefs refused to continue using force against protesters, effectively abandoning President Sánchez de Lozada to his own fate. With demonstrators marching through the streets of La Paz, Sánchez de Lozada had no option but to tender his resignation and flee the country on 17 October 2003.

Confrontations between the security forces and the protesters created further grievances that heightened political antagonism and left no shared political space for dialogue or negotiation. Following the confrontations of 20 September, the government hardened its own position, refusing to recognize the main union leaders, Felipe Quispe, Jaime Solares and Evo Morales, as legitimate interlocutors. For their part, union and Indian leaders escalated both their calls for action and their rhetoric, calling for a general strike of indefinite duration and telling their followers to defend themselves in any way they could. Evo Morales's statement that 'we are not going to have dia-logue with murderers of the people' (Pion-Berlin 2007: 11) is illustra-tive of the hardening of the protesters' position. A further issue that arose from the confrontations is that there is a clear but difficult-to-set political threshold for the legitimate use of force under democracy. Both excessive weakness and excessive force de-legitimize governments. It may not be easy to establish universal criteria for the proportionate use of state force but any democratic government that inflicts casualties on unarmed protesters risks breaching it and falling into a spiral of de-legitimation. In the case of Bolivia, a country that has a long history of violent repression of popular protest, the killings of October 2003 evoked memories of past massacres. It broke the link between legality and legitimacy (Bonifaz 2008) of President De Lozada's administration and made it untenable for the president to hold onto office.

Inter-civil society conflicts in Bolivia

The emphasis in the civil society literature on conflicts between CSOs and the state overlooks the confrontations within civil society that played a major role in the unfolding of institutional crises. Most analyses of civil society mobilization in Bolivia have focused on social movements traditionally aligned with the left, such as the trade unions and indigenous organizations. The country, however, also has a tradition of right-wing social mobilization which developed around demands for regional autonomy.

Conservative civil associations, known as *comités cívicos* (civic committees) and *movimientos cívicos*, were set up in the 1950s by regional elites, particularly in the province of Santa Cruz, to resist the MNR-dominated central government. Right-wing social mobilization had gained new impetus by the turn of the century when radical protests threatened the political and economic interests of regional elites at a time in which traditional parties, upon which conservative forces traditionally depended to protect their interests, were fast losing their political dominance.[10] The anti-free market backlash of 2000–3, the demands for the nationalization of the oil and gas industry and for the redistribution of rents from the hydrocarbons-rich lowlands to the poorer highlands activated a reaction from conservative political and economic forces of the so-called *medialuna* (crescent) of lowland states. The counter-offensive was headed by regional civic committees formed by an alliance of the local political elite, business associations and other local social movements. The committees coalesced around calls for regional autonomy, an ambiguous term whose meaning ranged from direct elections for regional political authorities to regional control over natural resources. Demands included the right to retain control of up to two-thirds of all tax revenues generated in the department and the authority to set policies other than in defence, currency, tariffs and foreign relations (Eaton 2007). Although elite-dominated, the committees enjoyed genuine popular support in their heartlands. In 2004, the Comité Pro Santa Cruz (CPSC) collected approximately 500,000 signatures in support of a referendum on autonomy and in November 2004 it led a civic strike in an attempt to force the national government to hold a referendum on the issue.[11] In addition to promoting street protests and civic strikes, the CPSC moved unilaterally to create a departmental assembly (which was not allowed within Bolivia's constitution) and symbolically declared its own president as governor of Santa Cruz. In January 2005, at the peak of the confrontation between the popular organizations and the government of president Carlos Mesa, the CPSC mobilized hundreds of thousands of supporters on a right-wing platform called the 'January Agenda', in contraposition to the so-called 'October (2003) Agenda' raised by the popular movements that ousted Sánchez de Losada (Eaton 2007; Spronk and Webber 2008).[12]

The committees' campaign for regional autonomy continued after Morales's electoral victory in December 2005. In 2005–6, they collected half a million signatures and put tens of thousands of people in the streets to pressure the government to hold a referendum on regional autonomy (Hochstetler and Friedman 2008: 11). In May and June 2008, autonomy referenda were held in four eastern departments, where their citizens voted to declare themselves autonomous from the central government. President Morales deemed the referenda illegal and separatist. In September 2008, anti-government protests escalated into violence in the east and north of the country. Protesters blocked roads, stormed public buildings and clashed with riot police in Santa Cruz, Beni, Pando and Tarija, with 30 people killed in the worst-affected region, the northern province of Pando. The government condemned the unrest as 'a civil coup'.[13] Following international mediation by other Latin American governments that strongly backed President Morales, the government and opposition reached a compromise on a draft new constitution that was ratified by a referendum on 25 January 2009. While the new constitution was passed with over 60 per cent of the national vote, a majority in four out of the nine provinces voted against it, showing the still considerable level of popular opposition to the new institutions in these regions and the underlying fractures in Bolivian society.

Conclusions

This chapter has looked at the politics of mass protest, leading to the interruption of presidential mandates. By analysing the political role of CSOs at such crucial moments in a country's history, we sought to address more general questions about civil society's relation with weakly institutionalized democracies, an issue already explored by Samuel Huntington's 'mass praetorianism' argument. We framed our enquiry on the apparently contradictory views of civil society: on one hand, as an arena of toleration that promotes civic values and, on the other, as a source of unmanageable conflicts that can threaten political order in a democratic polity.

It could be suggested that in order to further a democratic culture, civic habits of association, trust and compromise must be developed along three dimensions: inwards (inside social organizations), outwards (in the links across different social movements) and upwards (in the relations between civil society and the state). To emphasize the three-dimensional nature of civicness is not to claim a naive view of a conflict-free society where CSOs interact in a political vacuum. On the contrary, conflict is the essence of a healthy democracy. As Larry Diamond (1996: 230, cited in Salman 2007: 114) argues, the establishment of channels other than political parties, such as an active and independent civil society, is helpful in this regard. Not only can it foster respect for opposing viewpoints and weaken the principal polarities of political conflict, it can also enhance political institutions' accountability and inclusiveness.

The cases of presidential crises analysed in this chapter suggest that, while democratic continuity has allowed a considerable development of associational practices that have led to the emergence of powerful new social movements, these practices did not expand horizontally throughout civil society as a whole or vertically in the dealings between CSOs and the state. Instead, social mobilizations revealed deep social divisions and exposed the breakdown of trust between CSOs and political institutions, as well as among competing social organizations. This brings us to the question of why the breakdown of trust between society and governments reached such extremes in the cases under consideration. In his analysis of the relations between social movements and the state in Bolivia, Salman (2007: 13) argues that the protesters' radicalization was not a manifestation of their lack of democratic maturity but rather the product of political learning, nurtured by a long history of the official promotion of democratic values, such as trust in the politicians' integrity and good intentions and the importance of compromises, that worked systematically against the poor. As he put it, in Bolivia the political system's failure to address societal frustration hindered the societal capacity to translate demands into political choices. Instead, a process of *deconsolidation* took place in which the positive feedback between effective societal control, capable participation and a genuine social mandate, on the one hand, and the state's responsiveness to it, on the other, was broken. A similar line of argument is advanced by Zamosc (2007: 25) to explain CONAIE's apparent lack of commitment to democracy, as shown by the organization's involvement in the civil society coup against President Mahuad of Ecuador. He claims that time and again indigenous militants had decried what they viewed as a corrupt democracy, characterized by institutions colonized by governments that benefited the elites and discriminated against the common people. Moreover, indigenous activists were not alone in their disrespect for the rules of democracy: indigenous activists have 'learned the ropes' of practical politics within a system of interactions in which the prevailing attitudes were not characterized by reverence for constitutional conventions. The episodes of mass mobilization in Ecuador and Bolivia examined in this chapter appear to give substance to the argument that the politics of mass protest are the manifestation of crises of representation. The argument, however, requires at least some qualification. As Scott Mainwaring (2008) points out, Bolivia and Ecuador saw a massive expansion in both the quantity and quality of political representation in the 1990s. Constitutional reforms improved and expanded the electoral process by, among other measures, introducing new forms of local democracy. Restrictions to suffrage based on literacy were abandoned, enfranchising members of ethnic minorities who suffer from high rates of illiteracy. Urbanization and education limited the political influence of urban patronage and rural *caciquismo*. What accounted for the crises, according to Mainwaring, was not so much the inability of representative institutions to give voice to hitherto excluded sectors, but the inability of the state to address the citizens' demands for public goods, such as economic well-being, jobs, public security, education and clean government. In other words, failures in state capacity rather than truncated representation best explain the breakdown of trust between citizens and political institutions.

The cases of civil society strife in Bolivia add a further dimension to our analysis of the politics of mass protest, concerning the erosion of trust within civil society organizations. Arguably, civil society alone cannot generate the civic values that are essential for a healthy democracy. The aggregation of interests and the mitigation of polarities that are supposedly mainly promoted by Civil Society I-type relations are political operations that require political mediation. If political institutions fail to perform these functions, civil society becomes not a school of civicness but an arena of naked power struggles. In the absence of a capable state and of strong political institutions, societal relations are in danger of falling into a Hobbesian dystopia rather than a De Tocquevillian town-hall arcadia.

3

POPULISM AND THE RETURN OF THE POLITICAL

Twenty-first century populism in Latin America: Characterizing the politics of redistribution and recognition

In the previous chapter, we looked at how newly activated and mobilized popular movements re-politicized social relations and challenged the status quo from below. In this chapter, we look at processes of politicization from a different perspective, that of political leaders rather than grassroots movements, and at the relations between the two. In the depoliticized notion of democracy that characterized the Miami Consensus of the 1990s, institution building and good governance were supposed to limit the role of charismatic leaders that has been traditionally associated with Latin America's long history of populism. Contrary to the assumptions of those who believed that liberal democracy and free market economics were about to become the foundations of a new regional order, populism never really went away in the region. In a direct challenge to the Miami Consensus in the first decade of the twenty-first century, populism became part of the political appeal of a distinctive group of leaders that advocated political alternatives to liberal democracy and economic alternatives to both the Washington Consensus and its post-Washington Consensus variations.

The claim that Hugo Chávez, Evo Morales and Rafael Correa are 'populists' has revived the debate about what is populism and why it is so prevalent in Latin America. This debate has three interrelated aspects: theoretical, empirical and normative. Theoretically, populism is one of the most highly contested concepts in political analysis. Attempts at defining the concept often mix historical, political and economic elements without a clear insight into what blends them into a unified concept. Empirically, the term has been used to qualify leaders, parties and governments, adding to the conceptual confusion in the use of the term. Moreover, most of those leaders who are said to be populist reject the qualification, a reaction that has to do with populism's negative normative bias (Castañeda 2006).

In an attempt to lift the conceptual fog that envelops the term, some scholars either reject the notion that governments, such as those of Chávez, Correa and Morales, should be labelled as *populist* or, while agreeing that they are indeed populist, they have welcomed the transformative democratic power of radical populism. Based on an empirical study of grassroots organizations and everyday politics in Venezuela, Sara Motta (2011) denies that Chávez is in any way a populist and argues instead that new grassroots forms of organizing power and authority have broken with traditions of Venezuelan politics, of both the left and the right, in which leadership, political lines, and political hierarchy were dominant. However, Ernesto Laclau (2006: 60), who is also sympathetic to Chavismo, believes that the Chávez phenomenon bears all the marks of a populist rupture and that this rupture is positive for the advancement of democracy in the country. The fact that scholars sympathetic to Chávez's government could have such different views about the government's populist condition or otherwise highlights the politically ambiguous and theoretically problematic nature of the term. In order to limit the confusion arising from the use of the term for understanding important aspects of contemporary left-wing Latin American politics, it is thus necessary to briefly discuss the meaning of populism and place it in the context of Latin American history.

Before its current revival, populism was associated with a number of political leaders who dominated the region's political landscape between the 1930s and the 1960s, prominent among them Lázaro Cárdenas in Mexico, Juan Domingo Perón in Argentina, Getulio Vargas in Brazil, Carlos Ibañez in Chile, Juan Velasco Ibarra in Ecuador and Víctor Raúl Haya de la Torre in Peru. Populism, however, has always been about more than just some strong leaders. Studies of populism associated it with a crisis of early to mid-twentieth-century liberal oligarchic political order in the region, provoked by the inability of its institutions to integrate the new industrial working class (Germani 1979). Populist leaders challenged the status quo by constituting new popular identities in antagonism to both the laissez-faire liberalism of the time, dominated by landowning interests, and the political order hegemonized by self-perpetuating political elites. In the discourse of populism, the people was the embodiment of the

69

nation denied political rights and social justice by domestic oligarchies and foreign interests, hence its characterization as 'national
popular'. The strongly personalistic relationship between charismatic
leaders and the people went together with a systematic process of
political organization and mobilization of the popular sectors which
resulted in some of the most important popular movements of twentieth-century Latin America. In this early version of populism, political and economic nationalism went hand in hand. The nation-state
was at the centre of populism's political and economic institutions.
When in control of the state, populist leaders used its resources to
both organize and control their followers in corporatist-style arrangements. The state was also at the apex of the then new economic model
of import substitution industrialization, directly undertaking economic activities, subsidizing domestic industry and allocating rents
between different social sectors. As discussed below, there are significant differences between mid-twentieth-century populism and its
early twenty-first century manifestations but the legacy of the national
popular populism of the twentieth century constituted a repository
of ideational frames (Jobert 1989) and political practices that strongly
influenced its twenty-first century's manifestations.

Interest in populism waned in the 1970s and 1980s, as Latin
America went through a decade of military dictatorships in the 1970s,
followed by processes of transition to democracy in the 1980s. The
dismantling of the corporatist structures that characterized the populist state, the exhaustion of the ISI (Import Substituting Industrialization)
model of economic development and the distinctively more liberal
and pluralist values of the processes of transition to democracy,
appeared to confirm the historically dated nature of Latin American
populism. The theoretical and political onslaught against the ISI
model with which populism was associated meant that the term
mainly came to signify an economic strategy that had failed throughout the region, thus reaffirming its negative normative bias (Dornbusch
and Edwards 1991). Two developments, however, made the assumption about the historically dated nature of populism difficult to
sustain. Firstly, a growing body of academic literature showed that
populism was not exclusive to Latin America and could not be confined to a specific period in the history of the region (Canovan 1999;
Kazin 1998; Laclau 1977; Panizza 2005; Taggart 2000; Weyland
2001; Worsley 1969). Second, news about the death of populism in
Latin America appeared to have been greatly exaggerated, as new
and different varieties of populism became evident in the 1990s.
Moreover, the populism (or neopopulism as it was also labelled) of

the 1990s, associated with leaders such as Carlos Menem of Argentina, Alberto Fujimori of Peru and Fernando Collor de Mello of Brazil, showed its ideological malleability by being articulated to neoliberalism, the economic project that aimed at dismantling ISI (Panizza 2000; Weyland 2004).

From its historical ubiquity and geographical spread, it is clear that populism is not bounded by history or location. From its ideological turns, it is also clear that it has no distinctive ideology, as it effectively incorporates a wide range of diverse and often contradictory political beliefs. In this chapter, we adopt a specifically political definition of populism, broadly shared by a number of scholars, who with slight terminological variations define it as a direct appeal to the people (as the underdogs) against a dominant 'other' (a political or economic elite, a social group, a party system or an economic model) (Canovan 1999; de la Torre 2008; Knight 1998; Laclau 1977, 2006; Peruzzotti 2008; Roberts 1995, 2007). The politically constructed identity of the people depends on a constitutive outside against which a homogenous popular identity is formed. Political antagonism consolidates collective identities because, as Glenn Bowman (2005) put it, in oppressing all of them, the oppressor simultaneously renders all of them 'the same'. The 'other' of populist identities is as diverse as the identity of the people, from liberal Washington insiders or financier plutocrats, according to the US's conservative and liberal variances of American populism (Kazin 1998), to welfare recipients and immigrants in its right-wing, European version and the *partidocracias* (partycracies) in a contemporary version of populism in Latin America. From this notion of populism, it is easy to understand its anti-institutional bias and also the crucial role that leadership plays in processes of populist identification. The plurality of actors who constitute the people in populist discourse is held together not just by their common opposition to an oppressive *other* but by their identification with a leader whose political persona becomes the nodal point of what are otherwise heterogeneous social identities, a role that in other political contexts is mainly played by institutions.

There are three important points that need to be made before we proceed to the empirical study of twenty-first century populism in Latin America. Firstly, the anti-institutional bias of populism refers to its appeal against the *established* political order. But, as Paul Cammack (2000: 152) notes, the moments of unmediated populist appeals to the people are short-lived. Implicit in the populists' critique of existing institutions is the redemptive promise (Canovan 1999) that, once the enemies of the people are deprived of their institutional means of domination, a new political order will emerge in which the people will have an, unmediated, effective and lasting power (Aboy Carlés 2003; Barros 2005). More pragmatically, when populists succeed in gaining office, as Perón did in Argentina in the 1940s and Chávez in Venezuela in the late 1990s, they must set up new institutions based on principles other than those of liberal democracy and shape new political forces in order to consolidate their rule (Panizza 2000). Thus, paradoxically, institution building, or what we call populism's *foundational* drive, is very much part of its supposedly anti-institutional political make-up. Second, the importance of the direct relationship between populist leaders and their followers does not tell us the entire story about the specific nature of the relation, and more specifically the extent to which it is of a top-down nature or a more complex one and about the levels of organization and mobilization of the people. Thirdly, a purely formal theory of populism underplays the normative elements that sustain populism's claims to legitimacy. In populist discourse, the institutional order is fundamentally unjust because it does not represent the people and excludes them from some fundamental cultural, political or material rights. The alleged exclusion at the centre of populism's normative claim could be of a socio-economic nature (an unjust social order; the people exploited by an economic oligarchy), a cultural one or a political one (ethnic discrimination; the sovereign people denied voice in the political community; the corrupt and unrepresentative nature of the party system). In practice, however, the economic and political dimensions of populism are difficult to separate as they express two commonly interrelated dimensions of populist politics: the politics of redistribution and the politics of recognition.

Notions of popular sovereignty raise questions about the relationship between populism, institutions and democracy. Margaret Canovan (1999), by no means an apologist for populism, highlights populists' view of themselves as true democrats, voicing popular grievances and opinions systematically ignored by governments, mainstream parties and the media. She reminds us that many so-called populist leaders favour 'direct democracy', political decision making by referendum and popular initiative, all of which are part of the political baggage of democracy. As she rhetorically asks (1999: 7), if notions of popular power and popular decision are central to democracy, 'why then, are not populists acknowledged as the true democrats they say they are? How is it that they can be often seen as dangerous to democracy: all the more dangerous, indeed, in so far as they get popular support?' (7). An obvious answer to her question lies in the anti-institutional, illiberal nature of populism. The unrestricted exercise of popular sovereignty and the conception of the people as a homogenous collective actor are at best compatible with a majoritarian, Rousseaunian, notion of democracy that leaves little room for political pluralism and the protection of individual human rights. The antagonism between the people and its oppressors that characterizes the discursive logic of populism can potentially justify the exclusion and even the prosecution of those members of the political community that are considered enemies of the people. Moreover, as Arditi (2004: 143) notes, the centrality of the leaders and their direct rapport with the 'common man' transform them into something akin to infallible sovereigns, in that their decisions are unquestionable because they are theirs. And yet populism in Latin America has often voiced legitimate demands for social justice, and populist movements have effectively sought the political inclusion of previously discriminated social groups.

To sum up, populism is not an ideology but a political strategy that, paraphrasing Michael Kazin (1998), is available to any political actor (a leader, a party, a movement) operating in a discursive field in which *the notion of the sovereignty of the people and its inevitable corollary, the conflict between the powerful and the powerless*, are core elements of its political appeal. This strategy has a formal dimension (the antagonism between the people and its oppressors), a political one (its anti-institutional bias) and a normative one (the demands for social justice and political recognition).

What, if anything, is 'populist' about the politics of Chávez, Morales and Correa? As a political strategy, populism is part of the strategic repertoire of political leaders who may not usually be regarded as populists but who occasionally make populist appeals. In the same vein, so-called populist leaders are never entirely defined by their populism and may effectively combine it with non-populist appeals or abandon it in favour of alternative strategies. Many political leaders use the dichotomist populist discourse of the people against the system as well as practices of compromise and accommodation according to the circumstances of time and place. In this sense, it can be argued that Hugo Chávez, Evo Morales and Rafael Correa are populists to the extent and only to the extent that they appealed directly to the people against their countries' political and economic orders, divided the social field into antagonistic camps and promised redistribution and recognition in a newly founded institutional order.

Radical populism in twenty-first century Latin America

We have now the conceptual building blocks to understand the populist revival in contemporary Latin America. Radical left populism emerged in twenty-first century Latin America some twenty years after the start of the longest wave of democratization in the region. It did so in a context of intense electoral competition in institutionally unstable and socially exclusionary democracies. For all the progress made in advancing civil and political rights and in enacting the processes and procedures that are part of a democratic polity, scholars have argued that this was a depoliticized, low quality democracy. In a democracy, politics is about exercising choice and effecting change. Both entail contestation concerning public priorities and policy options (Linz and Stepan 1996: 12). A common critique of the democratic order of the 1990s was that transition to democracy was made at the cost of too many compromises with powerful economic, political and military establishments. The consequence, as Laurence Whitehead (1992: 148–9) put it, was a lowering of popular expectations of what could be achieved through political action that favoured neoliberal (or at least low participation) forms of electoral politics.

The paradox of a depoliticized democracy can be further understood from three interrelated analytical perspectives. The first one was the blunting of political antagonisms, which is central to the political game. Of course, the 1990s were far from being a conflict-free decade. But conflict was certainly more constrained than in the past, and perhaps necessarily so. The polarization between the radical left and the extreme right in the context of Cold War politics in the 1960s and early 1970s significantly contributed to the wave of military dictatorships of the 1970s. When the region started its transition to democracy in the 1980s, the main political actors involved in the negotiations were conscious of the importance of moderation and consensus to secure still fragile democracies (O'Donnell, Schmitter and Whitehead 1986; Przeworski 1991).[1]

The second aspect of the depoliticization of democracy was top-down economic reform. Paradoxically, it was the change from the Import-Substitution-Industrialization (ISI) model of economic development of the 1970s to the free market economic model of the 1990s that contributed to the perception that democracy in Latin America had been hollowed out by the lack of choice concerning economic policy. Several aspects of this process of radical economic change contributed to this view. Firstly, given the depth of the economic crisis of the 1980s and particularly the onset of hyperinflation in several

74

countries of the region, the adoption of free market economics was not seen as the result of political choice but rather of the lack of alternatives. Second, external actors played a crucial role in determining the direction of change. The International Monetary Fund's (IMF) abuse of conditionality to push through free market reforms was perceived less as a voluntary agreement between equal partners than the heavy-handed imposition of economic reform by a democratically unaccountable foreign organization controlled by the advanced industrial economies. Thirdly, many fundamental reforms were enacted by presidential decrees that bypassed Congress and provided for only minimal deliberation.

The third element of the democratic settlement of the 1980s that marked the retrenchment of politics was the retreat of the state and the deactivation of civil society. The state, which was the nodal point of both political and economic activity under the ISI economic model, was now conceived as having a more limited, less political and more technocratic role (Leftwich 2000). The weakening of the trade unions and other social movements as a result of the processes of privatization and de-industrialization limited the ability of increasingly fragmented subordinate sectors to mobilize in defence of their demands. Political parties went through similar transformations, as the weakening of labour movements and the shift away from the mass-based party organizations typical of the ISI era caused party systems to converge on elitist organizational models during the neoliberal era (Roberts 2002: 3).

The implications of the moderation of political antagonisms, the retrenchment of the state and the deactivation of social movements in the context of radical processes of free market reforms are captured in the argument put forward by Huber, Rueschemeyer and Stephens (1997: 338) that strides towards introducing and consolidating formal democracy in Latin America were combined with a move away from more fully participatory democracy and equality. To the political constraints and institutional weaknesses of liberal democracy in Latin America in the 1990s should be added the political repercussions of its economic failures which, as noted in the Introduction, were particularly felt in Bolivia, Ecuador and Venezuela. Market reforms fragmented societies between a rather narrow social strata that had the education, capital and job opportunities to benefit from the economic opening and a much larger social group that suffered from increasing inequalities and lack of protection from the force of the markets (Roberts 2007: 330). Economic and political dislocations provided the political opportunity for the re-politicization of collective grievances in antagonism to neoliberal economics and the parties that had dominated the region's political landscape for most of the 1990s. In challenging the depoliticized democracy of the Miami Consensus, radical left populism re-politicized economic policy, denounced *partycracies*, unified fragmented popular identities and mobilized the popular sectors against both the political and the economic order. The following section examines three representative cases of radical left populism in contemporary Latin America.

Bolivia: Re-founding the nation

In the first decade of the twenty-first century, Evo Morales, the leader of Bolivia's largest political movement, the Movimiento al Socialismo (MAS), became the country's first indigenous president. The Movement's political base combined coca farmers, historically excluded but newly politicized indigenous groups, urban informal workers, industrial trade unions and disenchanted members of the progressive middle classes into the largest and best organized party in the country. How did Morales, the leader of a group of small farmers that cultivated an illegal plant (coca), manage to set up such a powerful coalition in a relatively short period of time? To understand how MAS became the largest party in Bolivia, and Morales the country's first indigenous president, we need to look at Morales's political strategy within the context of social and political dislocations resulting from uneven processes of democratization and economic reform.

In Bolivia, the association between re-democratization and neoliberal reforms became probably stronger than anywhere else in Latin America. The country regained its democracy in 1982 but many Bolivians felt that it was only after the 1985 elections that the new democratic era really started in the country (Salman 2007). Just months after the inauguration of the new coalition government headed by the veteran leader of the 1952 nationalist revolution, Víctor Paz Estenssoro, the government enacted one of the earliest packages of structural adjustment and free market economic reforms in the region, the so-called New Economic Policy (NEP). Among other measures, the reforms included a reduction in public spending, the closure of inefficient state-owned tin mines and the promotion of foreign direct investment, trade liberalization and the privatization of public enterprises. The reforms were highly successful in restoring political and economic order after the social unrest and hyperinflation that characterized the administration of Paz Estenssoro's predecessor, President Hernán Siles Zuazo (1982–5). The vanquishing of hyper-inflation gave the new economic policy substantial political support but the reforms also incurred considerable social costs that were burdened on the industrial working class (thousands of whom lost their jobs in the mining industry) and the poorest sectors of society. In the 1990s, successive governments built on the NEP's initial success and on the strong elite consensus behind the reforms by continuing to advance free market economic policies together with attempts at reforming the country's political institutions, particularly during Gonzalo Sánchez de Lozada's first presidency (1993–7).[2] However, the close association between democracy and neoliberalism meant that a crisis of legitimacy of one was always likely to contaminate the other.

Politically, Bolivia appeared to be for a time an unlikely success story of democratic consolidation and economic reform. Under the country's distinctive presidential system, if no presidential candidate obtained a majority of the popular vote, the president was chosen by Congress, which made the creation of governmental coalitions a political necessity. 'Pacted democracy', as the system came to be known, provided governability to a country that had a long tradition of being ungovernable. However, pacted democracy did little to eradi-cate a patrimonialist and in many ways corrupt political culture in which parties traded political support for public jobs and state rents. The underside of pacted democracy was that it came to be perceived by many ordinary citizens as little more than self-interested agree-ments cemented by nepotism and the shared spoils of office, com-bined with a lack of responsiveness to citizens' demands (Assies and Salman 2003; Salman 2007: 118; Tapia and Toranzo Roca 2000).[3]

The perception of governmental coalitions as unprincipled alli-ances was reinforced by the formation of unlikely partnerships between parties that had been bitter political enemies in the recent past, such as the alliance between former left-winger Jaime Paz Zamora's Movimiento de Izquierda Revolucionario (Movement of the Revolutionary Left – MIR) and former right-wing dictator Hugo Banzer in 1989 and the 2002 alliance between the Movimiento Nacional Revolucionario (National Revolutionary Movement – MNR) and MIR that elected Sánchez de Lozada for a second mandate. As a result of the agreement, Sánchez de Lozada took office, having polled just 22.5 per cent of the vote which seriously dented his legiti-macy before large sections of the citizenship. While the succession of constitutional governments elected in free and fair elections gave

Bolivia its longest uninterrupted period of democracy since independence, support for democracy fell by almost 20 per cent between
1996 and 2004. In the same year (2004), just 16 per cent of Bolivians
said that they were satisfied with the way democracy worked in their
country, putting the country among the four lowest in the region in
the ranking of satisfaction with democracy. More tellingly, only 37
per cent of Bolivians (the lowest percentage in Latin America) believed
the way they voted could change the future (Corporación
Latinobarómetro 2004).[4]

Popular perceptions about the working of Bolivian democracy in
the 1990s matched academic criticisms of the depoliticized democracy outlined in the previous section. Elite consensus on free market
economics was construed by those opposing neoliberalism as evidence that all parties were the same, that governments ignored
popular grievances and that politicians made empty promises and
offered no genuine solutions to the popular sectors' continuous hard-
ship. There was, however, little appetite in Bolivia for the return of
military governments and, more generally, for political authoritarianism. Rather, public opinion's discontent with the political system
showed in the short-lived emergence in the early 1990s of a number
of populist alternatives (Conciencia de Patria, CONDEPA and Unidad
Cívica Solidaridad, UCS) of no particular ideological leanings and,
later in the decade, by the growing electoral support for radical non-
traditional parties, MAS and MIP (Movimiento Indígena Pachakuti)
that challenged the prevailing political and economic order in more
fundamental ways.

Paradoxically, the looming crisis of representation of Bolivia's traditional party system was exacerbated by reforms aimed at strengthening the legitimacy of the system and promoting popular participation.
The reforms were consistent with second-generation market reforms
(Naim 1994), goals of decentralizing economic resources, empowering civil society, addressing social deficits, promoting multiculturalism and fostering good governance and accountability. Most of
these reforms were passed during the first presidency of Sánchez de
Lozada.[5] They included a constitutional reform that established the
pluri-cultural nature of Bolivian society, laws of popular participation
(LPPP 1551) and administrative decentralization (LDA 1654) that
enhanced the political role of social organizations; the creation of
uninominal electoral districts and the setting up of a Defensoría del
Pueblo (office of the Ombudsman). Political and administrative
decentralization and electoral reform increased the political salience
of local politics, particularly in rural areas, opening institutional

spaces for the politicization of the rural–urban cleavage (Zuazo 2009) in which the rural dimension heavily overlapped with indigenous and peasant (*campesinos*) identities. Thus, the unintended outcome of the reforms was not the consolidation of the party system but rather the deepening of the crisis of representation of the country's traditional parties. The parties' loss of support resulted from the higher political legitimacy endowed to social mandates based on indigenous and regional affiliations over traditional party political representation (Fundación UNIR Bolivia 2010), combined with the lack of real impact of the new participatory structures on macro-political and economic decisions. The crisis of the traditional political order opened political opportunities in the new local structures for anti-systemic and non-traditional candidates and for the radicalization and politicization of ethnic identities beyond the ideological limits of cultural multiculturalism.[6]

While it is true that the free market reforms did not generate enough economic growth to lift substantial numbers of Bolivian citizens out of poverty, they nonetheless prompted a process of accelerated regional economic development centred on the agriculture, oil- and gas-rich eastern provinces, the so-called half moon of the country. The regionally lopsided and socially narrow nature of this process of modernization exacerbated regional, class, ethnic and cultural divisions in Bolivia that crystallized into two historically rooted antagonistic and mutually reinforcing political narratives (Eaton 2007: 79–80). One of these narratives, enunciated by dominant political and economic groups of the eastern region of the country, particularly in the provinces of Santa Cruz and Tarija, contrasted the entrepreneurial, culturally modern, economically prosperous, ethnically white and mestizo lowlands, the so-called 'Nación Camba', with the underdeveloped, indigenous-dominated, culturally backward-looking and economically parasitic highlands.[7] The second narrative, dominant in the highlands, had its roots in the resurgent indigenous nationalism of the 1980s and 1990s, as elaborated by aymara intellectuals and political leaders, particularly Felipe Quispe (Sanjinés 2004). Of particular importance for the resurgence of indigenous nationalism were revisionist accounts of the five hundredth anniversary of Spanish colonization of what is today Latin America that gave new political salience to the historical grievances of indigenous peoples (Mayorga 2009; Zuazo 2009). In a mirror image of the discourse of the 'Nación Camba', it presented the history of Bolivia as the unfolding of 500 years of oppression and exclusion of its indigenous majority by the Creole-mestizo elite, and of subordination of the national interests to the dictates of colonial and neocolonial powers, of which neoliberalism was only its latest manifestation.[8]

It is in this highly fragmented and divided social context that the political strategy of Morales as the leader of the Movimiento al Socialismo (MAS) party should be considered. The triumph of Morales in the 2005 presidential election reaped the legacy of struggle of the rural *sindicatos* and of the mass popular protests that exposed the gap between legality and legitimacy at the heart of Bolivia's political institutions (Bonifaz 2008). But, as Sven Harten (2008) notes, the 'unified people' that arose from the articulation of coca farmers' grievances and mainly urban anti-privatization protests of 2000–5 was not the result of spontaneous actions but a product of the political strategy by Morales and other rural union leaders of construction of a new political force, the MAS party, that originated in the rural areas and expanded to the cities. The party had its roots in a tightly organized and highly politicized social group, the rural unions (*sindicatos*) of the coca growers ('cocaleros'), peasants of the trópicos region, who lived on the fringes of the country's legal and political order and had a long history of confrontation (and mostly failed) negotiations with the state.[9] MAS, under Morales's leadership, managed to appeal to Bolivia's indigenous majority while transcending its rural and ethnic origins to represent a broad popular coalition. The original political organization evolved out of a movement set up to defend the interest of the coca farmers in a powerful political force that articulated the country's militant rural and urban social organizations behind a political project for re-founding the nation, setting up new political institutions, effecting agrarian reform, establishing state control of natural resources and promoting the redistribution of wealth. Morales's political discourse drew from the country's rich *nacional popular* tradition associated with the 1952 revolution (Céspedes 1956; Montenegro 1990) and combined it with new ideological elements that reflected the country's social and political changes of the 1990s. Economic nationalism, understood as the public ownership of national resources and the centrality assigned to the state in economic development, was at the heart of the 1952 national popular revolution's political programme and was also integral to MAS's political project. But in a new take on Bolivia's tradition of economic nationalism and anti-imperialism, Morales was able to link successfully the *cocaleros'* struggle against the US-sponsored campaign to eradicate coca plantations with the popular mobilizations against the privatization of water and gas. The party of the coca growers was thus able to position itself as the defender of national sovereignty and natural resources against the *politicos vendepatrias*. The defence of coca production as a matter of sovereignty against US impositions also allowed MAS to attack the Bolivian state as a neocolonial state ruled by the country's traditional parties, including the MNR (the party that led the 1952 revolution) which, MAS argued, had long betrayed its anti-oligarchical and anti-imperialist origins (Costa Benavides 2005; Harten 2008; Stefanoni 2003).[10]

While Morales's discourse drew ideological elements from the MNR's national popular tradition, there were clear political dividing lines between MAS and the MNR. The main differences between the two parties concerned their imagining of the people, their social bases of support and the relations between the political parties and their allied social movements. 'The people' of the MNR's 1952 national popular discourse was conceived as a multi-class alliance in which a shared national identity and common economic interests bound workers, peasants and the middle classes in a homogenous popular identity that did not allow for cultural or ethnic differences: in the vocabulary of the 1952 revolution, the words 'indio' and even 'indigenous' were replaced by the term *campesino* (peasant) (Salman 2007: 118). Whatever ethnic, linguistic and cultural differences were still apparent, these were to be homogenized by cultural nationalism, education and economic progress. MAS's conception of the people as the incarnation of the nation also includes a multi-ethnic and multi-class social alliance. But while the core of the MNR's social base of support was the industrial (mining) working class organized in the powerful Central Obrera Boliviana (COB), the social base of MAS is concentrated in the rural *sindicatos* of the region of the trópicos and the informal workers of the sprawling city of El Alto, near La Paz, many of them indigenous rural migrants.

Morales's cultural construction of popular identities is based on the exaltation rather than on the erasing of cultural and ethnic differences and grounded in indigenous rather than mestizo nationalism. For its ethno-nationalist political construction, Morales drew on the intellectual output of a new generation of aymara and quechua intellectuals and political activists, many of whom were active in the Katarista movement that emerged in the 1970s. The MNR's leadership was composed of middle-class Creole intellectual and politicians, such as Hernán Siles Suazo and Víctor Paz Estenssoro, and industrial union leaders, such as Juan Lechín. In contrast, in MAS's twenty-first century ethno-nationalism, the emphasis is in the self-representation of the indigenous and peasant communities with grassroots union

81

and community leaders, such as Morales himself, assuming positions of political leadership and being elected to Congress and later, during Morales's presidency, to positions in the Executive.

As noted above, the politicization of ethnic identities gave MAS a strong base of support among the country's indigenous people but at the same time it made potentially more difficult the constitution of a broader popular identity that transcended ethnic differences. Raúl Madrid (2008) shows how broader identification was made possible by what he terms an inclusive ethnic nationalism. He argues that low levels of ethnic polarization and the ambiguity and fluidity of ethnic identification in Bolivia meant that MAS could appeal not only to self-identified indigenous people (as was the case with the Katarista parties) but also to people from other ethnic groups who supported the party based on its positions on non-ethnic issues. Morales's personality, charismatic leadership and political appeal were crucial to this purpose. He was an Indian but he was also a politician and a union leader. The campaign for the recognition of the cultural, political and social equality of Bolivia's indigenous majority was a dominant feature of his political discourse. It is striking from reading his speeches to note how they are dominated by moral and political universals: 'dignity', 'equality', 'sovereignty', 'justice', 'liberation'. The reason for this emphasis lies, according to Morales (2006), in the history of cultural and racial discrimination, political exclusion and economic exploitation of Bolivia's indigenous majority. But the terms also reflected the broader themes of social justice and political and economic nationalism common to large sections of the population. Madrid also shows how self-representation of ethnic communities was tempered by the incorporation of non-indigenous representatives to MAS congressional and ministerial ranks and by the nomination of a prominent white intellectual (Álvaro García Linera) as Morales's vice-presidential candidate (Madrid 2008: 488).

The politics of recognition and the politics of redistribution went hand in hand in the political construction of populist antagonisms in Bolivia. This was attested by MAS's original campaign to increase oil and gas companies' royalties paid to the state and by subsequent confrontations between the central government and the gas- and oil-rich 'half-moon' provinces of Santa Cruz, Beni, Pando and Tarija over the allocation of rents. Morales (and MAS) articulated economic and political grievances about the government's neoliberal economic policies, the appropriation of water, oil and gas resources by foreign companies, the US-imposed eradication of coca plants, political corruption and violent military responses to set up a political dividing line between the popular movements and the country's traditional political parties. Thus, historical grievances about the plundering of the country's silver and gold deposits by Spain's colonial power resonated with contemporary grievances against predatory multinational companies to legitimize a populist political rupture with the country's political order, history and institutional heritage (Panizza and Miorelli 2009).

As noted in the introduction to this chapter, the other side of populism's anti-institutional appeal is its foundational aspirations. The redemptive promise of MAS's populism is explicit in the party's calls to re-found the Bolivian nation on new normative, cultural, political and economic principles that would, in Morales's own words, 'end the colonial state' and 'reach true equality for all Bolivians'.[11] Calls for a Constituent Assembly were meant to materialize the foundational project and restore the lost legitimacy to the country's political institutions to process political conflicts (Fundación UNIR 2010). However, the process of discussion and approval of the new constitution in the Constituent Assembly exposed populism's own fault lines. Political battles over the rules for the election of the Constituent Assembly, its terms of reference and the majorities required for the approval of the new constitution exposed the populist illusion of a fully reconciled people in which the underdogs of populist antagonism become the true holders of sovereignty. It was thus not surprising that in Bolivia the Assembly set up to reconcile the people and re-found the nation became instead the focus of deep polarization and political strife. The Constitutional Assembly faced questions as to whether claims for regional autonomy by the provincial governments of the eastern regions should be regarded as legitimate democratic demands (and therefore as part of the process of constituting a plural demos) or whether provincial autonomist movements were to be treated as the political expression of an anti-national and anti-popular other, alien to the people and a threat to its unity.[12]

The conflict brought Bolivia to the brink of civil war and was eventually defused by political negotiations and international mediation. A draft constitution was eventually agreed by the country's main political parties in October 2008 and approved by over 60 per cent of the popular vote in a referendum in January 2009. The new constitution, however, was rejected in four of Bolivia's nine provinces, showing the continuous polarization of Bolivia's society.[13] Nonetheless, the strong majority in favour of the new constitution, together with Morales's re-election in December 2009 with over 60 per cent of the vote and MAS's victory in the congressional elections of the same date, suggest that the new institutions enjoy considerable levels of popular support and political legitimacy. While conflicts and political tensions have far from disappeared, particularly around the implementation of the constitution's dispositions on territorial and ethnic autonomy, the process of political incorporation headed by MAS that started in the coca-growing region of the tropics appears to have entered a more institutional phase.

The political rise of MAS and of its leader, Evo Morales, allows us to reconsider the nature of populism and the combination of populist and other non-populist strategies that characterized Morales's political campaign. If, as argued by Roberts (2007), populism is understood as top-down individual leadership that directly appeals to unorganized members of the popular sector, it is clear that Morales does not fit the picture. Morales's leadership had strong 'caudillista' elements, with roots in traditional forms of indigenous leadership and other historical forms of popular representation. In a political system in which there was little trust in institutions, trust is bestowed in leaders rather than in parliaments or parties (Zuazo 2009: 41), which reinforced the personalist elements of Morales's political appeal. But his political ascendancy was the result of a bottom-up process of political mobilization rooted in highly politicized and strongly organized rural unions and Morales's political trajectory cannot be understood without reference to his position within these organizations. While personalistic leadership is a crucial element in the anti-institutional appeal of populism, successful cases of populism require the organization and mobilization of its supporters. MAS was such an organization. In this process, Morales provided strong leadership and became the nodal point for the unification of highly fragmented popular actors into a new common popular identity.

The denomination of MAS-IPSP as the so-called 'political instrument for the sovereignty of the people' crystallizes several elements of the populist mode of identification: the notion that political parties are divisive of the people, the mistrust of *partidocracias* and the quest for the unmediated representation of the people to ensure the exercise of their sovereign rights. The corollary of this mode of political identification is a majoritarian rather than a pluralist understanding of democracy, grounded in the notion of an oppressed people denied their human, cultural, social, economic and political rights. Yet, the new constitution retains important elements of liberal democracy combined with new participatory structures that at least on paper reinforce rather than erase institutional arenas for the autonomous expression of regional and ethnic autonomies.

MAS capitalized on the intense anti-systemic protests that led to the fall of Sánchez de Lozada and Mesa to polarize the citizens against the traditional parties but neither MAS nor Morales were complete outsiders. While backing mass popular mobilizations, they also worked within the country's political institutions (Hochstetler and Friedman 2008: 9), often mediating between formal and informal institutions, and taking advantage of the electoral processes to expand their appeal.[14] The combination of institutional and extra-institutional action was maintained during the process of constitutional reform in which MAS's representatives to the Constituent Assembly overrode procedural rules but subsequently negotiated amendments that made it acceptable to the main opposition forces. The pattern of anti-institutional and institutional strategies and the combination of political antagonisms, together with the acknowledging of differences that characterized Morales's (and MAS) political strategy, have continued in office. It shows that, except in exceptional circumstances, populism is always combined with other, non-populist, political strategies available to political actors in weakly institutionalized democracies.

Ecuador: A long tradition of populist politics

The rise of Correa to the presidency should be placed in the political context of a country with one of the strongest traditions of populism in the region. It is a tradition rooted in the historical legacy of former president José María Velasco Ibarra that gained renewed salience between 1996 and 2008, a period in which politics in Ecuador went through a protracted process of deinstitutionalization. *Velasquismo*, the political movement named after its leader, was the most important political force in Ecuador for over four decades. Velasco Ibarra himself was five times president of Ecuador (1934–5, 1944–6, 1952–6, 1960–1 and 1968–72) but his political legacy was not so much the product of his years in office but the fact that he created a template for Ecuadorian politics to the present.[15]

Two political elements mark the populist legacy of Velasco Ibarra. The first one was the framing of politics as an irreconcilable struggle between two sides, in his case, the Liberal *oligarquía* and the Velasquista *pueblo* (de la Torre 2004: 695). The second element of *Velasquismo* was that it was the leader of the people mobilized in the streets rather than elite-dominated formal political institutions that claimed to best represent the people's democratic demands. As Carlos de la Torre (2006: 32, cited in Montúfar 2008: 294) put it, in Ecuador the mass popular occupation of public spaces by protesters (streets, public squares, etc.) continues to be a source of political legitimacy often more powerful than the rule of law and representative institutions.

The weak legitimacy of Ecuador's representative institutions and the claims of populism to represent the sovereign people outside formal institutions was vividly exemplified by Colonel Lucio Gutiérrez's justification of the forced resignation of president Jamil Mahuad in January 2000 by an alliance of mobilized indigenous organizations and a military revolt. The revolt leader, Colonel Gutiérrez, justified the deposition of Mahuad in the following terms: 'Sovereignty is rooted in a people whose will is the basis of authority and who by exercising that right, in a sovereign manner, democratically majoritarian and direct, has elected its representatives.' Answering Mahuad's allegations that he had effectively headed a military coup, Gutiérrez further stated: 'It is a sovereign election, it is a direct election, it is a majoritarian election' (Herrera Aráuz 2001: 62–4 and 96, quoted in de la Torre 2007).

Mass popular protests and populist leaders of both the left and the right overshadowed institutional politics in Ecuador in the second half of the 1990s and the first decade of the new century. In a context of high electoral volatility, party political fragmentation and the progressive loss of support for the country's traditional political parties, mass protests led to the impeachment or forced resignation of three constitutionally elected presidents between 1996 and 2005, exposing the weak legitimacy of the country's political system.[16] However, weak political institutions masked the still considerable influence of the traditional political parties and the armed forces. Political outsiders or pseudo outsiders won elections in 1996 (Abdalá Bucaram) and 2002 (Lucio Gutiérrez) but, once in office, they depended on the support of the parties that controlled Congress to ensure governability. As Ana María Larrea (2005) put it, the people in the street deposed presidents, the military arbitrated the conflict and political parties decided on the succession, leading to a new phase in the cycle of conflict between politics and institutions. As noted below, this pattern has only been broken by the election of Rafael Correa.

There are obvious parallels between mass protests and political deinstitutionalization in Ecuador and in Bolivia. Politicized social movements played a significant role in the mass protests that led to the resignation of President Jamil Mahuad in 2000 in Ecuador and of President Sánchez de Losada and Mesa in Bolivia in 2003 and 2005 respectively (see chapter 2). But while in Bolivia organized popular movements continued to play a major role in the setting of MAS and in the campaign that led Morales to office, populist leaders in Ecuador did not establish organic links with social movements. Instead, Abdalá Bucaram, who won the presidential election in 1996, and the right-wing millionaire businessman Álvaro Noboa, who unsuccessfully contested the elections of 1998, 2006 and 2009, relied on extensive networks of patronage that linked their political campaigns with the voting poor through material benefits in exchange for political support (Freidenberg 2008).

When links between politicized social movements and populist leaders were established, they proved fragile and short-lived, as was the case of the alliance between Colonel Lucio Gutiérrez and the indigenous party Pachakutik in the 2002 presidential election. Following the failure of the 2000 coup, Gutiérrez was briefly imprisoned and, after benefiting from an amnesty, he came out of jail to campaign in and win the 2002 presidential election in the second round. His first-round political campaign combined military, ethnic and popular elements in an attempt to articulate new popular identities (Montúfar 2008: 300). As was the case with another military officer turned politician, Hugo Chávez, in Venezuela, his military investiture and the failed military coup that he led in 2000 were central to his political campaign.

However, once elected president, Gutiérrez distanced himself from the popular sectors that had backed his presidential campaign and broke with Pachakutik. Instead, he sought to gain the support of some of the country's traditional parties, as well as of the US government and the business elite. He abandoned his economic nationalist programme and followed orthodox free market economic policies, becoming a close political and military ally of the US. It was only towards the end of his presidency, when he was under threat of impeachment for attempting to control the Supreme Court, that he returned to his populist roots. He began to attack the so-called 'oligarchy', a term that had been largely absent in his presidential campaign. He assimilated the oligarchy to the political parties, the so-called *partidocracia* that wanted to throw him out of office. He unsuccessfully sought to promote plebiscitarian mechanisms to legitimize his attempts to concentrate power in the Executive by restructuring the country's political institutions. To prevent Congress from impeaching him for violating the independence of the judiciary, he mobilized his followers in the streets to confront, often with the use of violence, mass protests against his government. To shore up his political support among the poor, he used the Ministerio de Bienestar Social (Social Welfare Ministry) to set up a patronage network for the distribution of social benefits. Political polarization spilled onto the streets of the capital, Quito, with confrontations between supporters and opponents of the president (Montúfar 2008). Eventually, mass popular protests made it evident that Gutiérrez had lost the battle of the streets and the military withheld support, forcing him to flee the country.

Rafael Correa, who succeeded Gutiérrez after the interim presidency of Alfredo Palacio (2005–7), shows how the anti-institutional strategy of the politics of antagonism can be used to set up new political institutions. Populism's anti-establishment message of the politics of anti-politics can under the right conditions be an effective electoral strategy. As shown by the case of Gutiérrez, once in office populist leaders face a number of options. On one hand, they can either radicalize the populist strategy of the 'politics of anti-politics' and continue their attacks against the political establishment with the intention of bypassing other state institutions and rule with the support of mobilized public opinion (as Collor de Mello did in Brazil). On the other hand, they can seek the support of the political establishment, thus losing their status as political outsiders and risking becoming entangled in the same discredited web of pacts and compromises of the 'politics as usual' they had denounced while in opposition (Panizza 2000: 187–8; Freidenberg 2008). Alternatively, they can seek to promote new institutional arrangements that consolidate their rule while depriving the opposition of their previous institutional strongholds. While Gutiérrez followed the strategy of accommodation with the establishment and lost power, Rafael Correa chose the foundational path and won re-election.

Correa was the political heir of the so-called 'movimiento forajido' (the 'outlaws movement') whose mobilizations brought down President Gutiérrez in 2005. It was different to the demonstrations led by indigenous parties and social movements that had forced the resignation of President Mahuad in 2000, as the *forajidos* were mainly middle-class urban citizens who had few organized links with popular movements, relying instead on radio programmes and other means of communications, such as mobile phones, to coordinate their actions. In their social make-up and the targeting of the political class under the slogan 'everybody out' (*que se vayan todos*), they resembled more the people in the streets of middle-class neighbourhoods of Buenos Aires in 2001–2 than the urban and rural poor and organized social movements that constituted the bulk of the protesters in Bolivia's water and gas wars.

Correa was a political outsider. He is a technocrat (an economist by training) with no previous party affiliation whose only experience of public life was a brief stint as economic minister of Gutiérrez's interim successor, Alfredo Palacio. He positioned himself as the leader of a second independence movement in a political narrative that blended traditional historical figures from the nineteenth century, such as General Eloy Alfaro, with contemporary revolutionary ones, such as Che Guevara (de la Torre 2010). In contrast with Morales, he did not have an organized power base within the country's social movements and, in contrast with Chávez, he did not seek to build one once in office. In his first presidential campaign, he captured the spirit of the *forajido* movement by placing himself at the head of what he called 'a citizens' revolution' against the political parties and the country's allegedly corrupt political elite. The expression did not convey the notion of citizens as holders of political rights acting individually within the institutional rules of the game, but the promise of a clean sweep of the country's extant institutions to displace traditional power holders from their positions of power and give voice directly to the citizens in a new participatory institutional setting. His programme defined the new constitutional order as 'an active radical and participatory democracy'. To this purpose, Correa embarked on a high-risk political strategy that entailed a series of rapid-fire plebiscites and elections that crystallized political antagonisms with the traditional parties, performing as instances of majoritarian inclusion and giving him the legitimacy to redraw political institutions without too much consideration for the letter of the law (Conaghan and de la Torre 2008).

In a period of four years between 2006 and 2009, he entered five major political campaigns: to win the presidency, to win the right to call for a Constituent Assembly, to elect his candidates for the Assembly, to have the constitution approved and to win re-election. Throughout his campaigns, Correa used confrontational tactics to target the political order (the *partidocracia*) and what he called 'the long and dark neoliberal night' (Pachano 2008). In the presidential and congressional election of 2006, he refused to present a slate of candidates for Congress to distance himself from the party system. Instead, he ran an intensely personal campaign, calling for a Constituent Assembly that would radically redistribute power away from the political parties and towards the people. Using a pun on his name (Correa = Whip), he often campaigned with a whip in hand, threatening to smack his political opponents (Conaghan and de la Torre 2008). After winning the 2006 election, he said that 'Ecuador had voted for itself' (*'Ecuador votó por si mismo'*) (de la Torre 2010).

Once in office and without parliamentary representation of his own, Correa upped the ante by radicalizing his confrontation with the country's traditional parties and institutions. When Congress refused to sanction a plebiscite to call for a Constituent Assembly, he waged a legal and political campaign against congressional opponents, as a result of which 57 congressmen were stripped of their mandates, along with members of the Constitutional Court who were accused of obstructing the electoral process (Conaghan and de la Torre 2008). The moves were of an extremely dubious legal foundation but were effectively legitimized by a massive 'yes' vote in the plebiscite to call a Constituent Assembly in April 2007, which further widened the gap between legality and legitimacy in Ecuadorian politics. The plebiscite effectively sealed the defeat of the country's traditional parties and gave Correa a popular mandate to reshape the country's political institutions.

Correa's style of government has been labelled as 'permanent campaigning' (Conaghan and de la Torre 2008) but can be equally labelled as permanent antagonism, as he systematically attacked the press, his internal political adversaries and the US and Colombian governments, as well as the IMF and the World Bank and, of course, his *bête noire*, 'neoliberalism'. He combined the politics of antagonism with the policies of economic redistribution. Already in the 2006 electoral campaign, Correa launched a programme to register voters as potential beneficiaries of his prospective welfare policies (ibid.). In his first months in office, he doubled poverty assistance payments, doubled credits available for housing loans and reduced electricity rates for low-income consumers (Feinberg 1997; Pachano 2008). He complemented his redistributionist policies with high-profile confrontations with multinational companies, including a Brazilian construction company, and in 2008 defaulted on what his government considered the 'illegitimate external debt'. For Correa, the politics of antagonism and the politics of redistribution delivered the goals of accruing his political capital, weakening his opponents and reshaping the country's political institutions. Just 29 months after he was first elected, Correa won re-election on 26 April 2009 with an absolute majority of votes, becoming the first president of his country to secure a second consecutive term since the nineteenth century.

If the plebiscitarian politics of his first three years in office crystallized the majoritarian elements of populist democracy, the new constitution, approved in a referendum in September 2008, is an expression of its foundational promise. Economic dispositions seek to replace the market economy with a 'social solidarity economic system' (art. 283), based on economic redistribution, planning, national control over natural resources and the state allocation of key economic resources. The new constitution tightens state control of vital industries, such as mining and telecommunications; allows the state to expropriate and redistribute idle farmland; bans large landholdings and mandates that older citizens should enjoy free health care. It includes an extensive list of individual and social rights and acknowledges a plurality of legal sources, particularly indigenous groups' legal traditions (art. 171). The new political institutions strengthen presidential power, allowing Correa to stand for a further four-year term in office after his re-election in 2009. It weakens political parties and the National Assembly and sets up a number of decision-making bodies with the direct participation of the citizens and representatives of social organizations. Correa's constitutional changes and electoral victories appear to have put an end to a long decade of political instability in Ecuador. However, Ecuador remains a divided society, ethnically and geographically.

President Correa does not have the strongly organized support base of President Morales. What distinguishes Correa from the other cases of radical populism analysed in this chapter is his distance from some of the country's most powerful social movements, which he regards as defenders of corporatist interest rather than the national interest. During his first years in office, he clashed with teachers, public employees, some ecological movements and above all the formerly powerful indigenous organization CONAIE (see chapter 2). He transferred control of bilingual education from the indigenous movement back to the state and cut state funding to several public bodies controlled by social movements (de la Torre 2010; *The Economist* 2009) and he relies more on the politics of redistribution than on the politics of recognition to secure support, which makes him vulnerable to a downturn in the country's economy.

91

Venezuela: Radical populism and twenty-first century socialism

President Hugo Chávez of Venezuela is widely regarded by scholars as the most representative case of populism in contemporary Latin America (Laclau 2006; Roberts 2007; Weyland 2003, 2007). His politics encapsulate some of the key features of populism that are the subject of this chapter, particularly the populist rupture with the previous order, the politics of antagonism, the centrality of charismatic leadership and the foundational drive to set up a new political and economic order.

Politically, the riots that rocked the country's political order in February 1989 and the considerable popular support for the failed military coup of 1992 (see chapter 1) fit the argument that populism emerges as the product of a crisis of representation. Chávez's charismatic leadership also appears to correspond with the notion of populism as a direct, unmediated, relationship between leader and followers. Last but not least, the government's role promoting and funding regime-friendly social organizations tallies with Roberts's (2007) notion of populism as characterized by the top-down mobilization of followers. All these aspects are integral to Chavismo but arguably, important as these are, Chávez's appeal is grounded in more than the crisis of traditional parties that he hastens to promote and on his use of oil money to fund ambitious social programmes and pliant social movements. In line with our analysis of populism, it is necessary to look at the politics of recognition of Chavismo, to Chávez's personal leadership and to the institutional foundations of Chávez's Bolivarian revolution, later redefined as twenty-first century socialism.

Hugo Chávez was first elected president of Venezuela in 1998. Between 1998 and 2009, the Venezuelan citizens have been called to vote a record number of times in national and local polls, elections for a Constituent Assembly and a number of plebiscites and referendums, including a recall referendum and two plebiscites to allow Chávez to stand indefinitely for re-election. Of these, Chávez only lost the December 2007 plebiscite on a constitutional amendment that would have allowed the president to stand for re-election indefinitely, which was subsequently passed when the question was put again to the electorate in February 2009. While there are legitimate reservations about the broader political context in which these polls took place, particularly on the use of state resources to favour official candidates, pressures on public sector employees to support the gov-

92

ernment and low-level harassment of opposition candidates (Hidalgo 2009; Petkoff 2008), voting has been considered by observers on the whole to have reflected the will of the citizens, an assessment that is confirmed by the high levels of support for Chávez regularly reported by independent opinion polls throughout most of the period (Ellner 2010; see also chapter 4).

For Chávez's detractors, his popularity has been premised on the redistribution of oil rents towards the popular sector. Chávez's position would therefore be little more than a 'petro-populist' who has used the oil price boom of the early 2000s to finance material benefits for his supporters (Weyland 2007). In this sense, Chavismo represents less an historical break with past Venezuelan politics than a continuity with the tradition of rentier state politics (Karl 1997), in which the party that controls the state uses oil rents to shore up political support by distributing patronage among its followers. Given the highly volatile evolution of the price of oil, it is *fortuna* rather than *virtú* that accounts for Chávez's success: he came to power on the back of an economic crisis shaped by a long period of low oil prices and consolidated his rule on the extraordinary revenues accrued by historically high ones. His political economy of (probably) unsustainable redistributive policies is thus in line with notions of economic populism (Dornbusch and Edwards 1991). In defence of Chávez's politics of redistribution, some scholars note that he has distributed oil rents towards the poor more than previous governments. Buxton (2009a) claims that, in contrast with the *Punto Fijo* governments, Chávez's core support group (the poor) *do* feel that they have received their rightful share of national wealth and social investment, which has brought accusation of economic populism and the counter-argument that, if by populism one means worrying about how the bottom two-thirds of the population fares, then it may not be a bad thing (Stiglitz 2006).

There is no question of the importance of high oil revenues in explaining Chávez's popularity (Coronil 2008b; Hidalgo 2009; Riutort 2007; Weyland 2007). There are also strong arguments that Chávez has mismanaged oil revenues and that his economic policies are unsustainable in the long term and may ultimately undermine his social base of support. Legitimate questions can also be asked as to whether his social policies are addressing the underlying causes of poverty and exclusion in the country (Penfold-Becerra 2007; Riutort 2007). What is important to question, however, is the crude economic reductionist account of popular support for Chávez, as the exclusive result of social handouts that bribe the poor into supporting him. If political conflict in Venezuela in the 1990s and 2000s had been defined only by struggles over the distribution of oil rents, it is unlikely that it would have led to such a radical rupture of the political order as represented by the Bolivarian/twenty-first century socialism revolution. Chavismo cannot be fully understood without an appraisal of how the politics of redistribution have gone hand in hand with the politics of recognition in the making of the Bolivarian Revolution. There was relatively little change in economic policies during the first years of Chávez's presidency. After starting as a vague 'Third Way' economic reformer, it was not until January 2005 that Chávez formally embraced socialism (Capriles 2008; Ellner 2008). It was only in 2003–4, when faced with the impending revocatory referendum to terminate his presidency, that the government concentrated on social programmes aimed at the poorest sectors of society and their most urgent concerns for health and education, the so-called *misiones*.

A full account of Chavismo requires focusing on its political elements as much as on the economic ones. Historical ruptures often divide people and polarize political discourse (Coronil 2008a: 3). The populist rupture of Chavismo with Punto Fijo democracy was rooted in an already fractured society but cannot be accounted for by economic factors and political alienation alone. Chávez's leadership played an active role in framing disparate grievances in a common political discourse, redefining political frontiers, organizing and mobilizing the popular sectors and constructing a new institutional order. What made Chavismo such a radical rupture in Venezuelan society are its political, normative, cultural and institutional dimensions, which combine a populist strategy of dividing the political space into two antagonistic camps with elements of national popular, participatory democracy and socialist discourses.

Significantly, Chávez's first major political initiative after winning the 1998 election was to reform the country's constitution rather than its economic model. As Julia Buxton (2009b: 2) put it, 'Crucially, Chávez was elected because he promised to create a completely new form of democracy, a qualitatively distinct model of institutional and constitutional organization and a new type of political engagement for Venezuela's citizens.' The target of the constitutional reform and the defining antagonism of the time were the traditional parties and Punto Fijo's pacted democracy rather than capitalism or even neoliberalism. Legitimizing Chávez's goal of ending Punto Fijo democracy was the normative claim of ending the historical humiliation and neglect of the Venezuelan people at the hands of the elites and the need to regenerate Venezuelan society guided by different principles and through different means (Coronil 2008a: 3). In accordance with this redemptive pledge, the goal from the outset was not to make small, pragmatic changes to an already existing political system but the creation of new forms of political and social participation that could assist the rebirth of Venezuela (Zuquete 2008: 112). Chavismo's rupture with the country's political order is grounded in a reinterpretation of Venezuelan history that links Chávez's project with the country's historical myths. They include those regarding Venezuela's national identity and the cult of Simón Bolívar. Thus, the initial definition of Chávez's foundational project was Bolivarian rather than socialist. Chávez drew from the populist tradition the notion of a virtuous people rising from a long period of oppression in a never-ending struggle for social justice and, from the military tradition, the notion of himself as a selfless patriot willing to sacrifice his own self-interest and well-being for the people of his country (Capriles 2008: 9). His political discourse is aimed at making his followers feel that they are participants in a long-running struggle for the liberation of the Venezuelan people. Chávez claims that, because he has always been unwavering in his loyalty to the homeland and has never once caved in to the interests of factions, he has been the victim of systematic persecution. Spending time in jail has only invested his narrative with authenticity and made him ever more closely identified with the oppressed and the downtrodden (Zuquete 2008: 98).

Chávez's political strategy is defined by the politics of antagonism. If the struggle to emancipate the people from all powerful internal and external oppressors is an ongoing one, the target of his polarizing rhetoric has changed according to political circumstances and the radicalization of the Bolivarian revolution. So, while the *partidocracia* were the enemies of the people in his 1998 electoral campaign and in the first two years of his first presidency, President Chávez subsequently attacked the business organization, FEDECÁMERAS, the opposition-dominated trade union umbrella organization, the CTV, the private media, the hierarchy of the Catholic Church, US imperialism, President Bush, and, more consistently, neoliberalism as enemies of the people and thus of the nation.[17]

The centrality of President Chávez's leadership in the Bolivarian revolution, his anti-party rhetoric and his ability to reach the people though bypassing existing institutions downplays the importance of political organization in the understanding of Chavismo. Perhaps more than any other contemporary Latin American populist, Chávez has been conscious of the need to both organize and mobilize his supporters to defend and consolidate his project. Personalist leadership, plebiscitarian and grassroots forms of political participation and new forms of political organization combine to provide a more complex set of political relations between Chávez and his followers than the simplistic notion of populism as a top-down, unmediated relationship between leader and followers. There is a process of popular incorporation, organization and mobilization in the *Chavista* movement that is not captured by notions of top-down populism or economic handouts. Already during the initial years of his first presidential mandate, Chávez needed active and not just passive support from his followers because, as shown by the failed military coup of April 2002, with only passive support he would have been ousted by the mobilized middle classes and the military (Ellner 2010). Since then, the politics of street mobilization have combined with a strategy of political organization of the popular sectors that includes channels for political participation for his supporters and barriers for the representation of his adversaries. The mass participatory institutions framed by the new constitution, the promotion of grassroots organizations, such as the Círculos Bolivarianos and the Communal Councils, and the setting up in 2007 of the Partido Socialista Unificado de Venezuela (PSUV) as a mass political party attest to Chávez's organizational drive. While there is need for more empirical work on Chávez's attempts at promoting political participation from subordinated groups, it seems clear that he has given political voice to sectors of Venezuelan society that felt unrepresented by the old parties, particularly women, the poor and ethnic groups (Ellner and Tinker Salas 2007: 11; Motta 2007; Panizza 2009).

Organization, however, is not the same as accountability and civil society participation does not guarantee political autonomy from the state. While empowering the people at local level, the Chávez government has adopted many of the positions and policies that represented a dramatic leap forward in the 'revolutionary process' with little or no previous discussion within the *Chavista* movement or the nation as a whole (Ellner 2008: 16). An empirical study of the allocation of social funds for the *misiones* programmes show how, given increased levels of electoral competition and weak institutional constraints, the government used these funds clientelistically, even while distributing oil income to the very poor. While some of these programmes were influenced by poverty considerations, they were also allegedly used to maintain support among *Chavista* voters at local level (Hawkins and Hansen 2006; Penfold-Becerra 2007: 4, 63–84).

The rhetoric of popular sovereignty and participatory democracy raises important questions about the reach and limits of political participation under Chavismo and about how participatory democracy can be compatible with the concentration of power in the Executive that characterizes the everyday working of the Bolivarian revolution. At a macro-institutional level, the institutional arrangements that characterize the Bolivarian constitution do not do away with liberal democratic institutions, such as parliaments, elections and parties, but these are subordinated to Chávez's presidential power and to other institutional arrangements which are supposed to promote forms of direct and participatory democracy (Motta 2007). Clientelism, corruption and personalism are not exclusive to Chavismo and have a long history in Venezuela and elsewhere in Latin America. Chavismo, however, has been characterized by the colonization of the state by the ruling party and the systematic erosion of the checks and balances that characterize democratic pluralism. Control of the state without pluralist checks and balances leads to abuses of power, to new forms of political exclusion and to a deficit of accountability which are a part of the democratic deficit of Chavismo.

Critics of Chavismo have stressed its authoritarian elements and questioned Chávez's democratic legitimacy:

> [F]rom a conceptual point of view, the Venezuelan political regime is autocratic. All political power is concentrated in the hands of the president. There is no real separation of powers. This enormous power is not exercised 'for now' in a brutally dictatorial fashion in the style of Fidel Castro or Pérez Jimenez; there is no state terror, and this is not a police state in the Cuban or Soviet sense. But this simply means that the regime is much more oppressive than repressive. (Petkoff 2008: 12).

Petkoff's views reflect the extreme polarization of Venezuelan politics and the absence of a middle ground in which to assess the politics of Chavismo. Venezuela, however, retains a strong democratic culture. Venezuelan citizens record the strongest support for democracy in Latin America and rank the country second in terms of whether they consider it to be a democracy, a fact that cannot be dissociated from feelings of empowerment associated to new participatory institutions (Ellner 2010). A large majority of the Venezuelan people (80%) believe that voting is the most effective way of contributing to changing things and 76% (the second highest rate in Latin America) believe that, without political parties, there can be no democracy. As regards opinions about the actual working of democracy, Venezuela is a divided country, as one third of the population believe that it works worse than in the rest of the region, another third considers that it works better than in other Latin American countries and the remaining third consider it to be on a par with the rest of the region. Further, reflecting the strong polarization that characterizes public opinion, just over a third (35%) of Venezuelan citizens believe that the country is being governed for the good of all people and the people are finely divided in terms of approval of government performance (48%) and satisfaction with democracy (49%) (Corporación Latinobarómetro 2008). The persistence of democratic contestation in Venezuela is partly because Chavismo operates in a society with strong democratic traditions and within a region in which democracy has become the only legitimizing principle for holding power. It is also partly because Chavismo has never been defined by a totalizing ideology but is a project in the making in which many of its political and economic principles remain ill-defined and there are conflicting views about the long-term political and economic goals of the revolution within the Bolivarian Revolution (Ellner 2008).

Conclusions

The analysis of the cases of Bolivia, Ecuador and Venezuela throws light on the making of radical left populism in contemporary Latin America. In its political dimension – the politics of antagonism and its normative core, the politics of recognition and redistribution – the rise of radical left populism in the twenty-first century cannot be separated from the achievements and limitations of the process of democratization of the past thirty years. If, in the vision of the Miami Consensus, democracy appeared to be defined by institutions rather than by politics, in radical populism politics took precedence over institutions. The primacy of politics was manifested, among other aspects, in the key leadership role played by Morales, Correa and Chávez in processes of radical change in the three countries. Leadership went together with the organization and mobilization of the popular sectors and with a strong foundational drive to redefine their countries' political and economic orders. As seen in this chapter, there are significant differences in the relations between the three leaders and the popular movements of their countries, including the strength of the organic links between leaders and their organized base of support and the degree of control and accountability involved in the relationship. While personalist leadership remains a constitutive element of populism and this entails a top-down dimension, the relation between leader and followers cannot be defined simply as a

98

one-way imposition from above (it never was). Morales is clearly the leader more closely bound to powerful popular movements while Correa has distanced himself from Ecuador's social movements and his leadership style better captures the notion of a direct and unmediated relationship between the leader and the people. Chávez leadership fits the picture of top-down leadership more closely than other leaders but the notion of a one-sided vertical relationship with the popular organizations fails to capture the dynamics of Venezuela's highly mobilized popular sectors. To different degrees and through different mechanisms, Morales, Correa and Chávez have to listen to their supporters and account for their decisions to their followers and to the extent that elections remain free and fair to the citizens at large. What is key in the three cases is the leading role they played in unifying divergent and fragmented popular demands in a common antagonism against *partycracies* and neoliberalism and their subsequent drive to set up an alternative order to the Miami Consensus.

If politics matters for the understanding of populism, so does history. In many aspects, twenty-first century populist incorporation evokes the national-popular populism of the mid-twentieth century wave of popular incorporation. Economic nationalism and state interventionism are back on the agenda of the governments of Bolivia, Ecuador and Venezuela: 'Braden (the then US ambassador to Argentina) or Perón,' the option that General Perón put to the Argentinian citizens in the 1945 electoral campaign, became 'Bush or Chávez' in the Venezuelan campaign of 2006. President Chávez has followed the Punto Fijo tradition of colonizing the state and using oil rents to consolidate his political base of support. The nationalist legacy of the MNR in Bolivia and the anti-institutional populist politics of Velasco Ibarra in Ecuador have shaped the politics of Morales and Correa even if both have rejected substantial aspects of their countries' political legacy, including that of their populist predecessors.

But there are also significant differences between the two populist waves. With all its flaws and shortcomings, democracy is stronger in Latin America than it was sixty or more years ago. As explored in more detail in previous chapters, the social and political polarization that characterizes the politics of antagonism in both populist waves is less likely now to end in the military interventions that brought down populist governments in the 1950s and 1960s. The popular sectors, including members of the urban informal sector and politicized ethnic groups which constitute the social bases of contemporary populism, are more culturally and socio-economically fragmented than the working class of the new industrial belts of the Latin American cities of the 1940s and 1950s, but also more autonomous from state control and more conscious of their political rights.

If the national popular ideology of classical Latin American populism has influenced the discourse of twenty-first century populism, it may be worth remembering that classical Latin American populism was explicitly set up as a bulwark against what was then perceived as the threat of a socialist revolution. Today, the governments of Morales, Chávez and Correa define themselves as twenty-first century socialists. Ill-defined as it is, the term alludes to the ideological influence of the socialist tradition and the political influence of Cuban socialism, particularly in Bolivia and Venezuela. This marks a clear difference between the two populist waves and should be taken as a note of caution about the extent to which the term 'populism' defines an entire project or, as suggested in the introduction to this chapter, just a political strategy that can be articulated to very different substantive contents.

The same caveat applies to the new political institutions. Populism's foundational drive has crystallized in new constitutional orders. But it is wrong to argue that populism alone is what defines the new orders. The new institutions combine elements of representative democracy with different levels of concentration of power in the Executive (including presidential re-election in political systems in which the president can command state resources to further his political campaign) and the setting up of autonomous and participatory institutions. The apparently contradictory mix of personalism and participationism of the new political order reflects how contemporary populism has incorporated elements of participatory democracy that have gained political force over the past decades. Apparently, the two are incompatible, as populism favours top-down personalist leadership and participatory democracy bottom-up civil society representation. However, the redemptive promise of democracy as empowering the people to exercise their democratic rights without representative mediations is a promise shared from very different standpoints by populism and radical-participatory versions of democracy. In common, populism and participatory democracy blur the distinction between the public and the private realms that is at the heart of representative democracy and regard political parties as divisive and opaque forms of exercising voice.

Finally, it is necessary to briefly address the vexed question of the relation between populism and democracy. As Ellner (2010: 79) rightly notes, behind contrasting claims about the democratic nature of the government of Hugo Chávez (and in a more limited way those of Morales and Correa) lay two distinctive concepts of democracy: liberal democracy, with its emphasis on checks and balances and the rights of minorities, and radical democracy that stresses majority rule and the direct participation of the people in decision making. It is clear that the three regimes fare better when judged by the radical democracy criteria than under those of liberal democracy. But, while it is wrong to pretend that there is a single model of democracy, it is equally wrong to ignore that there should be some common criteria to evaluate different models of democracy. Among these should figure the extension of voice and accountability to wider sections of the population, together with the principle of equality before the law and the genuine contestation of power. The new political order has weakened the opposition and provided short-term political stability but it is not clear whether the new institutions command enough consensus to gain long-term legitimacy and thus close the gap between legality and legitimacy that undermined the old order, and whether their representative, personalist and participatory elements will in time improve the quality of democracy or rather reflect an unstable arrangement which will lead to further political turmoil.

— 4 —

PERSONALISM, PLEBISCITES AND INSTITUTIONS

There is one significant way in which the presidencies of Chávez, Morales and Correa can be put in a different category to any others in the region. This is their aggressive use of plebiscitary tactics to re-found national constitutions and assert the primacy of the presidency over the legislature. There is a certain logic to the use of plebiscitary tactics in weakly institutionalized systems as they have been a possible means of decisively changing national political institutions without democratic breakdown as such. Admittedly, other presidents in the past used plebiscites for this purpose, but those tactics have been mainly associated with the political right. The cases of Pinochet and Fujimori come to mind. What we might call socialist plebiscitarianism is genuinely something new. Moreover, the potential potency of the tactic has been implicitly recognized by its opponents. In Honduras in 2009, as we have seen, President Zelaya's attempt to hold a non-binding plebiscite on presidential re-election was treated as sufficient ground for his overthrow. His opponents specifically linked plebiscitary tactics to *Chavista* politics of centralization and redistribution.

We have to be aware that we are dealing with an unfinished process. There is a lot about any government that only becomes clear when it has left power, partly because of limitations on information and partly because incumbency itself changes political behaviour – sometimes drastically so. Nevertheless, it does seem likely that the establishment of a more powerful presidency backed by a more mobilized civil society will remain relevant in these countries for a long time.

All three leaders have continued to rely on personalist appeals, confrontational tactics and political centralization – though it must be said that the opposition has on occasion been quite confrontational itself. All three have sought to use the state as a whole to further their policy goals, which can be described in shorthand as 'twenty-first century socialism'. Although this socialist aspiration should be taken seriously, it also coincides in these cases with more than a suggestion of machine politics and a self-evident lack of political impartiality. Chávez, more than the others, has a bombastic and occasionally wild speaking style that at times makes him sound even more arbitrary than he probably is. He has also at times been rather bullying in his treatment of the opposition and sometimes intimated that their election victories would not be respected (Hidalgo 2009). In Venezuela at least, the judicial system has also been heavily politicized in the government's favour, as has been the pattern of public spending. This, though, has been nothing new. State bias in favour of government supporters was noteworthy in all three countries long before the rise of Chávez, Morales and Correa and indeed played an important part in the process of institutional discrediting that facilitated their rise.

There may be cultural aspects to the emergence of this kind of politics. In much of South America, systems of presidential government tend to coexist with widespread popular suspicion of the workings of 'horizontal accountability' institutions – such as political parties, courts and legislatures (Lagos 1997; O'Donnell 1999; Seligson 2008; Weyland 2002). There are often good reasons for this suspicion, but this nonetheless may make it easier for personalist politicians to establish themselves as leader figures, especially at times of crisis. Moreover, it is not difficult to detect intellectual influences on the three leaders that are profoundly anti-pluralist and yet rooted in the history of the region. The late Luis Castro, in his time perhaps Venezuela's leading public intellectual, once complained that 'the trouble with Venezuela is that Bolivar read Rousseau' (personal communication). There is certainly no doubt that Chávez admires Bolivar for his leadership qualities and does not greatly value checks and balances for their own sake and it is also clear that Chávez's own career has influenced the tactics adopted by Morales and Correa.

Culture probably matters but it is not the whole story. Popular preference for decisive leadership at times of crisis is clearly not peculiar to South America or sub-regions within it. There are many non-South American cases in which a deeply frustrated or frightened public opinion has looked for a leader to solve its political problems. The ascendancy of General de Gaulle in France in May 1958 would be an obvious example, as would the reassertion of presidential power in Russia under Vladimir Putin. Some of the uglier events in Continental Europe during the 1920s and 1930s are relevant as well. There is no doubt either that there is often a pro-status quo orientation behind the advocacy of 'checks and balances'. It is generally the case that radical social change requires a centralization of power, and it is this successful self-identification with change that has underpinned the electoral successes of Chávez, Morales and Correa.

Therefore the focus of this chapter is on institutional and not cultural aspects of government. It makes three claims. One is that traditional presidential/congressional systems have tended to deadlock in South America and would almost certainly have generated some kind of crisis in our three cases, no matter what tactics Chávez, Morales and Correa might have adopted. More specifically, the opposition to Chávez in 1998 was already planning to respond to his expected victory in presidential elections by seeking to establish itself within competing power bases. Chávez's answer to this threat, later copied by Morales and Correa, was to use plebiscites in order to enhance presidential power. The second is that the plebiscitary process has indeed conferred some degree of legitimacy on all three. Plebiscitary outcomes cannot be dismissed as the pure reflection of pro-incumbent state bias. Indeed, the opposition has resorted to recall voting in some circumstances in both Venezuela and Bolivia. Moreover, from a comparative point of view, where plebiscites have been held in other parts of South America they have mostly not simply rubber-stamped executive wishes. The third claim is that issues of democratic institutionalization cannot be isolated from broader issues of ultimate political purpose. The election of governments openly calling for socialist transformation, twenty-first century or otherwise, was bound to have had institutional as well as policy aspects, and centralizing ones at that.

It is quite understandable that the opposition should have offered institutional critiques of this kind of politics. Political scientists such as O'Donnell (1994), Linz and Stepan (1996) and Zakaria (1997) have each set out important principles of democratic institutionalism, which together make the argument that the health of autonomous institutions is necessary for democratic viability. Voting is not enough to establish a liberal democracy and over-reliance on elections may distort and ultimately even threaten democracy itself.

This critique of excessive personalism makes perfect sense in theory. However, relevant too is Brecht's point that democracy is about voters choosing the government and not about elites choosing the electorate. It is pointless to regard democracy as a set of procedures (no matter how neatly drawn up or precisely measured) that have little to do with what people want and are prepared to vote for, or to set out didactically the kind of system that people 'ought' to support. Voters in all three countries had many opportunities to vote for candidates advocating some form of checks and balances pluralism. In the end, the three electorates decisively rejected them.

No matter how one may try to account for voter choice, popularity must be a legitimate currency of politics in any democratic system. Chávez, Morales and Correa have not only won democratic elections repeatedly but also been generally successful at retaining their popularity during their mid-term periods. Moreover, contrary to a number of South American cases – including pre-Chávez Venezuela and pre-Correa Ecuador – where 'mandate-breaking' has occurred (Stokes 2001), none of the three presented themselves to the electorate in any obviously dishonest way. What the electorate saw and voted for is mostly what they got – even though it is true that Chávez has become more assertively socialist since winning re-election in 2006. A supporter of these three would also claim that the undoubted gains in political and social inclusiveness that have occurred in all three cases are more important in the eyes of the electorates themselves than state impartiality and individual autonomy (Lazar 2006). This may be a dangerous argument because it ignores the way in which the character of a state can change over time, but it is one that has resonance with public opinion in all three countries.

There has certainly been a lot of voting under Chávez, Morales and Correa if we include presidential elections, plebiscites, local and regional elections and legislative elections. There has as yet been no convincing suggestion of actual ballot rigging though the state has undoubtedly been used for partisan political advantage. We need, however, to be aware that some of the opposition to Chávez and Morales (less obviously Correa) has at times shown itself to be questionably democratic. In the case of Venezuela, there was the Carmona coup attempt of 2002, the deliberately damaging PdVSA strike of 2003 and the opposition's boycott of congressional elections in 2005. In the Bolivian case, there were racist as well as separatist overtones to at least some of the opposition activity in Santa Cruz in 2008, as well as an outright call for a military coup. Some leading figures in the Bolivian opposition have personal antecedents that go back to earlier periods of military dictatorship, and anti-government extremists have both advocated and practised political violence against government supporters. One factor that has made things difficult for moderate opposition figures in all three cases is a fear that they may end up playing into the hands of an outright dictator. This is not a possibility that can by any means be dismissed outright.

The problem: Presidential weakness in South America

Having made these general observations, we turn to institutional specifics. The next part of this chapter addresses the topic of presidentialism and claims that Chávez, Morales and Correa – despite their strong initial popular mandates – would probably not have been able to address their radical social and economic agenda without confronting Congress in some direct way. The South American presidency, contrary to some perceptions, tends to be a weak institution and this weakness often leads to presidents disappointing their electorates (Valenzuela 2008).

The idea that presidentialism in South America is vulnerable to institutional crisis is quite a familiar one, and relevant to this discussion. Linz (1994) has famously claimed that relations between president and Congress in presidential systems are complicated by the fact that both can claim a legitimate mandate based on direct popular election. The resulting 'dual legitimation' can make conflicts, when these develop, hard to resolve according to agreed institutional criteria. The result need not be the end of democracy but may well be a tendency towards institutional polarization, executive weakness and political deadlock. Linz's claim has been contested in a good deal of political science literature. We now have quite a lot of empirical evidence on this point and it may be best to look directly at the historical record rather than revisiting all the literature. Linz's key prediction that major conflict can occur between president and Congress in South America (and, for that matter, Central America) has been significantly verified.

There have been fifteen cases since the onset of 'third wave' democratization in which Latin American presidents were removed or decided to resign before the end of their terms of office. This has happened seven times in our three countries – once in Venezuela, three times in Bolivia, and three times in Ecuador. Outside of our three countries, there are eight cases of premature presidential removal or resignation since the mid-1980s. They are – in chronological order – Alfonsin in Argentina (1989), Collor in Brazil (1993), Serrano in Guatemala (1993), Cubas in Paraguay (1999), Fujimori in Peru (2000), both De la Rua and Rodriguez Saa in Argentina (2001) and Zelaya in Honduras (2009). There was also one case in which a president used the military to close the National Congress – this was Peru in 1992 – and Colombia's Samper narrowly survived impeachment by Congress. Overall, that is quite a long list.

Nor have Latin American presidents been safe following impeachment or resignation. Seven former presidents – Pérez in Venezuela, Cubas and Gonzalez Macchi in Paraguay, Fujimori in Peru, Collor in Brazil, and Bucaram and Gutiérrez in Ecuador – were subsequently charged with criminal offences (Argentina's De la Rua is still under investigation) though only Fujimori and Pérez have so far served significant prison sentences. Fujimori is currently serving twenty-five years. A seventh ex-president – Sánchez de Lozada – avoided arrest only by seeking political asylum in the United States. Bolivian efforts to secure his extradition have so far been unsuccessful. Argentina's Menem and Peru's Garcia, though their presidential terms were not truncated, had to face criminal proceedings after leaving presidential office. In the case of Menem, these are still alive.

These removals, resignations and prosecutions are not all purely the result of undue executive weakness or evidence of institutional failure. Some of the removed presidents (by no means all) do seem to have cases to answer in terms of personal conduct. In some cases, it could be argued that presidential impeachment proved that the system worked. However, the overall pattern surely indicates executive vulnerability. When making this regional comparison, what is unusual is that Chávez, Correa and, to a significant degree, Morales have been able to strengthen their executives at a time when most conflicts between president and Congress have resulted in presidential defeat.

The general pattern of conflict in executive–legislative relations seems to indicate that Latin American presidentialism has generated different outcomes from presidential systems in other parts of the world. In the United States, presidential removal from office has been rare. In more than two hundred years, only one US president was forced to resign to avoid removal by Congress, and two others faced serious though ultimately unsuccessful congressional attempts to remove them. In the United States, elected representatives have mostly accepted Hamilton's original stipulation that impeachment should be considered only for serious criminal offences and not on the basis of political disagreement (Whitehead 2002: 102). However, in Latin America it has become common enough for president and Congress not to check and balance each other, subject to overriding regulation by the courts, but to fight to the political death (see also Cox and Morgenstern 2001).

It may well be that there are narrowly defined institutional arrangements that help us explain why this has tended to happen so often in Latin America. Constitutional arrangements involving such issues as the timing of presidential and congressional elections, the existence (or lack of one) of a vice-president, and the length of presidential-term limits may explain some of the higher incidence of presidential resignation or impeachment in South America (Haggard and McCubbins 2001). The common Latin American pattern of having the presidency elected on a 'first past the post' basis and having Congress elected via some form of proportional representation is also blamed by some for executive–legislative deadlock (Foweraker 1998). Moreover, Latin American party systems are often weak and this, too, is a contributory cause of unsatisfactory governance (Mainwaring and Scully 1995).

Institutional issues of this kind are no doubt relevant but it is not convincing to locate ultimate explanatory power in the formal rules without at least asking who benefits from them. Constitutions are not immutable, and well-organized political forces can either adapt to the rules or negotiate changes to them in order to improve their political prospects. Constitutional change in the region has been common enough. There have been quite a number in Latin America since the 1980s. There is an apocryphal story of a man going into a bookshop in Latin America to ask for a copy of the national constitution and being told that the shop does not stock periodicals. The overriding issue here surely has to do with institutional weakness in general rather than with any specific problems caused by the 'rational choice' implications of a particular set of rules. The key fact is that, in Latin America, institutions can often be the servants of political contestation rather than the arbiters of it. Informal elite-level bargaining has tended to play a significant part in conflict resolution and, when this bargaining fails to deliver a satisfactory outcome or breaks down in disarray, the outcome can be politically destabilizing.

The Venezuelan 'solution': From partidocracy to presidential rule

We can now see how some of this played out in Venezuela during the decisive period surrounding the initial election of Chávez. The decision to change the date of the congressional and state governorship elections of 1998 gives us an insight. For most of the period after 1958, presidential and congressional elections in Venezuela were held at the same time. However, exceptionally in 1998, the elections for Congress and state governorships were held in November, with presidential elections held in December. Although the official rationale was that the change would avoid overloading the electoral machinery in December, since otherwise the vote for state governorships, regional assemblies, Congress and the presidency would have to be held at the same time, the real rationale was believed to be more political. After all, there were no major problems when megaelections were held in 2000 under the new constitution. It has been suggested – and was commonly believed by political observers at the time – that the dates of the 1998 elections were changed in the expectation that this would disadvantage the candidacy of Hugo Chávez (Lalander 2004: 221).

The anti-Chávez majority that still controlled Venezuelan politics at the time when the elections were rescheduled had a lot to gain from such a change. By the mid-1990s, it had become clear that Venezuela's two-party system (involving Acción Democratica (AD) and COPEI) had lost much of its credibility. Opinion surveys showed an accelerating fall in the proportion of voters expressing sympathy for AD or COPEI (Molina and Pérez 2002). Nevertheless in 1998, the ruling 'partidocracy', though electorally in decline, still had enough votes in Congress to try to use institutional processes to weaken the presidency before Chávez took office.

The traditional party leaders had good reason to believe that their parties – which still enjoyed residual strength as political machines even though largely discredited with the wider public – would perform better in congressional and regional elections than in presidential ones. That is how it turned out. In the November governorship and congressional elections, the pro-Chávez Polo Patriótico polled well. Even so, while enjoying a plurality in the Chamber of Deputies and getting close to one in the Senate, the Polo Patriótico could still be outvoted in Congress if AD and COPEI joined forces. In the December presidential elections, however, the major parties performed much worse than they had in November and Chávez won with 56 per cent of the vote.

Had AD in particular not experienced a disastrous final few weeks of campaigning, it would have hoped to hold Chávez to below 50 per cent of the vote in the presidential elections. The opposition could then have claimed that Chávez did not have a mandate for radical change and hoped to use its potential majority in Congress for blocking purposes. As we have seen, a hostile congressional majority can be a real obstacle to a South American president.

As it happened, the traditional parties severely lost credibility after November and the collapse in their support left them in no position to mount an effective blocking strategy. Given their lack of public support, they had no prospect of being able to call on either broader political society or indeed the military to stop Chávez. Meanwhile, following his election, Chávez refused to deal at all with the 'November' legislature. Instead, he adopted the tactic of calling for a plebiscite to vote on the proposition that there should be a new Constituent Assembly. The vote was held on 25 April 1999 and Chávez's allies (the 'Patriotic Pole') won 66 per cent of the vote and took 121 of the 128 available seats – i.e., 93 per cent. The Assembly met for the first time on June 25, formally stripped the existing Congress of its powers and then drafted a new constitution. This new constitution was approved by plebiscite in December 1999, after which the existing Congress was formally dissolved. In order to validate the new constitution, Chávez stood for the presidency again and won with a broadly similar share of the vote to that achieved in December 1998.

Plebiscitary politics in Ecuador and Bolivia

There is little doubt that Chávez's use of plebiscitary tactics to confront the National Congress influenced Morales and Correa. Correa won presidential elections in Ecuador as an outsider in 2006. He made a point of standing for the presidency without presenting any candidates for Congress at the same time because that would (he said) dilute the force of his promise to create a new constitution if elected (Conaghan 2008). While there was no 'Correa party', there were understandings and alliances involving the parties of the left, who enjoyed significant though not majority representation in Congress. Like so many other presidents in Ecuadorian history, therefore, Correa was elected without a congressional majority. However, Correa, like Chávez but unlike some of Correa's Ecuadorian predecessors, responded combatively rather than seeking to negotiate with his opponents. He would have been aware that his three presidential predecessors were all weak figures who mostly failed to adhere to their electoral mandates. They also all failed to complete their terms of office.

Correa's plan, like that of Chávez, was to use the undoubted popularity of his proposal for a new constitution to press ahead regardless. The opposition initially offered to bargain by promising to agree to a new constitution subject to the stipulations that this would be allowed to change neither the presidential term nor the role of Congress. This was unacceptable to Correa who went ahead with a plebiscite on the need for a new constitution. The vote was held on 15 April 2007 and the government won with over 80 per cent of the votes cast. Despite a series of legislative manoeuvres, which resulted in inconclusive legal challenges, it was this popular vote that proved decisive in winning the day for Correa.

Elections for a Constituent Assembly were then held in September 2007 and the government won a majority of over 60 per cent. A new constitution was duly drawn up and itself submitted to popular vote. Rather like the Venezuelan constitution of 1999, the new constitution was centralizing in political terms but symbolically inclusionary in broader social terms. Incumbent presidents were allowed a second term and the government was also given the right to appoint judges. The plebiscite to approve the new constitution was held on 28 September 2008 and supported by more than 60 per cent of the vote.

Fresh presidential elections were then held in April 2009, which Correa won with 52 per cent of the vote. His margin of victory was reasonably convincing, even though his party did not win an outright majority in the newly elected legislature and a leader of the conserva- tive opposition won mayoral elections in the second city, Guayaquil. The new Ecuadorian constitution gives significantly more power to the presidency than the old one, enabling Correa to rule to a signifi- cant extent by decree.

In Bolivia, Morales was elected to the presidency at the end of 2005 with an absolute majority of the popular vote but without an overall majority in Congress. His immediate proposal to set up a Constituent Assembly received the agreement of both the ruling MAS and the oppositional PODEMOS. However, PODEMOS made its support conditional on an agreement that the Constituent Assembly would need a two-thirds majority to approve any new constitution. The opposition also stipulated that Constituent Assembly elections be held according to a system of proportional representation, which made it virtually impossible for any single party to gain the required two-thirds majority. When elections for the Assembly were held in July 2006, they gave the right-wing opposition an apparently blocking minority, which it was prepared to use to water down much of what the government supporters wanted to put into the constitution.

There was then a considerable period of political conflict before the new constitution was voted through at the beginning of 2008 via some doubtfully legal tactics from Morales supporters. There followed several more months of tense confrontations and negotiations before the new constitution was finally put to a vote in January 2009. Once put to the popular vote, it was passed with just over 60 per cent of the vote but with some important regions of Bolivia voting against it.

There were many constitutional issues that caused controversy, including the enhancement of indigenous rights, but the most polarizing dimension of politics has been regional. Bolivia is substantially polarized between the highlands, which are dominated demographically by indigenous peoples, and the lowlands, which are dominated (though not exclusively peopled) by people of European origin. Complex patterns of human settlement make these divisions rather untidy but they do matter in terms of political organization. The main sources of Bolivian raw material wealth are to be found in the lowlands, where the dominant political culture tends to be market-oriented in contrast to the greater collectivism of the highlands. There was also racial prejudice on the part of some lowlanders, which threatened to become ugly when political tensions rose during 2008.

Once it had failed to block the consolidation of a left-wing government in La Paz, the opposition changed tactic and started to champion the cause of regional autonomy. The opposition-run state of Santa Cruz unilaterally decided to have an autonomy vote, which it held in May 2008. The states of Pando, Beni and Tarija, all of which were controlled by the opposition, followed suit. This was an unprecedented move, without formal legal sanction, but it was a political fact of some significance. It seems that the right-wing opposition was using the plebiscitary tactics originally introduced by Morales, but with the ultimate threat of some kind of secession if this tactic failed. Nevertheless, despite the fact that the conservative opposition in Bolivia was far more politically prepared than the anti-Chávez opposition in Venezuela, the outcome was still a new national constitution and elections planned to be held under its terms.

Plebiscites in regional context

The main reason why Chávez, Morales and Correa won their confrontations with Congress, when so many other South American presidents did not, was their use of plebiscites to overcome opposition. Plebiscites are defined here as direct popular votes on matters

112

of constitutional importance, in contrast to referendums which are defined as direct popular votes on issues of government or policy. All plebiscites are therefore referendums but referendums are not necessarily plebiscites. The use of plebiscites evidently ties in with a central theme of this book which has to do with the dilemma of democracy as majoritarianism versus democracy as pluralism.

The most drastic criticism of plebiscites is that they can overstrengthen incumbent governments, in the extreme case even appearing to legitimize dictatorship. A more moderate criticism is that the extensive use of plebiscites damages the principle of political representation and weakens democratic institutionalization generally. This moderate criticism also involves the claim that plebiscites can be polarizing because they bypass the brokering, negotiation and compromise that are a necessary if occasionally disreputable part of the democratic process. Brokering deals is an essential part of what political parties and legislators do. Replacing their services with frequent popular voting can lead to excessive partisanship. Voters need a certain amount of respite from political competition. In systems where constitutional governance is already weak, an excess of partisanship can be especially polarizing because it encourages a kind of politics in which intransigence develops on both sides, and the state is used as an instrument of politics.

The literature on democratic consolidation has been sceptical, implicitly rather than explicitly, of the value of plebiscites in Latin America. In comparison with the abundant literature on presidentialism, party systems and executive–legislative relations, the literature on plebiscites (and even referendums) in Latin America is comparatively scarce (exceptions are Alberts 2008; Breuer 2007, 2008; Conaghan 2008; Payne et al. 2002). Where existing institutional systems have not worked well, political scientists have tended to turn their attention to the improved design of representational systems rather than ways of organizing the direct popular vote.

In contemporary Latin America, as in the broader democratic world, the practice of direct voting varies considerably from country to country. The majority of Latin American countries have used referendums to decide some issues. Some countries, such as Argentina, have used them rarely – in fact only once since 1980 and then on a consultative basis only. Others, such as Uruguay, use them frequently. Uruguayans voted directly on no fewer than ten initiatives between 1980 and 2004. Referendum practice similarly varies both within Europe and in the US – with Switzerland and some US states allowing quite a lot of direct voting while some US states forbid this entirely

113

and many European countries use referendums sparingly or not at all (Butler and Rannay 1994).

There is enough evidence from the holding of plebiscites in Latin America as a whole to contest any idea that they are always a reliable asset to incumbents. This is so even with plebiscites held by actual dictatorships. The most relevant such cases are the 1957 plebiscite in Venezuela, the 1978, 1980 and 1988 plebiscites in Chile, the 1980 plebiscite in Uruguay and the 1993 plebiscite in Peru. Of these six, three were won by incumbents, two by the opposition, and one – in which the government declared victory – soon led to regime change when suspicion of ballot rigging led to military intervention against the incumbent. This suggests, on the whole, a roughly even split.

This first of these plebiscites occurred under the last Venezuelan military dictator, Pérez Jiménez. Pérez Jiménez had seized power with others in 1948 and was subsequently 'elected', without opposition, to a six-year presidential term in 1952. He attempted in 1957 to use a plebiscite to confirm himself in office for a further presidential term. Voting was indeed held and Pérez Jiménez declared himself the winner, but allegations of ballot rigging, plus the suspicion that he was not as popular as he had claimed to be, led to unrest within the military. This unrest found an echo within broader civil society, and civil–military opposition finally led to his overthrow at the beginning of 1958. The post-1958 democratic political order reacted against institutions of direct democracy to the point that for a time it avoided holding direct elections for state governorships and municipal authorities. Municipal elections were not held until 1969 and direct elections for state governorship were not held until 1989.

In Chile, General Pinochet used a snap plebiscite early in 1978, with a notoriously loaded question, to consolidate his position at the head of the ruling military junta. The plebiscite was aimed as much at his fellow officers as at the general public, and it marked the moment when a collective military dictatorship started to give way to a personalist despotism. Pinochet then ordered a plebiscite to be held in 1980 in order to ratify the constitution that his supporters had drafted. This led to a substantial positive vote in favour of provisions that – among other things – gave Pinochet an eight-year term of office as president with virtually no checks and balances. There was intense state repression in the years before the 1980 plebiscite but the stronger factor involved in producing a positive outcome was probably an economic boom, although a short-lived one. It is likely that the 1980 vote helped Pinochet's regime survive the severe economic downturn that followed because his opponents were divided on whether the 1980 constitution should be used as a basis of negotiation or rejected outright. The Chilean electorate in 1988 was given a further opportunity to vote, this time on Pinochet's possible re-election to a further term of office, and on this occasion it rejected the proposal. The military accepted the outcome and the Pinochet regime gave way to democracy. A further plebiscite was then held to approve the democratic transition.

The Uruguayan military dictatorship in 1980 submitted its constitutional plans to a plebiscite and suffered rejection. The proposed constitution would have allowed a considerable period of military rule behind the scenes in the context of a long period of dictatorship. The rejection of these plans led to a slow transition to democracy, with full elections being held in 1984. As in the Chilean 1988 plebiscite, state repression had been harsh in previous years but some campaigning was allowed ahead of the plebiscite itself. In fact, it seems that the vote genuinely surprised the authorities. Finally, in Peru, Fujimori's success in getting the 1993 constitution approved – albeit with a narrow 53–47 per cent vote split – allowed him to run for the presidency again in 1995.

The overall picture of plebiscitary results under authoritarian governments in Latin America is therefore mixed. Incumbents have sometimes won plebiscites and authoritarian regimes have sometimes successfully counterfeited some of the advantages of democratic legitimation as a result of winning them under questionable circumstances. The Pinochet regime in 1980 and Fujimori in 1993 are clear examples. However, plebiscites do not invariably rubber-stamp incumbent preferences, even under dictatorships. Presidential popularity is the key issue, and unpopular authoritarian systems have lost plebiscites more than once.

Some other Latin American experiences show that plebiscites and referendums do not generally offer much comfort to weak or unpopular democratic governments either. Ecuador provides us with a good example of this. Between 1978, when a plebiscite approved the transition from military to democratic rule, and the election of Correa in 2006, there were four referendums. In one, the executive's proposals were rejected outright. The government won the other three but the effect was not to strengthen the presidency. Incumbent presidents were overthrown in 1997, 2000 and again in 2005.

In Bolivia, a pre-Morales experiment with a policy referendum was a narrowly defined success in terms of voting but a failure for the incumbent in broader terms. Faced with popular mobilization in

September 2003, incumbent president Sánchez de Lozada offered a referendum on the issue of whether to go ahead with a proposed pipeline that would export gas to Chile, which had been the subject of popular protests (see chapter 5). This involved an implicit deal that would have exchanged a referendum (which the government would almost certainly have lost) for the ending of anti-government mobilization. The dissidents were unimpressed and Sánchez de Lozada fell. However, his successor, Carlos Mesa, sought to defuse the difficult political situation by asking Congress to approve the holding of the original referendum. In February 2004, in the context of political turmoil, Congress approved a constitutional reform package, which specifically allowed the holding of referendums on policy issues. As was expected, this led the Mesa government to call for a referendum on future gas policy (Breuer 2008). Later in the year, an ambiguously worded referendum was passed with a high degree of popular support. The popular 'yes' vote, however, soon gave rise to issues of interpretation and Mesa's attempt to use the referendum result as a basis for fresh legislation on the gas industry led to the Bolivian Congress passing a more thoroughgoing nationalist law than Mesa wanted. Mesa did not long survive this outcome and resigned when faced with popular demonstrations in 2005.

Taking these examples together, it is clear that the plebiscitary option only works with popular – or at least reasonably popular – governments. Authoritarian incumbency would seem to help at the margin, but incumbent victories cannot be taken for granted. Chávez, Morales and Correa mainly succeeded because the three were able to tap into and organize important sources of popular support. Without this, they would almost certainly have failed.

The opposition responds: Recall votes under Chávez and Morales

The opposition has also sought to use direct voting as a tactic, mainly in the form of recall referendums. The idea of a recall vote, though well established in some US states, is relatively new in South America. Some provision for this exists in Colombia, but the only occasions where recall votes have been used at national level have been in Venezuela in 2004 and Bolivia in 2008. In Venezuela, the idea of a recall vote was actively pursued by the opposition, whereas in Bolivia the opposition agreed to a proposal that it did not initiate. Nevertheless, at least in two of our three countries, the opposition has responded to the success of ideas of direct democracy by attempting to use a similar idea against the incumbent.

By the end of 2003, Venezuelan politics had become acutely polarized, with a coup attempt in April 2002 and an oil workers' strike starting at the end of 2002. These are both discussed in other chapters. Following these events, the opposition sought to make use of a proviso in the 1999 constitution, according to which elected officials could be recalled to seek a fresh mandate if a sufficient number of signatures requested this. In the case of a presidential recall vote in Venezuela, nearly 2.5 million signatures were required – a formidable requirement (Hellinger in Ellner 2007). When the Venezuelan opposition initially presented its petition, there were many disputes about the authenticity of signatures and court proceedings were invoked. Amid the claims and counterclaims, a sufficient number of signatures was ultimately accepted as valid and the vote went ahead, with Chávez once more emerging victorious with just under 60 per cent of the vote. Although Chávez did win the 2004 recall referendum, he evidently did not welcome the need for one and probably did not expect (any more than most others did) that the terms of the 1999 constitution would lend themselves to the opposition's own plebiscitary tactics.

This was not the case in Bolivia where Morales's party was the first to call for a recall vote, in the context of controversy over Morales's attempt to secure approval for the new Bolivian constitution. This proposal was initially rejected by the opposition, which however then changed its position and agreed to a recall referendum for the president, vice-president and departmental prefects. The recall vote was witnessed by international observers, and its legitimacy was generally accepted. Morales won his recall vote with a somewhat higher proportion of the vote than he achieved when a presidential candidate in 2005 but opposition governors won re-election in the four eastern states most identified with autonomy demands. It could be argued that the Bolivian recall vote essentially confirmed what was already known, namely that Morales was popular in Bolivia as a whole but very unpopular in some significant parts of the country.

The idea of a recall vote was to enable the popularity of a political incumbent to be tested between elections. Broadly speaking, this is in fact what happened. Both Chávez and Morales resubmitted themselves to the electorate. Both won the resulting votes and both outcomes were verified by international observers – though, at least in the Venezuelan case, not without some discussion. Whatever the shortcomings of these processes, they do provide further evidence

117

that direct democracy in these countries has been significantly institutionalized.

Too much presidential power? Democracy and presidential re-election

The final issue to be considered in this chapter is presidential re-election. This has been a major item of dispute between Chávez, Morales and Correa and their political opponents. A key constitutional provision in all presidential systems stipulates the length of the presidential term and the possibility – or otherwise – of re-election. Most presidential democracies put some term limits on presidential re-election, even though this is not in principle a necessary feature of a democratic process. Many people do believe that it is good democratic practice to limit the re-election of chief executives. However, the United States until the late 1940s permitted indefinite consecutive presidential re-election. Franklin Roosevelt was elected to the presidency four times and eventually died in office.

Presidential re-election has been an especially sensitive issue in a number of Latin American countries where there is a reasonable concern that incumbent executives may use their powers to bias the state in order to remain in office. We have already seen that popular leaders who overstep their powers can in practice be difficult to check. Restrictions on presidential re-election are therefore seen as a crucial backstop, given the general weakness of checks and balances. This backstop is not altogether satisfactory because there are ways in which incumbents can find their way around the spirit of the restrictions, notably by pressing the cause of close relatives. Argentina's Perón nominated his third wife, Isabel, as vice-presidential candidate in 1973 and she – disastrously – succeeded to the presidency upon Péron's death the following year. More recently, in 2007, Mrs Cristina Kirchner of Argentina was elected to the presidency upon the expiration of her husband's first term as president.

However, the issue still remains controversial. Popular but autocratic leaders who can stand for re-election do face the temptation to engage in measures that bias the state in favour of incumbents. Behaviour of this kind is not unknown in much of the world, but it has a particular salience in Latin America, where practices of this kind have become historically notorious. There are several national variants on the saying that 'when in power, one does justice to one's friends and applies the law to one's enemies'. There is a very real fear that an unscrupulous elected government might use a temporary period of popularity to bias the state against opposition to the point that the necessary condition of maintaining some kind of democracy – a genuinely competitive electoral process – is not met.

There is also a fear that an opposition movement, unable to remove an entrenched president due to re-election provisions, will move beyond the role of a loyal opposition and adopt more desperate measures. There is little doubt that this kind of thinking did exist in the cases considered here. It is hard to imagine that the Venezuelan opposition would have planned a coup against Chávez in April 2002 if his presidential term had been due to finish in early 2004 with no immediate re-election permitted, which is what the 1961 constitution would have required. In fact, Morales's promise made in late 2008 to stand down in 2014 if re-elected in 2009 played an important part in making opposition to his government less intense and thus permitted the vote on the new constitution to go ahead. It is, of course, too early to be sure of what will actually happen in 2014. Correa, too, has promised not to seek further re-election after serving two terms under the 2009 constitution.

In general, even though there is no purely logical reason to regard a presidential system that permits re-election as necessarily less democratic than one that does not, there is a genuine popular ambivalence about the indefinite re-election of incumbents in several Latin American countries. The most famous 'no re-election' slogan in fact comes not from South America at all but from the Mexican Revolution. At the beginning of the 1990s, the majority of Latin American countries had restrictions on presidential re-election, either prohibiting immediate re-election or in some cases re-election at any time.

Nevertheless, under 'third wave' democracy there has been a general change in the direction of facilitating presidential re-election in South America, even though not in Central America or Mexico which have tended to keep their restrictions. Today, most countries in South America permit immediate re-election to a second term of office. Only Paraguay, Chile and Uruguay still forbid any immediate re-election. The restrictive Chilean system can be seen as part of a reaction against the long incumbency of Pinochet and the similarly limiting Paraguayan system as part of a reaction against Stroessner. In fact, Paraguay's former president Duarte did attempt to change the national constitution to permit re-election but was in the end unsuccessful. A system, similar to the US, in which incumbents are permitted a second term but not usually a third, has tended to become the norm in most of South America. Chávez has, however, made clear his desire for indefinite re-election and this opens the way, in principle, to a presidency for life. This, indeed, makes him an outlier and raises issues of democratic stability.

By way of conclusion

Chávez, Morales and Correa have already had an impact that would probably survive to a significant degree even if they were to abandon office tomorrow. Institutionally, the key issue is the combination of presidentialism and plebiscites. Plebiscitary tactics may in the future continue to exercise significant influence, in different ways, in other Latin American countries. Not only may popular incumbents seek to use this means of converting potentially short-term popularity into longer-term institutional advantage, but opposition politicians may take a keen interest in suppressing the plebiscitary route, even at the risk of total confrontation with the presidency. Something of this kind happened in Honduras in 2009, where one can see a clear connection between institutional conflicts and conflicts of political philosophy.

There may be some reason for democratic concern about another institutional development, namely the relaxation of rules on re-election. Given the way in which incumbents can bias the state in their own favour, there must be a real issue connected with the dangers to democracy of a 'presidency for life' in the Latin American context. We saw in chapter 1 that Fujimori's quest for a third presidential term brought that country close to democratic breakdown. If Chávez seeks to follow the 'third term' path in 2012, then one can anticipate serious problems.

However, the re-election issue – unlike the plebiscitary one – does not divide our three cases neatly from the rest of the region. Morales and Correa have promised to limit their incumbency to two presidential terms. On the other hand, Argentine President Kirchner sought to undermine restrictions on presidential re-election by supporting his succession by his wife. Furthermore, both Argentina's Menem and Colombia's Uribe looked seriously at the possibility of a third term, though ultimately drawing back. Full discussion of political succession issues in Latin America would require another book, but there may in fact be good reason for believing that presidential re-election rather than plebiscites or socialism may be the Achilles heel of Venezuelan democracy.

This, though, is an issue for the future. For the present, whatever reservations may be relevant, one cannot dismiss plebiscites, recall votes and some relaxation of re-election rules as simply undemocratic. If Pinochet could be defeated in a plebiscite, then the same must surely be true of Chávez – who was indeed initially defeated in a 2007 referendum on extending presidential re-election provisions. Some degree of bias within an essentially democratic process is not at all the same as downright falsification of the popular vote. In Venezuela, Bolivia and Ecuador, there have been many opportunities for the democratic will to express itself. Institutional weaknesses in all three countries clearly remain but they have led to more political conflict (and more 'politics' generally) rather than less.

When commenting on broader philosophical issues, we cannot get away from the point that democracy has to do at some level with the will of the majority. Critics who claim that – for example – Chávez's government 'has deteriorated into a simulacrum of democratic rule' (Schamis 2008: 58) give insufficient weight to this point. Even the opposition has acknowledged the authenticity of Chávez's re-election in 2006. His domestic opponents and foreign critics did themselves no favours by 'crying wolf' too early, too often, with too much hyperbole and insufficient understanding of how discredited the 'ancien regime' had become. The uncompromising view that Chávez was heading an illegitimate regime per se led to such self-defeating moves as the 2002 coup attempt and the opposition boycott of legislative elections in 2005.

It also seems that the style of politics adopted by Chávez, Morales and Correa is in one key respect less dangerous than it would have been prior to 'third wave' democratization. In the past, left-wing political leaders in South America who polarized the political process risked overthrow by the military. Venezuelan history over the past half-century itself illustrates some of the consequences of this, at the time quite reasonable, concern. In Venezuela, 'pacted' Punto Fijo democracy was seen as being (and to some extent was) a plausible answer to the question of how to sustain some kind of democracy in the US backyard at a time of intense Cold War politics. Whatever its faults, this form of democracy mostly respected civil rights and was never overthrown by a Pinochet figure. However, the 'low intensity' (Gills and Rocamora 1992) character of what gradually turned into a rather elitist kind of democratic system involved real shortcomings in respect of excessive clientelism, corruption, weak law enforcement and a general failure of representation.

Now times have changed. As we saw in chapter 1, dictatorships have become much harder to impose. If one no longer has to worry so much about a Pinochet-style reaction, then one kind of objection to 'twentieth-century socialism' – namely that it may create the kind of polarization that could lead to the collapse of democracy itself – loses some of its force. The alternative danger, that extreme presidentialism may ultimately lead to the total undermining of effective democratic contestation, cannot be dismissed completely but it does reflect a somewhat pessimistic view of the significance of domestic public opinion.

In institutional terms, the issue of political centralization cannot be separated from broader questions of political ideology. What significantly differentiates our three cases from other presidents who have used plebiscites – especially Pinochet and Fujimori – has been their general political orientation. Both Pinochet and Fujimori were clearly right-wing politicians. In both cases, plebiscites were part of a broader strategy of political demobilization backed by the military. Chávez, Morales and Correa have been much more mobilizing, with a participatory and socialist ideology. The use of plebiscites in a left-of-centre context may indicate an area of political vulnerability. If public confidence in Chávez, Morales or Correa becomes decisively undermined (due to failures of economic management, external setback or some other cause), it seems entirely likely that they will pay the appropriate political price. Socialism, meanwhile, clearly has an institutional and not simply a policy context. Even in its most moderate and democratic manifestation, it is ultimately about using the power of the state to combat social elites and empower the economically excluded. It is not a political philosophy that is to everybody's taste. It is certainly not a feature of the Miami Consensus. However, democratic socialism (so long as it is indeed democratic) is a potential alternative to checks and balances democracy and one that has clearly resonated with many people in three Andean republics. While there are certainly many grounds on which 'twenty-first century socialism' may be criticized – there have been some significant policy failures – it raises institutional issues that should not be reduced to the simple idea of elective dictatorship.

— 5 —

THE POLITICS OF OIL AND GAS: TWENTY-FIRST CENTURY SOCIALISM IN PRACTICE

Broadly speaking, the 1990s were a decade of low commodity prices. This was an important part of the explanation for why some quite bold economic reforms undertaken in the context of the Miami Consensus and, more narrowly, the Washington Consensus did not achieve the hoped-for results. By the late 1990s, a note of disappointment was creeping into official reports about the region's economic progress (IDB 1997) and the political outlook was starting to look less settled. The 1990s was certainly a decade of low international oil prices, whose renewed weakness in 1998 led the Venezuelan government to cut public spending in an election year. This was greatly to the advantage of Hugo Chávez, who was then in the process of emerging from a political outsider into a serious presidential candidate.

The first decade of the current millennium was a period of much higher oil prices. These provided enormous windfall gains to the Chávez government, and enabled it to use selective inducements – low-cost oil, soft loans and some grants – to pursue both domestic policies of redistribution and (as we shall see in the next chapter) a broadly anti-Miami Consensus foreign policy. Chávez promised, and to an extent delivered, quite generous amounts of help to his foreign allies, including most prominently Cuba but also Bolivia. *Chavista* foreign policy has not invariably succeeded, but it has not failed completely either. One reason why Chávez has enjoyed at least limited success in frustrating the free trade objectives of the FTAA (Free Trade of the Americas) has been his ability to back its opponents with money. Moreover, one dramatic act of expropriation in Bolivia, Morales's seizure of the gas export pipeline to Brazil in 2006, was to an extent influenced by Chávez.

Venezuela's commodity wealth plainly offers some protection against the constraints that might otherwise impose some binding limits on unorthodox forms of economic management. However, dependency on oil and gas exports represents a different source of domestic vulnerability. It is one thing to redistribute income from high commodity rents but, as the historical record of Latin America has shown repeatedly, quite another to turn the benefits of a temporary commodity boom into sustainable economic development or even sustained macroeconomic stability. (The occasionally expressed hope – or fear – that one day a commodity boom will last for ever has so far not been borne out.) According to the criterion of turning oil revenues into sustainable development, Chávez has not succeeded.

It would be much too simple to claim that Chavismo could not survive significant economic setback. Argentina's Perónism, to make an obvious comparison, has survived many. However, the more intangible issue of international prestige is associated with economic performance, and here the perception of success is of broader importance. For a small country such as Bolivia, it may well be feasible to deal with any negative results from over-bold policy making by an unobtrusive change towards pragmatism, but it would be much harder for Venezuela to evolve in this direction due to its far stronger international profile.

Oil and gas issues: An overview

This chapter deals with the politics of oil and gas in Venezuela and Bolivia. Because it may still be too early to assess the effect of Correa's oil policies, the chapter barely touches on Ecuador. Although all three countries are oil and gas producers, their relative dependency on resource rents varies. Venezuela is by far the most important oil producer of the three. It is an influential member of OPEC, an organization that it played a key role in setting up in 1960. It is dependent on oil for around 90 per cent of its exports and some 50 per cent of its fiscal income (a figure that does not count indirect effects). Bolivia is a regionally significant gas exporter but even the small Bolivian economy is not comparably dependent on gas. Ecuador is a small oil producer and exporter but one of local rather than regional or global significance. Some 40 per cent of Ecuador's total oil production is consumed domestically (BP 2009). Of the three, only Venezuela can be considered a hydrocarbon economy in the full sense of the term and much of Chávez's political orientation – both domestic and international – is based on this fact.

The long-term trend, though, is bleak. In 1950, Venezuela produced some 15 per cent of the world's total oil supply, which was much more oil than the rest of Latin America put together (Philip 1982: 68). However, Venezuelan oil production has suffered a relatively declining trend since the 1950s and an absolutely declining trend since around 1970. Today, Venezuela produces rather less than 3 per cent of world oil output. Meanwhile, non-oil industries have not expanded significantly to take the place of declining oil revenues. In comparison with Mexico, Brazil, and even Ecuador and Bolivia, the Venezuelan economy is much less diversified.

We have already noted that the Venezuelan economy as a whole underwent an absolute decline during 1980–2000. This outcome was quite disappointing in the light of expectations at the time. There is already a good deal of literature about whether, and if so how, a so-called resource curse operates in hydrocarbon-dependent economies (see, for example, Dunning 2008, Karl 1997 and, on Venezuela, Rodriguez 1991). This chapter addresses a different issue, but a potentially decisive one, which has to do with declining production.

An important reason for this decline has been the politicization of oil and gas production. Relevant to this broad theme is the way in which both Chávez and – at least initially – Morales adopted high-profile confrontational tactics in dealing with oil and gas issues. In this context, we need to draw a distinction between redistributive politics and oil and gas nationalism. The latter, defined as the use of the state to try to control domestic oil and gas resources, has been common enough in Latin America and indeed beyond. Prior to the 1990s, there were several Latin American cases of high-profile expropriations or extensions of state control, driven to an extent (though not usually exclusively) by internal politics. Cases include the Mexican oil expropriation of 1938, the 'O Petróleo é Nosso' campaign in Brazil in the late 1940s, and the confiscation of the US-owned International Petroleum Company by the Velasco government in Peru in 1968. The Bolivian nationalization of 2006 could be seen as another event in this tradition. It was actually the third nationalization of oil or gas in Bolivia, the previous ones occurring in 1937 and 1969. What is different about Venezuela is that the oil industry had already been nationalized, in 1976, and the main conflict involved the Chávez government and the managers of the state oil industry. What was at issue here was a conflict between two visions of state-led policy, one technocratic and rather respectful of state autonomy and the other redistributive and highly political.

It is no surprise that Chávez and Morales adopted oil and gas policies different from their predecessors which were somewhat pro-market in the case of Venezuela and decidedly so in the case of Bolivia. Public opinion across the region is probably more hostile to market-oriented oil policy than almost any other aspect of free market economics. Even during the 'Miami Consensus' period, when market reform was vigorously pursued in most Latin American countries, the reversal of previous oil nationalizations was not complete. For example, Mexico retained its state oil monopoly, despite adopting vigorous policies of market reform in other areas.

However, resource nationalism is one thing; policy making led by a mentality of capturing economic surpluses for redistribution is something different. Moreover, what distinguished Chávez and Morales (at least initially) from more moderate resource nationalists such as Brazil – in addition to a stronger redistributive mentality – was their greater aggressiveness. Both Chávez and Morales have tended to adopt the principle of 'he who is not with us is against us' in policy making as well as in their politics. Chávez and Morales, as well as their opponents, used oil and gas policy as a staging ground for confrontations designed to solidify their domestic political support – if necessary at an economic price. Both of these points relate to a broader theme of the book, which is the return of politics to issues that in the 1990s would have been seen in most of Latin America as being essentially matters for technocrats.

This discussion looks in some detail at two political issues in Venezuela that illustrate the general argument and then at one key decision in Bolivia. With Venezuela, the first of these two was the ending of the corporate independence of PdVSA. The claim being made here is that Chávez's treatment of PdVSA has closed off a state capitalist option that might have worked better for Venezuela than the options that it now has. This is not to deny that managing PdVSA raised serious policy problems for successive Venezuelan governments or that Chávez faced significant political provocations from PdVSA managers. However, Chávez preferred to adopt an essentially political approach rather than taking the trouble to balance the complex requirements of maintaining an efficient state company.

The second decision is Chávez's reinforcement of Venezuela's role in OPEC. This can be explained at one level in terms of Chávez's anti-US orientation and support for pro 'third world' forms of politics. However, it also shows *Chavista* policy to some advantage. It is indeed the case that there are circumstances in which commodity exporters can benefit from rejecting the principle of free markets in the interests of producer solidarity. Venezuela has surely benefited considerably from the fact that OPEC-led production cuts were effective in combating the sharp fall in oil prices at the end of the 1990s, and seem to have worked again in 2008–9. A possible conclusion would be that, in some short-term situations, Chávez's adversarial style of politics has something to recommend it. However, a long-run view may be less favourable. Despite an undoubted degree of short-term success, there may be longer-term problems stemming from Venezuela's vigorous policy of pro-OPEC solidarity. Significant future increases in oil production have now become less likely. Furthermore, Venezuelan exports have fallen (and domestic demand has risen) to the point where even relatively high international prices may not be enough for Venezuela to avoid economic problems.

The chapter then moves to Bolivia and discusses its gas nationalization of 2006. What is significant here is not only the fact of the nationalization, but the way in which it was implemented. Under some degree of *Chavista* influence, Bolivia may well have alienated Brazil in a way that has long-term significance for its chances of turning gas reserves into real development. This is another example of how a tactically effective act of confrontational political leadership in the short term may turn out strategically very questionable in the longer run.

Venezuela: The decline and fall of PdVSA

The most important single factor behind the decline of the Venezuelan oil industry under Chávez has been the PdVSA strike of 2002–3 and PdVSA's failure to recover from it. This strike may turn out to mark a major turning point in the economic history of Venezuela, and it was certainly a key event in the Chávez presidency. To understand the reasons for the strike and its outcome, we need some historical background.

When the Venezuelan oil industry was nationalized at the beginning of 1976, the 'partidocratic' political elite in power at that time was conscious of Venezuela's dependence on oil revenues and of the potential danger of putting Venezuela's leading industry into the hands of an inefficient state company. Mexico's Pemex, which had an unnecessarily large number of employees and a reputation for corruption, was seen as an example of what needed to be avoided.

One may note the irony that the Mexican government today regards PdVSA as an example of what Mexico needs to avoid.

PdVSA, in any case, needed to step up its level of investment almost immediately. By the end of the 1960s, high taxes on the private oil companies and low international oil prices caused oil production to decline to levels then considered dangerously low. In 1970, Venezuela produced some 3.8 million barrels daily (b/d). Disinvestment in the years leading up to the nationalization caused this to fall to 2.4 million b/d in 1976 (both figures from BP). The Venezuelan state in the mid 1970s therefore inherited an oil industry that needed to be turned around after a period of decline. Venezuela's entire economic outlook depended on PdVSA's ability to do this.

Given this background, a great deal of emphasis was placed from the start on maintaining PdVSA's corporate autonomy, which in practice meant the autonomy of the senior corporate executives who had stayed behind to run the new state company. Some initial political battles fought out between the state oil company and the Ministry of Mines and Energy – theoretically PdVSA's supervisor – were decisively won by PdVSA. By the end of the 1970s, PdVSA had established itself as a major power centre within the Venezuelan state and as a relatively efficient technocracy.

The fundamental dilemma of whether to maintain the efficiency of PdVSA by allowing significant corporate autonomy or to maintain tight control for political reasons long pre-dates Chávez. Several accounts of the post-nationalization period have tended to take a positive view of PdVSA's demand for autonomy and a negative view of subsequent 'political interference' by the government (Baena 1999; Coronel 1983). However, there is a case for taking a less positive view about state enterprise autonomy beyond a certain point because an over-powerful state enterprise can exploit weaknesses in accountability. The result may be too much spending on investment and corporate salaries and not enough emphasis on financial control.

PdVSA certainly increased its investment in the later 1970s. This rose (in current dollars) from $323.5 million in 1976 and $526.1 million in 1977 to $2,270 million in 1980 (Philip 1982). Even allowing for some dollar inflation, this was quite a large increase. It is true that, without a significant amount of public investment, oil production might have collapsed. Yet there was a legitimate question about whether PdVSA was over-investing (or simply spending too lavishly). Whatever the economic merits of these arguments, it would never be politically realistic to suppose that a country facing macroeconomic problems on the scale of those affecting Venezuela in the 1980s could allow a state company of the size of PdVSA to maintain complete operational autonomy. It was in principle quite reasonable for PdVSA's critics to claim that the company needed to be held more accountable. However PdVSA managers were not wrong either in their suspicions that, without a politically autonomous state company able to defend the interests of the industry, Venezuelan governments of any persuasion would concentrate too much on consuming oil rent and not enough on producing oil.

Some tension is inherent in the management of almost any state company – in South America as elsewhere – and PdVSA was no different. A fundamental problem has to do with issues of political loyalty. A successfully run state company has to train and retain staff who hope to be internationally employable. State oil company managers may find that close relationships with the private sector can enhance their employability. According to Hellinger (2000), literally hundreds of executives left PdVSA in the 1990s to find employment with foreign oil companies, who were by then allowed to operate in Venezuela. The potential market value of an engineer or geologist will also depend to some extent on the reputation of their current employer and, for a state company employee, the issue of corporate autonomy may be relevant. Professional employees loyal to their immediate employer won't necessarily be institutionally loyal to the government of the day. They may, rather, identify their own career prospects with maintaining some kind of distance from their own government, especially if the latter is seen as being as corrupt, inefficient and accident-prone as several Venezuelan governments were in the 1980s.

One factor making the issue of loyalty so important is asymmetry of information and subsequent problems of accountability. There have been many well-known cases even in first-world countries when experts have used privileged information to support a hidden corporate or personal agenda and distorted national policy as a result. In the case of Venezuela, the danger of this was much greater than it would be in a developed country, due to the weakness of the checking process. This was itself largely due to the clientelistic nature of the national public administration, the lack of expertise in Congress, and the relatively concentrated nature of knowledge about the oil industry. Some observers of the Venezuelan oil industry in the 1980s were surprised at the limited coverage of issues relating to oil in the print and broadcast media at that time. There seemed to be very little general curiosity about how this vital national industry actually operated.

In addition, there were political resentments. PdVSA managers came to be seen by their critics as overpaid, arrogant and doubtfully patriotic. They themselves were proud of running something close to a corporate meritocracy and had little respect for the efficiency of the rest of the public bureaucracy. It did not help that the economic decline affecting Venezuela in the 1980s reduced the budget of the Mines and Energy Ministry – to which PdVSA in theory reported – to the point that it lost most of the limited effectiveness that it had once enjoyed (Paris 2007). PdVSA, meanwhile, was mostly able to maintain the real value of its salaries during Venezuela's long period of economic decline in the 1980s and 1990s while most of the state bureaucracy, and even the military, were not. In 1999, at the very beginning of the Chávez presidency, the president of PdVSA was paid $25,400 per month, while the Minister of Mines and Energy was paid $1,100 (Hellinger 2000). In policy-making terms, PdVSA bosses also tended to go over the heads of ministry officials and approach the president directly.

Following the fall of Carlos Andres Pérez in 1993, PdVSA gained even more power and autonomy, due largely to the fact that the Venezuelan 'partidocracy' was in evident disarray. Moreover, unpopular though PdVSA was in some ways, it was probably less unpopular than the 'neoliberal' economic technocrats who had attempted to run Venezuela from 1989 to 1992. Once these had fallen from office under conditions that made their return unlikely, PdVSA's technocrats came to be seen as the only economic show in town. Some senior managers within PdVSA, anxious to avoid continuing dependence on the vagaries of Venezuelan politics, talked aloud about the gradual privatization of the company. The head of PdVSA in the 1990s, Luis Giusti, was also known to be politically close to the Acción Democratica establishment and was spoken of in some places as a potential presidential candidate.

When Chávez assumed the presidency, therefore, PdVSA was a big, powerful and significantly autonomous state company informally aligned with Chávez's political opponents. This was not a particularly stable situation. Chávez allowed it to be understood when campaigning for the presidency that he thought that PdVSA had become overmighty. This view was not confined to Chávez's supporters. The pro-market presidential candidate, Miguel Rodríguez, took a broadly similar view.

Chávez started with considerable caution in his dealings with PdVSA. His first appointment as head of PdVSA was of a highly qualified oil executive. He named an oil liaison commission while he was waiting to take power, and some of those who were most involved in this (notably Ali Rodríguez and Bernardo Alvarez) played a continuing role in making oil policy under the new administration (Paris 2007: 196). They were more moderate figures than some other Chávez advisers. Subsequently, though, there was a change in the political balance once the 1999 constitution was finally approved. This established oil and gas as state monopolies and also empowered Chávez to decree legislation. Chávez soon began to question the autonomy of the state company more aggressively. Higher taxes on PdVSA profits and closer official regulation of PdVSA business then followed.

In February 2002, Chávez, by this time showing signs of irritation with PdVSA's resistance to the kind of reform that he wanted, imposed a new board of directors – largely made up of political loyalists rather than industry technocrats – on the state company. PdVSA managers saw this as a deliberate blow to the principle of corporate meritocracy. Almost immediately, a group of top managers publicly denounced the 'politicization' of the industry. Their denunciation was quickly supported by leading Venezuelan business interests, who were by then moving into open conflict with the government. Chávez responded in a high-handed manner when he sacked seven named PdVSA officials on television, during his 'Aló Presidente' programme on 7 April. This triggered a strike involving PdVSA and a series of other events that led to the failed coup attempt on 11 April. Although Chávez defeated the coup attempt, his post-coup behaviour was for a short time more conciliatory. He reinstated the dismissed managers and appointed Ali Rodriguez – a close ally but a relatively moderate figure – head of PdVSA.

In December 2002, PdVSA officials went on strike once more. This time it was an openly political strike called by the 'Coordinadora Democrática'. The strike was part of a strategy designed to bring down Chávez by damaging the Venezuelan economy. The strike did enormous damage but eventually failed. Many of the strikers were dismissed and quite a number of people left the company. The company after the strike had lost a lot of its power and prestige. Neither investment nor production nor maintenance fully recovered. The loss of 18,000 employees who left the company – either of their own volition or otherwise – represented a real and sustained setback to PdVSA's productive potential. These people were hard to replace.

Instead of giving PdVSA a chance to recover via a period of rebuilding, Chávez's drive for political control over the company intensified. He moved Ali Rodriguez to another position and appointed Rafael

Ramírez, a close personal ally, in his stead. The company subsequently became much more political, with loyalty counting for more than efficiency. When the 2006 presidential election campaign was underway, Ramírez told PdVSA employees to support Hugo Chávez or their jobs would be at risk. When these remarks led to controversy, they were fully supported by Chávez himself. More generally, there is considerable evidence indicating that the human capital necessary to run a successful oil industry has been radically downgraded in favour of political loyalty. Open opponents of Chávez are no longer employable within PdVSA. While Chávez's desire to undermine a potential source of opposition may have been subjectively understandable, PdVSA's once-impressive resources of human capital were heavily depleted as a result.

The government also in 2004 started to set up a group of so-called Misiones – essentially state-sponsored social spending agencies – with direct access to PdVSA's resources, so that PdVSA was required to invest directly in social projects. Investment in the actual oil and gas industry was cut sharply. According to official figures, in 2006 PdVSA invested no more than $5.9 billion in the year, including $2.6 billion in exploration and production (*Petroleum Economist*, January 2007). The official figure for 2007, of $11bn invested in the whole oil and gas industry, seems more appropriate but still rather low given the lack of private capital entering the industry at that time. Moreover, while there may have been some financial savings generated by tighter political control of PdVSA, after the strike there were efficiency losses as well. It is difficult to quantify these because PdVSA's attitude to information has become much more opaque since the strike. This opacity has been quite deliberate and makes it hard to analyse the post-2003 oil industry with any degree of confidence.

Chávez also used PdVSA as an arm of what was in some respects a personal foreign policy. PdVSA has sent experts to help Evo Morales run the nationalized natural gas industry in Bolivia, and there have been plans for joint ventures in refinery construction in other friendly countries. At a more macro level, there have been some high-profile policies of offering oil to friendly countries at concessionary prices or as part of barter arrangements. The best-known of these programmes was the 'oil for doctors' exchange programme with Cuba. It is perhaps fortunate for Venezuela that some of Chávez's more imaginative ideas – including the construction of a transcontinental gas pipeline to Argentina – were dropped at a relatively early stage because of doubts about their economic feasibility. While this is not the place for a detailed discussion of the financing of such projects, one is left with the impression that PdVSA is being used for international as well as domestic political purposes in ways that seem hazardous to its commercial operations. Moreover, while not all of Chávez's many announcements of oil-related cooperation with his political allies have been backed by action, the effect of those that were further compromised PdVSA's operational autonomy.

The central point is that Chávez inherited a state company that – while not free of political and managerial difficulties – was an efficient oil producer. Venezuela in 1998 had the option of using PdVSA to spearhead a process of planned economic development while employing its negotiating skills to bring in private investment in a generally subordinate capacity. After 2003, this option had effectively disappeared and everything was instead largely subordinated to Chávez's social and political priorities, and indeed to Chávez himself. It is true that the PdVSA strikers were legally in the wrong for launching an openly political strike and maintaining it even after the Supreme Court declared it unconstitutional. The government undoubtedly had a legal right to dismiss them, but a more conciliatory attitude once the strike was over might have been wiser. One has the impression that conciliation, at least for any length of time, is simply not in Chávez's nature and that maintaining the efficiency of PdVSA in Chávez's eyes took second place to winning a political battle. However, without an efficient state company, Venezuela has had to choose between greater reliance on investment from outside Venezuela and accepting lower levels of oil production. So far, it has mostly been the latter.

Chávez's confrontational economic nationalism was also in evidence when renegotiating the terms on which foreign companies invested in Venezuela in the 1990s. The desire to renegotiate the contracts, in itself, was understandable enough. It could well be argued that the general increase in international prices after 2000 would have made it irresponsible to do anything else. However, what might have started as a reasonable fiscal strategy ended up being driven by an aggressive form of politics that often concluded in expropriation. An important set of contracts, involving strategic association between PdVSA and various transnational oil companies, was put on notice that it would be ended unilaterally when, during the course of a television programme in 2005, Chávez announced his intention to cancel it.

For political reasons, too, Chávez sought to reorient the character of foreign investment coming into Venezuela away from the mostly US-owned companies that made up the majority of non-PdVSA capital in the industry in 1998 towards investment from Russia, France and China. This attempt to diversify (rather than end) Venezuela's dependence on foreign partners makes sense in terms of Chávez's foreign policy preferences but is of doubtful help in solving the problems of oil production. It is true that, in comparison with earlier historical periods, today's more pluralistically organized world oil industry has given Venezuela a reasonably wide choice of potential partners. In political terms, investment from Russia, China or even France might be much more palatable to Chávez than investment by the major US- or British-owned transnationals. It is also just conceivable that a company from a friendly country might be prepared to offer slightly more favourable terms to the Venezuelan state than a company from a politically unfriendly one. However, Russian and Chinese companies can no more afford to lose money in Venezuela than US- or European-owned companies can. The issue of over-dependence on foreign oil investment has not gone away.

Venezuela's role in OPEC

Venezuelan policy towards OPEC was also very political but in a way more successful. The problems facing Venezuela with regard to OPEC were indeed significantly amenable to political action in the short run, though there are unresolved problems in the longer run. These do not involve Venezuelan relations with OPEC as such so much as the risk of 'locking in' inadequate levels of domestic oil production as a result of solidarity with the rest of OPEC.

Before discussing Venezuelan policy towards OPEC, it is necessary to make a preliminary point about the nature of the OPEC 'cartel' itself. Some readers may be puzzled as to how a product whose price fluctuates as much as oil's does can be said to be controlled by a cartel at all. In fact, it is more accurate to regard the international oil industry as only semi-cartelized. OPEC was in 2008 responsible for around 43 per cent of world oil production (figure from BP), and a significantly higher proportion of internationally traded oil. After a complex and incident-packed fifty-year history (on which, for example, Yergin 1991), OPEC today exerts a significant influence on the international oil market but does not really control it. It does set production quotas to which members of the organization are expected to adhere, though there is no real enforcement in the case of non-compliance. Oil producers that are not members of OPEC, for example Mexico and Russia, sometimes cooperate, tacitly or otherwise, with OPEC and sometimes don't. In the absence of cooperation from non-OPEC countries, OPEC members risk the problem of responsibility without power. They may hold back production and have non-OPEC exporting countries take advantage of higher prices without sharing the cost of production restrictions. When cooperation starts to fail, production discipline within OPEC itself can be lost. Something of this kind happened in the 1980s and led to the collapse of international oil prices in 1985.

Prior to the election of Chávez, Venezuela's degree of support for OPEC tended to fluctuate according to who was currently in power. There was an initial period of enthusiasm in the 1960s after Venezuela had played a major part in setting up the organization. Venezuela also pushed aggressively within OPEC for higher prices in the 1970s. When OPEC formally adopted production quotas at the beginning of the 1980s, Venezuela, like other OPEC members, faced a collective action problem. Would output restrictions, if seriously adopted by one country, effectively support the international price, or would rival producers simply dive in and pick up market share? There was for some time a debate within Venezuela between those who were mostly supportive of maximizing oil production and sceptical towards OPEC and others who tended to be more supportive of OPEC. Over time, as prices stayed low, the sceptics tended to gain in confidence. The state oil company, PdVSA, had a bureaucratic interest in scepticism towards OPEC since it had no desire to accept restrictions on its own investment and production. As PdVSA gained political strength within Venezuela during the 1990s, the anti-OPEC tendency of the Venezuelan government became stronger. After Caldera assumed the presidency at the beginning of 1994, Venezuela virtually ignored OPEC and simply sought to maximize production. This was seen by some as being an understandable temporary reaction to the Venezuelan banking crisis of that year, but production continued to increase during the whole of Caldera's term. In 1998, a decisive election year, PdVSA was fighting something close to an all-out price war with Saudi Arabia, so helping to push world prices down to historically low levels.

Chávez immediately reversed Venezuela's anti-OPEC policy and worked hard to build relationships with other oil-exporting countries. In his 1998 campaign, he declared that 'oil is a geopolitical weapon' (quoted in McBeth 2005: 13) and his opinion did not change thereafter. One of his first acts in office was to send his close political ally Ali Rodríguez to talk to Saudi Arabia and Mexico (both, along with Venezuela, major suppliers of oil to the United States) about jointly cutting production. Some restraints on production were indeed agreed and international prices, which in 1998 were at an all-time low, recovered somewhat in 1999. Chávez then went further and organized an OPEC summit in Caracas in September 2000. In the course of seeking support for the summit, in 1999 Chávez visited presidents Khatami of Iran and Saddam Hussein of Iraq in a new form of petro-diplomacy that clearly disturbed the US government (Jones 2008).

Chávez did indeed help to reinvigorate OPEC. Partly as a result, but for other reasons too, there was a sharp upward trend in international oil and gas prices between 2000 and 2008. International oil prices peaked in July 2008 and then plunged, falling from over $140 per barrel at its peak to as low as $35 a barrel early in 2009 before recovering. This collapse was part of the world recession that started in that year, and had little to do with Venezuela. Chávez, though, returned to his support for collective action through OPEC, although in far less propitious circumstances. He played a significant part in persuading other OPEC countries to meet on three occasions in late 2008 in order to cut back production. In return for promising to reduce its own production by some 350,000 b/d, Venezuela helped persuade OPEC as a whole to promise to reduce output by a total of 4.2 million b/d. Even though total cutbacks by OPEC did not achieve the promised total, they were large enough to make a real difference to the international price level. It is likely that, without the resulting restrictions on production – above all those carried out by Saudi Arabia and the Gulf States – the international price would have collapsed to a level even lower than actually reached, with disastrous consequences for Venezuela. To an extent, Chávez's view of oil as a geopolitical weapon was vindicated.

Yet, agreements to cut production – however helpful to exporters facing low prices in the short run – are likely to have less benign long-term consequences. The problem is that, unless Venezuela returns to its rather risky pre-Chávez policy of pretending to comply with OPEC restrictions while in practice violating them, it can no longer sell all of the oil that it could produce because its output is limited by quota. Renegotiating its quota upwards is a possible option, but this would depend on Saudi Arabia's willingness to cut production by even more than it currently has. This seems an unlikely outcome since Saudi Arabia is not an obvious sympathizer with the Bolivarian revolution. Venezuela's radical political allies such as Iran have too many internal problems to be of much help. Meanwhile growing domestic demand is increasing the gap between Venezuela's permitted production under OPEC quota and its level of exports.

136

Venezuelan oil prospects: An assessment

At the Summit of the Americas conference held in April 2009, Chávez publicly presented Obama with a copy of a book entitled *Open Veins of Latin America*, written by Eduardo Galeano (Galeano 1973). While containing much polemic, many errors of fact and significant hyperbole, Galeano's book makes the substantially valid point that the economic and social development of Latin America has been held back by dependence on exports of commodities. The general point that commodity dependency can have negative long-term developmental consequences, particularly when the commodity is owned or controlled by foreign interests, is quite widely accepted and not only by left-wing authors. Since Chávez evidently approves of Galeano's work, the criterion of commodity dependency might be a reasonable basis for evaluating Venezuela's development progress since 1998.

It is not necessary to be a 'neoliberal' to conclude that, in some ways, Venezuela's structural dependency has become worse. It has certainly not lessened. There are several possible ways of dealing with the problem of over-dependence on a single commodity. They include export diversification as practised by Mexico – which was in the early 1980s highly dependent on oil exports but is now essentially an exporter of manufactured goods. Another possibility is for government to lead a policy of resource-based industrialization (Auty 1990), including the expansion of domestic energy production. Morales's Bolivia seems to be attempting something similar though – as we shall see later in the chapter – its Chávez-backed nationalization of gas did not help its case. In fact, neither strategy is without problems or pitfalls, but they both offer potential exit options from at least some of the problems of commodity dependency. However, Chávez's Venezuela has made no progress in developing non-oil exports (the share of oil in total exports has actually increased since 1998) and the destruction of the professional ethic within PdVSA has made any kind of 'Petrobras style' of public–private cooperation unfeasible, which it was not in 1998.

When we move from this rather broad ground to the narrower issue of fiscal calculation, we need to confront a difficulty that both complicates and summarizes the general picture. This is that there are no commonly accepted statistics as to what Venezuelan oil production currently is. If we take a 'snapshot' of mid-2008, the International Energy Agency (IEA) and the OPEC secretariat both put Venezuelan production at around 2.4 million b/d – an estimate that includes Orimulsion as well as production from the once

137

privately operated companies that Chávez took over. This IEA figure refers to a period before OPEC agreed production cuts in the autumn of 2008. Subsequent to these cuts, the IEA in early 2009 estimated Venezuelan oil production at 2.1 million b/d. BP statistics are broadly compatible. These put Venezuela's oil production figure for 2008 as a whole at some 2.6 million b/d (BP 2009). The Venezuelan authorities, however, have continued to insist that national production amounted to some 3.2 million b/d before falling back below 3 million b/d, due to the OPEC production restrictions from late 2008. A discrepancy of at least 33 per cent on production figures makes for a pretty sharp difference as to how one assesses the Venezuelan oil industry.

This discussion assumes that the lower estimate is more likely to be correct. Of course, the IEA estimate could conceivably be wrong. The preference here for the IEA figure is partly based on the 'Caesar's wife' principle that notes the inability of the Venezuelan authorities to make their statistics sufficiently credible to be accepted by independent sources with no particular axe to grind. Official Venezuelan figures for domestic oil consumption also seem implausibly low which suggests doubt about the reliability of other figures. Scepticism about the government's figures is also partly based on the observation that, if the IEA is wrong about oil production figures in Venezuela to the extent claimed, then (on the double-entry principle) at least some other IEA figures would have to be very wrong as well. A discrepancy of nearly 1 million b/d can hardly be hidden in 'errors and omissions'. Furthermore, Venezuelan export figures to both the US and non-US markets (other than markets for oil on concessionary terms) fit IEA figures better than they fit government figures (see Espinasa 2009). These seem to be sufficient reasons.

Some confusion may have been caused by the fact that PdVSA operates refineries and marketing outlets overseas and supplies some of them by buying crude oil from outside Venezuela. It may therefore be that some government figures for Venezuelan oil production may somehow involve re-exports. However, the main explanation for the numerical discrepancies is probably a general tendency of the Venezuelan government to treat economic statistics as an instrument of politics.

If the lower figures are indeed correct, or close to being so, Venezuela is producing quite a lot less oil than it was a decade ago and less still than it was a generation ago. Production amounted to 3.8 million b/d in 1970, compared to a likely 2.5 million b/d in 2008. Even if these figures are somewhat approximate, there is clearly a problem of declining per capita oil production in the long term. While this is not particularly uncommon – US, British and Mexican oil production have all been on a long-term declining trend – Venezuela's greater dependence on oil exports makes the problem much more serious. Moreover, the problem in the case of Venezuela is not a lack of oil reserves. BP estimated Venezuela's total oil reserves at the end of 2006 at 80 billion barrels – some 6.6 per cent of total world oil supplies – with a reserve–production ratio of 77.6 years (BP). It is a problem to do with the quantity of investment and the efficiency of operations.

In addition to the problem of stagnating or falling production, we must also consider the increasing cost of the heavily subsidized oil sold on the domestic market. Venezuela's steadily growing population has led to an upward trend in the domestic consumption of oil products. According to most private estimates, at least 0.7 million b/d is being sold on the home market, including oil products smuggled to foreign markets. The local price of oil products was in 2008 so low as to be negligible – and clearly below the cost of producing and refining it. A figure of 0.7 million b/d for local consumption (there are higher estimates) would account for nearly 33 per cent of total production if the IEA estimate is right. This amounts to a drastic increase in comparison with the 6 per cent or so of total production sold on the home market in 1970 (Philip 1982). Unless the Venezuelan economy really collapses, or unless a Venezuelan government finally addresses the thorny political issue of domestic subsidies, this problem will tend to get worse as domestic oil consumption increases further.

The income forgone by Venezuela from selling subsidized oil to Chávez's political allies abroad is more difficult to evaluate. There have been many efforts to quantify the value of these subsidies but without much success – a lot depends on fluctuations in world price. Nevertheless, over 100,000 b/d goes to Cuba in return for medical services and a somewhat larger figure is in principle accounted for by the Petrocaribe arrangement that covers much of Central America and the rest of the Caribbean. Then there was Venezuela's offer of cut-price oil to US consumers via its refining subsidiaries in the United States. Despite the appearance of generosity in the headlines, it may be that the net cost of subsidizing 'political' oil exports is not very high. The Venezuelan authorities have deliberately been rather secretive in respect of some international ventures, but one suspects a tendency to over-publicize. We also need to remember that exports sold at below-market prices may still exceed the cost of production. If international prices fall, the subsidy element in the lower export price may also decline. However, even if there is not a very high cost to Venezuela of

Table 5.1 Venezuelan oil production in early 2009: million b/d

Total oil production capacity as of mid-2008	2.5
LESS	
Reduction in output due to OPEC quota restrictions	(0.35)
LEAVES	
Actual oil production in early 2009	2.15*
LESS	
Revenue shortfalls due to	
Domestic sales at below cost	(0.7)
Estimated subsidy element in total concessionary oil exports	(0.1)
LEAVES	
Income-generating oil exports	1.25

Source: Author's calculations on the basis of figures from the IEA and OPEC.

* The International Energy Agency in March 2009 estimated Venezuelan production at 2.1 million b/d.

subsidizing its oil exports, there will certainly be some additional effect on an already diminished export surplus.

A rough estimate as to how much crude oil Venezuela may be producing and exporting if the IEA figures are correct is presented in the table above, which is intended as a guide only.

One cannot move too confidently from oil production figures to a conclusion about Venezuela's long-term macroeconomic prospects. Other factors have to be taken into account, including most obviously the international oil price level. However, one can conclude that there is a real risk that Venezuela's oil export surplus will fall sharply in the years to the point that only dramatically high international prices would be enough to offset sustained economic decline. Many of the problems with Venezuela's oil economy that risk this negative outcome will be difficult to address. They include a long period of insufficient investment due to social spending commitments, inefficiency within PdVSA due to its loss of human capital, potential restrictions on output due to the OPEC quota, and the sustained growth in domestic oil demand due to subsidized prices.

Bolivia, Brazil, and the 2006 gas nationalization

Chávez, Morales and Correa all came to power in countries where there was significant private investment in oil and gas production.

All three sought to renegotiate oil and (in Morales's case) gas contracts. This was only to be expected. Certainly, the principle that host governments are entitled to amend contracts unilaterally, to the point of nationalization if desired, is no longer seriously disputed. Moreover, the upward trend in oil and gas prices during 2003–8 provided a potential surplus to which producer governments generally considered themselves fully entitled.

This does not, though, mean that nationalizing foreign oil and gas investments should be regarded as an invariably cheap and accessible source of ever-enhancing public revenues. Nationalization can be costly in the long run, especially if it is undertaken largely for internal political reasons. By far the most dramatic confrontation between host government and private companies in our three countries was the nationalization of oil and gas in Bolivia in 2006. To understand some of the issues that this raises, we need a little background in how the politics of natural gas in Bolivia differs from the politics of oil in Venezuela. The key issue is transportation.

Bolivia exports most of its gas by pipeline, and pipelines are expensive to build, capital-intensive to operate, and usually financed over long payback periods. Once a pipeline is built, both supplier and customer are locked into a long-term relationship that is dangerous to disrupt and costly to end. The relevant relationships therefore tend to be bilateral rather than global. For a small economy such as Bolivia, decisions about whether and where to build a pipeline can be of real geopolitical as well as economic significance.

Bolivia's policy environment stems in large part from its situation as a small country with larger and more powerful neighbours. Bolivia's relationship with most of its neighbours is complicated. Bolivia was twice defeated by Chile in nineteenth-century wars. As a result of its second defeat, it lost direct access to the Pacific. Bolivians still feel strongly about this loss. There was a war scare involving Bolivia and Chile as recently as the 1970s. Exporting gas to or via Chile would be bound to raise sovereignty concerns in Bolivia, as indeed it did when the Sánchez de Lozada government was rash enough to propose it. Meanwhile, Peru has a major gas industry of its own whose marketing plans certainly did not include importing from Bolivia. So where was Bolivia to sell its gas?

When internationally significant reserves of gas were first discovered in Bolivia in the 1960s, Brazil was seen as the largest possible market, and to that extent the most promising. The Brazilian government could possibly organize the financing of a large pipeline, which is something that Bolivia could not hope to do on its own. There was, though, a significant current of expert opinion within Bolivia that preferred to export mainly to Argentina. A small gas export pipeline to Argentina was initiated in the 1960s and completed in the 1970s. Subsequent commercial relations with Argentina did not run entirely smoothly. Argentina renegotiated the gas price downwards from the mid-1980s. In the 1990s, following some major gas discoveries, Argentina itself became a net gas exporter.

For Bolivia to export gas to Brazil was much more politically toler-able than exporting to or via Chile and more economically logical than exporting to Argentina – though perhaps less politically conven-ient. However, it was not completely straightforward either. Brazil, seen as an over-powerful neighbour by a significant number of Bolivians, is somewhat distrusted not least because it borders Santa Cruz where there is a powerful autonomist movement. As a result of these considerations, some Bolivians opposed exporting gas to Brazil because they feared over-dependence, while some Brazilians similarly feared over-dependence on supplies from Bolivia which were seen as potentially unreliable. A variety of issues on both sides held up devel-opment from 1973 (when the original project was first mooted) until the 1990s. When the building of the pipeline was finally agreed in 1994, this was seen as a significant triumph for the market reformers who at that time governed Bolivia. It involved a major commitment from Brazil, both financially and in terms of its willingness to depend to a significant degree on supplies of gas from Bolivia. The pipeline was a large and complex project, big enough to make a considerable difference to the Bolivian economy.

One of the fears expressed by the anti-pipeline Bolivians before construction began was that Bolivia might turn out not to have enough gas to comply with the requirements of the contract. Partly for this reason, the Bolivian government in the 1990s adopted an aggressive policy of attracting private investment into the gas indus-try. The policy involved a version of privatization for the state company YPFB. From some points of view, this policy was a success. Investments in Bolivian gas increased and major new gas reserves were discovered. According to BP estimates (BP 2007), Bolivian gas reserves increased nearly sevenfold between 1996 and 2005. However, there was also a short-term fiscal cost. The favourable terms of the new exploration contracts and the investor-friendly terms on which YPFB was broken up and semi-privatized had the short term effect of reducing the contribution of oil and gas revenues to the Bolivian state (Dunning 2008: 247). This was particularly resented because the Bolivian government sought to persuade the National Congress to adopt a series of tax increases to cover its fiscal deficit (Lechner 2006: 143).

When in opposition, Evo Morales demanded the nationalization of Bolivian gas, claiming that the contracts that the Bolivian government had signed in the 1990s were unfavourable to Bolivia and had not been submitted to the National Congress for approval as legally required. However, Carlos Mesa, who replaced Sánchez de Lozada as president after the upheavals of 2003, did not want to nationalize the sector completely. Instead, he called for a national referendum on energy policy. This took place in 2004 and slightly more than two million Bolivians (some 60 per cent of the electorate) voted. The voters were asked whether they wanted the 1996 oil and gas law repealed and replaced by a new law that Congress would pass. They were also asked whether YPFB should be returned back into a state-owned company, whether gas should be used to promote Bolivian industrialization, and whether gas should be used 'as a strategic mechanism to recover a sovereign port in the Pacific Ocean' (Velasquez-Donaldson 2007: 7). This referendum led to a resounding 'yes' vote except for the last question – which seemed intended to pave the way to an export pipeline via Chile. This passed only narrowly.

In 2005, the Bolivian Congress passed a new law which was more nationalist than Carlos Mesa wanted. It increased taxes on private oil and gas companies, returned formal ownership of oil and gas resources to the state and called for the renegotiation of all contracts. It did not formally require nationalization, in the sense that the industry had to be operated by a state-owned company. The legislative change did succeed in raising very substantial amounts of extra tax revenue, but this did not satisfy radical Morales supporters that enough had been done. Soon after taking power at the beginning of 2006, Morales acted in more dramatic fashion, issuing a nationalization decree and giving foreign companies 180 days to sign new contracts. The decree also imposed higher-profits taxes – raised from around 40–60 per cent to 82 per cent (Arriagada 2006) – though this new rate was to be subject to variation once the renegotiation of contracts with the private companies had been completed.

Morales had a legal right to issue the decree that nationalized the gas industry because this gave effect to the 2005 law that Congress had already passed. What mainly raised eyebrows was that Morales actually sent troops into the gas fields in May 2006 and formally reoccupied them on behalf of the Bolivian state. The seizure was intended to be the prelude to further negotiations, but it was a public relations gesture that caused a considerable reaction. The most seriously affected, and angered, party was Brazil because Petrobras at the time had significant assets in Bolivia and some of these were formally seized by the military. It did not help matters that Petrobras had already offered informally to accept some renegotiation of the initial investment terms in favour of Bolivia. Morales's use of troops to seize assets belonging to Petrobras was seen by some observers, not least Luis Ignacio de Silva's conservative political opponents within Brazil, as a humiliation.

To make matters worse, there was already a somewhat complicated relationship in foreign policy terms between Brazil and Venezuela (discussed in chapter 5). Brazil had elected Luis Inácio de Silva ('Lula') of the Brazilian Workers Party to the presidency in 2002 and there was some degree of rivalry between Lula and Chávez for leadership of the Latin American left. Chávez had also been a political ally of Morales long before the latter's election and Morales was expecting that YPFB, and Bolivia in general, would receive substantial help from PdVSA following the nationalization. Bolivia and Venezuela had already agreed a series of energy-related agreements, signed on the day after Morales's inauguration (Arriagada 2006). Given Chávez's strong political support for Morales before the latter's election, the Bolivian government seemed to have good reason to listen to him. It must have seemed that, if it came to a bidding war between Venezuela and Brazil, there would be no real contest. Until oil prices fell in late 2008, Venezuela could offer far more help to Bolivia than Brazil could afford or the United States had any desire to.

Moreover, Argentina seemed to give some kind of backing to the Bolivian nationalization. The Néstor Kirchner government, though by no means as left-wing as that of Chávez, wanted good relations with Venezuela, especially after the latter emerged as a significant buyer of Argentine bonds following the latter's debt default in 2002. In October 2006, Morales and Kirchner signed an energy accord, which included Argentine promises to build a second pipeline to import Bolivian gas and to finance an industrialization project in Bolivia. In return, Bolivia promised to increase its supply of gas to Argentina. These plans, though still alive and periodically revisited, have not yet come to fruition. Argentina has not yet found the money to build a new gas pipeline and Bolivia, post-nationalization, has not yet discovered enough gas to supply it.

In the short term, the nationalization was widely seen as a victory for Chávez and a defeat for Brazil. Brazil could not afford to discontinue its purchases of Bolivian gas in the short run. Around half of its consumption of natural gas was at the time accounted for by imports from Bolivia. It had little choice but to accept Morales's demand for an increase in the cost of gas being supplied to Brazil, which gave Bolivia quite a significant windfall gain. (The Argentine government accepted a similar price rise.) It also accepted that tougher terms would apply to Petrobras's investments in Bolivia. Petrobras also sold back two refinery plants which it had acquired under the 1990s privatization arrangements. The one short-term success of Brazil's policy of accommodating Morales was that the gas kept flowing, though Petrobras did retaliate indirectly by cancelling several gas projects at that time under negotiation with Venezuela.

Subjectively, Lula blamed Chávez for this state of affairs more than he blamed Morales, whom he tended to regard as an inexperienced leader being led astray. Nevertheless, since 2006, Brazil has actively been seeking to reduce its dependence on Bolivian gas. Pre-existing plans to expand the capacity of the gas pipeline were put on hold by Brazil (Arriagada 2006). Brazil instead intensified its investment in LNG import terminals that could receive supplies from Africa and also stepped up its investment in developing local natural gas. These new investments soon achieved results and in early 2009 Brazil cut its imports of Bolivian gas from 30 million cubic metres per day, first to 24 million cubic metres per day, and then to only 19 million cubic metres. The official reason given – which contains some truth – was that a recovery in rainfall in Brazil enabled that country to produce more hydroelectricity from internal sources. Brazil increased its purchases later in 2009 to 24 million cubic metres daily in line with its contractual obligations. However, while Brazil has not technically broken its contract, it is now much less dependent on imported gas from Bolivia than it was in 2006. To compensate for this decline, Bolivia was able to negotiate a limited increase in its gas exports to Argentina. That increase, though, was relatively minor and did not compensate for the reduction in Brazilian purchases. Unless and until a new Bolivian pipeline to Argentina comes onstream, the gas export outlook for Bolivia remains one of continued reliance on a large single customer which, having lost faith in its most obvious source of supply, is now successfully looking elsewhere.

The nationalization has also led to problems with gas exploration within Bolivia itself. Most of the private companies investing in Bolivia in 2006 chose to limit their investments – in some cases accepting nationalization – rather than continuing to operate on new terms. According to the *Petroleum Economist* in February 2008, investment in the Bolivian gas fields 'virtually ceased' after the nationalization while US Department of Energy figures put the total amount of investment in Bolivian oil and gas in 2007 at $149 million, which is a long way down from the $605 million invested in 1998 at the height of neoliberal rule. Despite some subsequent softening of policy, this decline in investment has led to production problems. Natural gas production stagnated between 2006 and 2009 and oil production actually fell.

As a result of this shortfall, Morales seems to have somewhat moderated his original line. The 2009 constitution involves some explicit softening of the legal terms of the 2006 nationalization, making specific mention of the validity of acquired rights. Morales has also engaged in some active courting of investment from countries such as Russia and Iran, though it is not yet clear whether this will yield significant results in the long term.

Some Bolivian nationalists have questioned the whole notion of producing gas mainly for export, arguing instead for a strategy of resource-based industrialization. They were keenly aware that Bolivia had for centuries been a producer and exporter of raw materials (silver and then tin) and yet the country remained very poor. They therefore had in mind some kind of policy of using Bolivia's abundant raw materials to build up a metal refining and possibly also a petro-chemical sector for export in order to enhance employment opportunities and value added. This argument has some merit and the Morales government was indeed able to negotiate a project to use local deposits of iron ore to develop a local steel industry.

A successful resource-based industrialization strategy for gas, however, would need a good working relationship with foreign companies. YPFB is a small company in a small country. It cannot unlock Bolivia's energy potential on its own. Unfortunately, too, concerns about corruption within the gas industry, which were part of the sub-text of Bolivian economic nationalism during the neoliberal period (Enron was one of the original shareholders in the Brazil gas pipeline project) have by no means gone away. From early 2006, when Morales first arrived in office, until the end of January 2009, no fewer than six different chief executives have been appointed to head the state company. In February 2009, there was a damaging public scandal within YPFB that Morales, implausibly, sought to blame on the CIA. The real problem seems to have been Morales's over-reliance on political appointees selected mainly on the basis of loyalty. However, this scandal led to a change of personnel at the top of YPFB and the energy ministry, which seems thus far to have led to a more businesslike atmosphere within the state company.

When evaluating the Bolivian case, it is important to remember that Morales has been in office for seven fewer years than Chávez, and his oil and gas policy has not been established with the same degree of finality. The Bolivian situation is therefore more fluid than that in Venezuela. Furthermore, there remains a possible Argentine market for Bolivian gas. Moreover, one has the impression that Morales is gradually becoming more pragmatic in oil and gas policy while Chávez has, over time, become more radical. Yet there is the same problem in both cases. Both governments deterred private investment and both state companies have been run in ways that made it impossible for them to fill the gap – both in quantity and in terms of the necessary accompanying expertise.

Concluding reflections

Both Chávez and Morales came to power in countries in which abundant endowments of raw materials had failed to relieve mass poverty. That is essentially why they came to power in the first place. However, winning election as a reaction to previous failures is one thing, and putting a country's economy on a viable footing is another. Judged by this latter criterion, Chávez has essentially failed, at least thus far. According to most independent statistical sources, Venezuela has become more and more dependent on exporting less and less oil and it also has a credibility problem with its broader economic management. The Bolivian case is less straightforward. It seems that Morales is still finding his way but his dramatic nationalization of Bolivian gas – his most overtly Chávez-influenced policy – was an act of hubris that may militate against the success of his more recent, more realistic, economic strategy.

Behind this failure there is a problem of socialism, as understood in much of Latin America and certainly by many Venezuelans. Classic Leninism certainly over-privileged production as opposed to consumption and redistribution. At the extreme, this led to terrible human suffering as when Stalin starved millions of peasants in the Ukraine as part of his industrialization policy. Few would recommend anything similar today. However, Latin American left-wingers have tended to go to the other extreme, excessively prioritizing consumption and redistribution over saving and investment. This has been true not only of socialists such as Allende but of left-wing nationalists such as Argentina's Perón, Mexico's Echeverria and Lopez Portillo, and (in his first term as president) Peru's Alan Garcia. Most cases in which consumption and redistribution have been prioritized have ended in disappointment and sometimes in disaster. What has tended to make things worse has been the effect of markedly volatile commodity prices in encouraging optimism and wishful thinking when things were going well and subordinating strategic policy to crisis management when things went badly. Chávez may, precisely, have fallen into this trap.

It is not just a matter of the volume of investment, but also of its quality. It cannot be said that public investment invariably works well but there are nevertheless parts of the world in which state enterprise has played a positive role in achieving economic progress (Evans 1979, 1985). Venezuela in 1998 was possibly one of them. It did have an efficient state company that was seen by some as being a potential leader of economic diversification – at least into related industries such as gas, coal and petrochemicals. At the very least, it was surely capable of ensuring that Venezuelan oil exports were maintained at the level of the late 1990s. Yet Chávez turned PdVSA into an instrument of redistribution and allowed oil production to fall. This was indeed a triumph of politics.

— 6 —

THE FAULT LINES OF LATIN AMERICAN INTEGRATION

Throughout this book, we have made repeated references to the so-called Miami Consensus to contrast it with the politics and policies of twenty-first century socialists. This chapter looks to the fate of the Miami Consensus in a broader regional context. We do it by mapping the political shifts and challenges to the Consensus expressed in subsequent western hemisphere presidential summits and by analysing the unravelling of what was the Miami Consensus's main resolution: a commitment to complete negotiations towards hemispheric economic integration by 2005. The new hemispheric trade area that was to be known as the Free Trade Area of the Americas (FTAA) was basically an extension to the rest of Latin America of the North American Free Trade Agreement (NAFTA), signed by the US, Mexico and Canada in 1992, which came into effect in January 1994 (Lettieri 2005). Although economic integration was defined in purely economic terms, it had clear political implications as, in the words of Mark Peceny (1994: 189), the spread of democracy, free trade and complex interdependency was opening a new era of unprecedented inter-American peace and cooperation with the potential of transforming the hemisphere into a Kantian liberal 'Pacific Union'.

As seen in this book, just over fifteen years after the Summit, Latin America's regional landscape looks very different to the one painted in Miami. Today free market economics are contested, hemispheric integration (at least in the shape of the FTAA) is dead and Latin America and the United States have once again drifted apart. And, as seen in chapters 3 and 4, while the region remains

149

overwhelmingly democratic, liberal democracy is being challenged by majoritarian and populist versions of democracy. In the introduction to this book, we pointed out that President Chávez saw himself as the leader of these transformations. As Michael Shifter (2009: 55) put it, he embodies the antithesis of the 'convergence' thesis of the Miami Consensus. The role of Chávez's highly activist foreign policy, backed by oil money (see chapter 5), in aborting the Miami Consensus and his considerable regional influence, grounded in a geopolitical vision that seeks to expand the Bolivarian revolution's influence in the region, is undeniable. But, as will be argued in this chapter, Chávez's leadership has been only one among a number of social, political and economic developments that changed the politics of regional integration from its formulation in Miami in the mid-1990s to a more fragmented set of initiatives based on alternative principles of political and economic integration by the end of the first decade of the twenty-first century.

In order to fully understand the changes in the regional landscape, it is thus necessary to broaden our focus beyond the rather narrow confines of Chávez's external politics. Over the past decade, Brazil and Venezuela have been part of a regional power game in a region in search of a new equilibrium in light of the declining US influence and the emergence of a more multi-polar world (Brun 2010). The two countries are engaged in relations of competition and collaboration that encapsulate shared goals of increasing South America autonomy from the US but also significant differences in their approaches to regional integration, international trade and other global issues. This chapter looks at the regional integration initiatives that crystallize Brazil and Venezuela's quest for regional leadership: the Mercado Común del Sur (MERCOSUR, the common market of the south), the Unión de Naciones Suramericanas (UNASUR, the union of South American Nations) and the Alianza Bolivariana para los Pueblos de Nuestra América (ALBA, the Bolivarian alliance for the peoples of our America).[1] We also look at how political changes in the region have affected relations between the US and Latin America since Miami. In doing so, we address some of the issues that cut across the different chapters of this book: the impact at regional level of the turn to the left in domestic politics, the relation between politics and institutions (in this case in processes of regional integration) and the extent to which alleged divisions between populist and social democratic left-of-centre governments in the region are reflected in competing projects of regional integration.

The unravelling of the Miami Consensus and the transformations of MERCOSUR

The idea of a free trade agreement ranging from the Yukon to the straits of Patagonia had first been floated by President George H. W. Bush in his 1990 Enterprise for the Americas Initiative but the impetus for its adoption in the 1994 Miami Summit was largely a Latin American initiative (Fishlow 1999; Wiarda 1995). The convergence between the Latin American countries' goals and aspirations and those of the US expressed in Miami was seen as a turning point in hemispheric relations but, as suggested in the introduction to this chapter, history would show otherwise (Feinberg 1997, cited in Palmer 2006: 27). Regional politics began to change by the turn of the century and, just over a decade after Miami, the goal of a western hemisphere free trade area was abandoned for all practical purposes. By 2005, the Miami Consensus had been broken by alternative projects of Latin American integration that incorporated more state-centred, protectionist and socially oriented elements, as characterized by the evolution of MERCOSUR and the emergence of ALBA, initially as a Cuban–Venezuelan project.

A brief analysis of the Declarations of the five summits of Western Hemisphere Heads of State and Government that took place between 1994 and 2005 maps the rise and fall of the Miami Consensus, as reflected in the rhetoric of presidential diplomacy. Four years after Miami, the Declaration of the Heads of State and Government participating in the Second Summit of the Americas that took place in Santiago de Chile in April 1998 still placed representative democracy, free market economics and hemispheric integration at the centre of the community of nations' goals. While acknowledging that the positive growth shown in the region in the past years had not yet resolved problems of inequity and social exclusion, the Declaration reaffirmed the member countries' commitment to 'sound, market-based economic policies' and claimed that steadfast and cooperative efforts to promote prosperity through increased economic integration and more open economies had resulted in faster economic growth, lower inflation, expanded opportunities and confidence in facing the global marketplace. The Santiago Declaration reiterated the determination of the member countries to conclude the negotiations of the FTAA 'no later than 2005', and made renewed commitments to uphold representative democracy (Second Summit of the Americas 1998).

In the Third Summit that took place three years later in Quebec City, Canada, in April 2001 the Heads of State and Government adopted a Plan of Action 'to strengthen representative democracy, promote good governance and protect human rights and fundamental freedoms' (Third Summit of the Americas, 2001).[2] The Declaration reaffirmed past Summits' beliefs in the benefits of 'free and open market economies'. It also directed its ministers to ensure that negotiations of the FTAA Agreement were concluded no later than January 2005 and 'to seek its entry into force as soon as possible thereafter, but in any case no later than December 2005'. Dissent, however, was already evident at the margins of the resolutions. Perhaps the most significant statement of the Summit was not to be found in the body of the Declaration but in its footnotes. Here, the Venezuelan delegation stated two reservations about the document revealed the first fault lines of the Miami Consensus. The first relates to alternative views of democracy:

> The Venezuelan delegation wishes to reserve its position on paragraphs 1 and 6 of the Declaration of Quebec City, *because, according to our government, democracy should be understood in its broadest sense and not only in its representative quality.* We understand that the exercise of democracy encompasses, as well, citizen participation in decision making and in government management, with a view to the daily formation of a process directed towards the integral development of society. *Because of this, the Venezuelan government would have preferred and thus requested that, in this Summit, the text of the Declaration would expressly reflect the participatory character of democracy.* (Third Summit of the Americas, 2001, emphasis added)

The second reservation referred to the Summit's commitment to conclude negotiations of the FTAA agreement by 2005. In it, the Venezuelan government rather cryptically states that 'consultations are taking place in various sectors of the national government dedicated to our internal legislation, in order to fulfill the commitments that would result from the implementation of the FTAA in the year 2005' (ibid.). The significance of the Venezuelan government's reservations could only be fully appreciated retrospectively. What appeared to be no more than a minor and uncontroversial political point on democracy and a cautionary reserve regarding the FTAA were effectively anticipating major domestic and international political changes in the region.

If the Quebec Summit sowed the seeds of change, the Fourth Summit that took place in November 2005 in the Argentinian seaside resort of Mar del Plata blew the Miami Consensus apart. The Summit reflected contrasting visions on economic development and integration. They varied from the US delegation's insistence on the benefits of the FTAA to the pre-Summit declaration by the Venezuelan Foreign Minister, Gustavo Márquez, that his country 'will defend regional integration, in contrast to the FTAA which represents a return to the Monroe Doctrine' (Lettieri 2005). It also contrasted a highly unpopular President Bush, who had depleted his political capital in a vain effort to push the FTAA negotiations forward, with a new wave of left-wing and left-of-centre presidents who had opposed them (ibid.). For many of the participants, not least for the host, President Néstor Kirchner of Argentina, the Summit provided a political platform to denounce the free market policies of the 1990s and an opportunity for President Chávez to attack US imperialism. Politically strengthened by his victory in the recall referendum of August 2004, Chávez embarked on a more radical political path, both internally and in his foreign policy (González Urrutia 2006). Chávez effectively overshadowed the other heads of state and became the main protagonist of the Summit. A parallel 'People's Summit' saw the Venezuelan president addressing tens of thousands of political activists in a soccer stadium (Meyer 2008). Among those attending the rally was the soon to be elected Bolivian president Evo Morales and Argentine football star Diego Maradona. 'Every one of us brought a shovel, because Mar del Plata is going to be the tomb of the FTAA', President Chávez said. 'The FTAA is dead, and we, the people of the Americas are the ones that buried it' (The *New York Times* 2005).

With less rhetorical flourish, the Summit's Declaration effectively sanctioned the end of the Miami Consensus and the demise of the FTAA. One of the most notable aspects of the Mar del Plata Declaration, titled 'Creating Jobs to Fight Poverty and Strengthen Democratic Governance', is the total lack of reference to the benefits of free market economies. Concerning economic development, the Declaration follows a post-Washington Consensus agenda (Panizza 2009) of 'sustained economic growth, with equity and social inclusion' (Fourth Summit of the Americas 2005), rather than the orthodox free market declarations of principles of Miami and Santiago. Instead of universal prescriptions for development, it states its 'support for a country's legitimate right to pursue and attain its development within the framework of its political, economic, social and cultural realities' (ibid.). It claims that economic growth is 'a basic, indispensable, but not sufficient, condition to address unemployment, poverty and the growth of the informal economy' (ibid.). In a reference to the erratic patterns of growth of the 1990s, it notes that 'in the recent past some countries of the Hemisphere have experienced periods of economic growth that did not translate into equivalent employment gains, compounding existing problems of high income concentration, poverty and indigence' (ibid.).

The main outcome of the Summit was a negative one. In a rather convoluted way, the Summit Declaration registered the end of what had been the cornerstone of the Miami Consensus, the FTAA. It states that, while some member states remained committed 'to the achievements of a balanced and comprehensive FTAA', others maintained that the necessary conditions were 'not yet in place for achieving a balanced and equitable free trade agreement...' (ibid., paragraph 19). The meaning of this statement was made explicit by the then Argentine foreign minister, Rafael Bielsa. Answering journalists' questions about whether he agreed with President Chávez's claim that the FTAA was 'dead', he stated: 'If a process of regional integration lacks equity, access to markets and the end to distorting subsidies, then it is effectively dead.'[3]

However, if the Mar del Plata Summit exposed the widening gap between the US and Latin America, it also made evident deep divisions between the countries of the region. A significant majority of 29 out of the 34 countries, including Mexico and most of the countries of Central America and the Caribbean, that attended the Mar del Plata Summit wanted the resumption of the FTAA negotiations, which were effectively blocked by the opposition of just the four countries of MERCOSUR (Argentina, Brazil, Paraguay and Uruguay) with the support of Venezuela (Sweeney 2005).

Politically, the Summit took place against a background of increasing domestic political instability throughout the region, particularly in Bolivia and Ecuador (Lettieri 2005) that are analysed elsewhere in this book. Also, political conflicts between Colombia on the one side and Venezuela and Ecuador on the other raised the danger of military confrontations between Latin American nations. Divisions between the countries of Latin America crystallized in the United Nations in 2006, as Latin America and the Caribbean was the only region of the world that was unable to select its candidate for a temporary seat at the UN Security Council by consensus (Hakim 2008; Shifter 2009).

The effective burial of the FTAA project in Mar del Plata brought to light not just the fragmentation of Latin America but also the proliferation of integration projects throughout the region. These comprise both bilateral treaties (mainly between the US and countries of South and Central America) and overlapping sub-regional agreements with different memberships, goals and methods of integration. Regional and sub-regional agreements also reflect competing projects of regional leadership in which Brazil and Venezuela have been the main actors.

While there is a long list of past and present projects of economic and political integration in South America, none equals the political and economic importance of the Mercado Común del Sur (MERCOSUR), the South American Common Market. MERCOSUR is the fourth largest regional market in the world, with a joint population of some 270 million and a GDP at market prices of US $2.4 trillion in 2008 (Council on Foreign Relations 2009). Its membership comprises Argentina, Brazil, Paraguay and Uruguay as full members, with Bolivia, Chile, Colombia, Ecuador and Peru as associate members and Mexico as an observer. In July 2006, Venezuela was admitted to MERCOSUR but at the time of writing this book its full incorporation is still pending parliamentary approval in Paraguay.

How have the political domestic and regional changes that led to the unravelling of the Miami Consensus affected MERCOSUR? MERCOSUR has always been more than just a regional trade arrangement. The consolidation of democracy was at the origins of MERCOSUR, as its inception marked the end of a long history of political and potentially military conflict for regional leadership between the two largest South American countries, Argentina and Brazil. After the two countries returned to democracy in 1983 and 1985 respectively, a key goal of the new civilian governments of presidents José Sarney of Brazil (1985–90) and Raúl Alfonsín of Argentina (1983–9) was to build up political trust between the two nations in order to weaken their military establishments and help consolidate the still fragile democracies of both countries (Cason 2000; Oelsner 2005).

If the new democratic environment constituted the political background for the emergence of MERCOSUR, the process of economic liberalization that gathered momentum by the late 1980s provided its economic context. While neither President Sarney nor President Alfonsín were economic liberals, and arguably MERCOSUR was originally a developmentalist project, the negotiations that led to the setting up of MERCOSUR by the Treaty of Asunción in 1991 were conducted by presidents Fernando Collor de Mello (1990–2) of Brazil and Carlos Saul Menem (1989–95; 1995–9) of Argentina, two presidents committed to the modernization of their economies at home and the promotion of the free market principles of the Washington Consensus in their trade relations (Cason 2000). Conceived as a project of open regionalism (Phillips 2003) to distinguish it from the more protectionist and trade-distorting regional projects of the past, MERCOSUR was part of a wider political and economic strategy aimed at locking in domestic economic reforms, attracting the foreign direct investment necessary to modernize the countries' economies and creating a regional market (particularly for high value-added goods) that would allow the progressive integration of the MERCOSUR economies in the fledging global order. The latter goal was to be facilitated by the negotiation of free trade agreements between MERCOSUR and other regional trading blocs, such as the European Union.[4]

Democracy, free market economics and regional integration grounded MERCOSUR on the same principles that were at the core of the FTAA's initiative, making the two part of the overarching regional consensus of the 1990s. Latin America in the second half of the 1990s appeared to be split between, on the one hand, the countries of MERCOSUR, characterized by democratic stability and a broad consensus on free market economic modernization, and those of the Andean region on the other, affected by the deinstitutionalization of democracy, social conflict, the rise of populism and stalled economic modernization. A crucial episode in MERCOSUR political history happened in April 1996 in Paraguay, when the then head of the army, General Lino Oviedo, threatened to oust the country's first civilian president in almost forty years, Juan Carlos Wasmosy. The intervention of Brazil on behalf of MERCOSUR, together with the United States, was crucial to aborting the coup (Cason 2000). In 1998, the implicit commitment to democracy that was at the origins of MERCOSUR was made explicit when the countries of MERCOSUR established in the Protocol of Ushuaia that democracy was a condition for membership of the trading bloc.

In spite of rapid progress in its early years, MERCOSUR's process of integration stalled in the new century. The lack of supranational mechanisms for the enforcement of the rules of MERCOSUR, the politicized nature of the state and the consequent lack of demarcation between state institutions (including the judiciary) and governments makes the latter permeable to pressure from lobby groups and special interests whenever competition from imports from member countries affect powerful interests (Guedes de Oliveira 2001; Mecham 2003). As a result, more than a decade and a half since its coming into effect, MERCOSUR has not yet become a fully functioning free trade area, let alone a customs union or a common market (Reid 2002). It remains an imperfect free market, an incomplete customs union and is almost as far away as it was in its inception from becoming a truly integrated common market (Flemes 2009).

The coming to office of left-of-centre governments in the four countries of MERCOSUR in the first decade of the new century appeared to create the opportunity to both expand and deepen MERCOSUR.[5] The new political direction of MERCOSUR was reinforced by Venezuela being admitted to the regional market.[6] The continent's third largest economy, Venezuela, offers the other countries of MERCOSUR an attractive market for their products and an economy that is complementary rather than competitive with the other economies of the region. The financial resources of the Venezuelan state could be used to finance projects in the areas of transport, communications and energy integration, as well as to provide financial assistance to other states, making them less dependent on private sector financing and multilateral lending from outside the region. A medium-sized, cash rich, regional economy with a government that pursues a high-profile, activist, foreign policy could also contribute to balancing Brazil's economic and political hegemony in MERCOSUR.

If and when completed, Venezuela's accession to MERCOSUR, however, is set to raise fundamental questions about the nature and direction of the regional market. As noted above, although not strictly speaking a 'neoliberal' undertaking, MERCOSUR, as a project of open regionalism and market-led economic integration, was a creature of the Washington Consensus (Kellogg 2007). In contrast, for Venezuela MERCOSUR is conceived as one among a number of instruments for the construction of a South American counterweight to US hegemony in the region (Shifter 2009: 57) and an alternative economic order to neoliberalism, if not to capitalism. Supporters of the Bolivarian revolution have questioned Venezuela's move to join MERCOSUR, arguing that it represents a free market strategy of economic integration that has opened the countries' economies to the penetration of multinational enterprises in the name of free trade. In December 2005, Chávez argued that MERCOSUR could, and should, be detached from its neoliberal roots: 'We need a MERCOSUR that prioritizes social concerns, we need a MERCOSUR that every day moves further away from the old elitist corporate models of integration that looks for...financial profits, but forgets about workers, children, life, and human dignity' (Kellogg 2007: 195). In July 2006, in the ceremony marking Venezuela's formal accession to

MERCOSUR, Chávez reiterated that Venezuela's 'road to liberation' lay with MERCOSUR and urged MERCOSUR to put aside internal squabbles and stand against the US-backed free market policies that, he said, 'enslaved' the region in debt to the International Monetary Fund.[7]

The model of regional integration favoured by Venezuela is state-centred and based on the creation of new regional public enterprises and joint partnerships between national state enterprises, which is far removed from the original model of MERCOSUR (Hart-Landsberg 2009). Trade relations are largely mediated by the Venezuelan state and based as much on political as on economic considerations. The access of Venezuela to MERCOSUR may also test MERCOSUR's democratic clause. Arguably, for all its faults, Venezuela remains a democracy and, in February 2007, Venezuela ratified the Ushuaia Protocol, which includes MERCOSUR's so-called 'democratic clause' (SELA 2007). Chávez, however, has rejected the notion of 'liberal' or 'representative' democracy that was the shared understanding of the meaning of democracy when MERCOSUR was set up in the 1990s. So far, the governments of the countries of MERCOSUR have failed to openly express their concern about Chávez's authoritarian drifts, particularly the cancelling of broadcasting permits to opposition radio and TV channels and the harassment of opponents to the government.

Beyond the rhetorical denunciations of neoliberalism, particularly by Presidents Néstor and Cristina Kirchner of Argentina and Chávez of Venezuela, the governments of MERCOSUR have adopted different mixes of continuity and change in relation to the free market model of the 1990s. Paraguay and Uruguay have remained open economies eager to expand trade relations with countries outside MERCOSUR (Panizza 2008).[8] Brazil continues its drive to become a global player (Flemes 2009) and has become a leading player in the Doha round of the World Trade Organization (WTO) negotiations aimed at expanding free trade worldwide. The country also strives to attract foreign direct investment. Argentina meanwhile has turned increasingly inwards in an economic project that has strong resemblances with the developmentalist model of the 1960s. The administrations of Néstor and Cristina Kirchner have implemented a policy of subsidies to public utilities and other productive sectors, price controls, external trade quotas and taxes and blocked market access to goods from other MERCOSUR countries (Riggirozzi 2009). Meanwhile, Venezuela has formally adopted a socialist economic model that includes the nationalization of the main economic sectors and pervasive state control of the economy (Buxton 2009a). Interventionist and protectionist economic policies interfere with the free movement of goods between the member countries, create new forms of protectionism and distort competition and prices. It is just not possible to envisage how a free market, let alone a customs union, could be established on these bases.

In short, the progressive abandonment of its founding principles has deepened MERCOSUR's crisis of identity. Political convergence on a left-of-centre outlook has done little to address MERCOSUR's fundamental problems of weak institutionalization and lack of macroeconomic coordination.[9] If anything, it has made MERCOSUR even more reliant on presidential diplomacy. As Andrew Hurrell (2008: 55) put it, MERCOSUR is now far more divided that at any time in its history. Its already weak institutional structures have not been strengthened, and it is difficult to believe that Venezuela's full accession will do anything other than weaken them still further. The sub-regional organization seems to have increasingly less and less to do with free trade and more to do with politics. It has shifted from a project of open regionalism, liberal democracy and convergence with the US to one of more inward-looking development with a larger role for the state and more diffuse notions of participatory democracy. The emphasis in the integration process appears to be changing from commercial integration through market forces to energy, infrastructure and productive integration politically mediated by state actors. This has increased tensions between the MERCOSUR members that are in favour of the original project of open regionalism, such as Paraguay and Uruguay, and those, such as Venezuela and Argentina, that want MERCOSUR to run on different principles with Brazil unwilling or unable to use its political and economic weight to help close MERCOSUR's fault lines.

Brazil and Venezuela: The politics of the new regional order

The failure of MERCOSUR to deepen economic integration and the switch from markets to politics as the main driver for regional integration was the context for the emergence of the Unión de Naciones Suramericanas (UNASUR), a community of twelve South American nations aiming at creating a common political and economic space in the region (Hurrell 2008). While MERCOSUR was a joint Argentine–Brazilian undertaking, UNASUR was very much a Brazilian initiative in which Venezuela played a secondary but significant role. UNASUR's constitutive treaty was signed in Rio de Janeiro in May 2008 by all the presidents of South America with the exception of those of the Guyanas.[10] Institutionally, UNASUR is to have a general secretariat based in Quito, and a South American parliament based in Cochabamba, Bolivia. In December 2008, the member countries of UNASUR approved the setting up of a South American Defence Council and a South American Health Council (Comunidad Andina, Secretaría General, 2008). Like other Latin American integration projects, its decision-making process is based on the principle of unrestricted respect for the sovereignty of the member countries, which precludes any move away from inter-state agreements towards supranational institutions. The prevalence of national sovereignty over collectively binding supranational decisions is highlighted by the principle that all norms of UNASUR are to be adopted by consensus (article 12) and by the provision that any member state may completely or partially refrain from implementing an approved policy, be it for a period defined beforehand, or for an indefinite period of time (article 13) (South American Union of Nations Constitutive Treaty 2009). The treaty stipulates that policy resolutions should be implemented following 'flexible and gradual criteria' (ibid.) (article 13) which may make it difficult to promote a rules-based process of integration. As in the case of MERCOSUR, UNASUR lacks an independent system for the resolution of conflicts, which makes its functioning over-dependent on presidential diplomacy papering over shallow resolutions and weak institutions.

The agenda of UNASUR comprises political dialogue, physical and energy integration and the promotion of agreements in the areas of the environment, justice, social inclusion and telecommunications. Article 1 of the UNASUR treaty lists as its objectives

to build, in a participatory and consensual manner, an integration and union among its peoples in the cultural, social, economic and political fields, prioritizing political dialogue, social policies, education, energy, infrastructure, financing and the environment, among others, with a view to eliminating socio-economic inequality, in order to achieve social inclusion and participation of civil society, to strengthen democracy and reduce asymmetries within the framework of strengthening the sovereignty and independence of the States.[11]

Its long-term goal is the unification of South America's two largest regional markets, MERCOSUR and the Andean Community of Nations. While UNASUR's goals include economic, social and ecological objectives, the organization has a strong political profile as a forum for political coordination and the resolution of disputes parallel to the Organization of American States (OAS) and autonomous from the United States.

The political dimension of UNASUR came into evidence in September 2008 when its then acting head, the Chilean President Michelle Bachelet, played an important mediating role in the conflict between President Morales and the opposition, which, as seen in chapter 3, brought the country to the verge of an armed confrontation (Peña 2009). In 2009, UNASUR also sought to mediate in the conflict between Colombia and Venezuela over the announcement that the Colombian government was to allow the US government to use military bases in its territory. Following the announcement, President Chávez and his regional allies, Ecuador and Bolivia, wanted a condemnation of Colombia. An extraordinary meeting of heads of state of UNASUR in Bariloche, Argentina, in August 2009 issued a face-saving declaration that allowed both parties to claim victory (Álvarez Valdés 2009).

As in the case of MERCOSUR, Brazil has played a leading role in the setting up of the new regional entity. The new organization reflects a long-term project of Brazilian diplomacy first expressed in the proposal in 1993 by the then foreign minister, Celso Amorim (who was also the driving force behind the setting up of UNASUR) to set up a South American Free Trade Area, comprising all the countries of South America (Botelho 2008). However, UNASUR is more than just another instrument in Brazil's long-term ambition of regional leadership by consensus (Burges 2006). It also reflects Venezuela's activist policy of regional integration both partnering and competing with Brazil for regional influence (Botelho 2008). Venezuela has given strong political and financial support to UNASUR. As the paymaster of regional integration, Venezuela has outbid the US economic assistance to Latin America and helped to ease the financial costs for Brazil of the drive towards regional integration. After some initial misgivings, Argentina has also been influential in the setting up of UNASUR, reflecting the political common ground between the three largest South American economies in force since President Duhalde of Argentina abandoned President Menem's strategic alliance with the United States.

Questions should be raised, however, about the relations between Brazil and Venezuela in terms of competing projects of regional integration and alternative leadership. Venezuela is the only country that is a member of the three regional bodies: MERCOSUR, UNASUR and ALBA. If MERCOSUR and UNASUR represent Brazil's steady rise as a regional leader, ALBA has become synonymous with the radical reforms underway in Venezuela and of President Chávez's ambition to promote 'twenty-first century socialism' and expand its influence throughout the region (Kellogg 2007). First floated by the Venezuelan government in 2001 as an alternative to the FTAA, ALBA was set up in 2004 by Presidents Chávez of Venezuela and Fidel Castro of Cuba (Hart-Landsberg 2009). According to the original joint Cuban–Venezuelan document: 'cooperation between the two countries will be based not only on solidarity principles...but also...on the exchange of goods and services that are most beneficial for the economic and social needs of both countries' (Kellogg 2007: 200). Since then, ALBA has evolved into a sub-regional integration and cooperation project comprising eight countries by June 2010: Antigua and Barbuda, Bolivia, Cuba, Dominica, Ecuador, Nicaragua, Saint Vincent and the Grenadines and Venezuela.[12] The initiative combines a strong anti-imperialist element and the promotion of an alternative model of integration to free trade based on non-market principles, such as the exchange of Venezuelan oil for Cuban doctors, with a more politics-based dimension. The latter is centred on Venezuela's petro-diplomacy, which involves the selling of oil at sub-sidized prices to the countries of ALBA in exchange for the importation of goods from the member countries (Serbin 2009).[13] Venezuela also provides financial support for social programmes, finances the setting of mixed enterprises and underwrites energy cooperation and infrastructure-building initiatives. In October 2009, ALBA heads of state agreed in principle the creation of a regional monetary unity of exchange, the sucre, to be used as common currency for electronic transactions amongst ALBA members in place of the US dollar.[14]

At the heart of the ALBA project is a state-centred development strategy involving managed trade based on the productive integration rather than competition between the countries' economic sectors, a dirigiste economic model and the creation of 'grand national enter-prises' (Hart-Landsberg 2009: 7). The term refers both to new regional public enterprises set up by agreements between national governments and to regional firms based on associations between national state enterprises. ALBA's constitutive agreements set up a broad range of goals for the organization. Among these are: to promote trade and investment between member governments based on cooperation, and with the aim of improving people's lives; to cooperate to provide free health care and free education to people across the ALBA states; to integrate the ALBA members' energy sectors; to develop basic industries; and to ensure land redistribution and food security (Hart-Landsberg 2009).

While ALBA claims to be a bottom-up model of integration in contrast to the traditional top-down models, the reality is rather different. ALBA has an advisory council of social movements that is supposed to provide direction and oversight to the process. Decisions, however, are made by a presidential council which are then formalized and implemented according to terms set up by a ministerial council. In practice, ALBA remains politically dependent on the decisions of the presidents of the participating countries and economically heavily dependent on Venezuela's funding (Serbin 2009). As Hart-Landsberg (2009: 9) put it: 'This means that activities are decided upon and implemented from the top down rather than the bottom up... This structure often results in a bias towards large-scale mega projects (construction of refineries, pipelines, transportation, infrastructure, resource extraction enterprises), many of which raise environmental and indigenous rights concerns.'

As part of its strategy of regional integration, the Venezuelan government, in addition to participating in both MERCOSUR and ALBA, has proposed, promoted and financed the setting up of a number of regional and sub-regional public enterprises in the areas of infrastructure, energy, finances, trade and telecommunications. In 2005, Chávez set up Petrocaribe, a programme to provide subsidized oil to fourteen Caribbean nations (Altman Borbón 2009). Also, as proposed by Venezuela, in 2005 Argentina, Brazil, Uruguay and Venezuela agreed to set up PETROSUR, a joint partnership aimed at setting up mechanisms for energy cooperation and integration among the state-owned oil companies of the four countries.[15] A regional TV network, Telesur, financed by Venezuela and with its headquarters in Caracas, was established in 2005 to compete with the US news networks. Also at the initiative of Venezuela, in 2007 seven South American countries set up the Banco del Sur, in Quito, Ecuador, which was a regional development bank intended as an alternative to borrowing from the International Monetary Fund (IMF) and the World Bank (WB). Brazil and Venezuela were to be the main providers of capital for this. In January 2008, the ALBA countries created an ALBA Bank with a capital of US$1 billion. The Bank's stated aim is 'to boost industrial and agricultural production among its members, support social projects as well as multilateral cooperation agreements among its members, particularly in the field of energy' (Hart-Landsberg 2009). Other proposals for joint public companies yet to be materialized cover the areas of air transportation and insurance.

The analysis of the still short life of UNASUR and ALBA shows the commonalities and differences between the Brazilian and Venezuelan governments' approaches to regional integration. Both governments follow a strongly nationalist foreign policy and agree on the strategic importance of South American integration as a condition for making the region more autonomous of the United States. They also share a strategic view of a multi-polar world in which South–South relations play an increasingly important role (Hurrell 2008). Presidents Chávez and Lula da Silva believe that it is to their countries' advantage to diversify relations, including trade and political relations with countries hostile to the US, such as Iran. However, for the Lula da Silva administration, regional autonomy was part of a broader strategy to consolidate Brazil as a global player, both in the political and economic scenes. To project itself into the international arena, Brazil seeks to be perceived as a moderating force within the region, as the basis for a collaborative relation with the US based on a shared interest in regional stability and on the US de facto recognition of Brazil's regional leadership. In contrast, for Chávez's Venezuela, the different projects of regional integration (MERCOSUR, UNASUR, ALBA) are instruments for the building of a broader anti-imperialist alliance and for the construction of an alternative order to capitalism. In order to achieve these goals, Chávez has actively supported grassroots opposition forces to centre-right governments in the region and clashed with the US allies in South America, particularly Colombia (González Urrutia 2006). Occasionally, Venezuela has also clashed directly with Brazil, most notably in May 2006 when President Morales of Bolivia nationalized the gas pipeline from Bolivia to Brazil. President Chávez angered the Brazilian government by encouraging the nationalization and promising that Venezuela's state energy company, PdVSA, would invest hundreds of millions of dollars in Bolivian gas production, though in this case the promise has not really been backed by action. In this regard, while Brazil's goal is preserving stability in the region, Chávez's strategy prioritizes political and ideological confrontation with those Latin American governments that he regards as allied to the United States, as a means of promoting region-wide political change (González Urrutia 2006). The next section examines how the politics of regional integration have affected relations between Latin America and the US in the context of wider global changes since the Miami Summit.

US–Latin American relations revisited

The unravelling of the Miami Consensus, the anti-imperialist rhetoric of Presidents Chávez, Morales and Correa, and the emergence of regional economic and political integration projects such as UNASUR and ALBA, autonomous of if not antagonistic to the US, have been presented as evidence that the US is in danger of 'losing' the region (Hakim 2006). For a country that historically saw Latin America through the frame of the Monroe Doctrine, this would not be a trivial development (Erikson 2008).

What explains this remarkable turn of events? Reviewing US–Latin American relations during the Clinton years, David Scott Palmer (2006: xi) accuses Clinton of failing to seize the opportunity provided by a strong collaborative environment based on the common goals of supporting democracy and overcoming Latin America's 1980s 'lost decade' for development to build and sustain an effective Latin American policy. This failure, he concludes, contributed to the renewed disquiet in the region over US policy. It is not the purpose of this chapter to examine the reasons internal to the Clinton administration (sporadic attention at the top, inadequate financial authorizations, conflicting national interests and shifting priorities) regarded by Palmer as responsible for the failures of his policies towards Latin America or indeed to qualify Palmer's generalization with a more nuanced analysis of Clinton's successes and disappointments in dealing with the region (Leogrande 2007). However, an overarching argument concerning US–Latin American relations throughout the Clinton–Bush eras is that the US neglect of the region has resulted in the waning of US influence in its former backyard. Assessing the George W. Bush administration's policies towards Latin America, Peter Hakim (2006: 39) claims that relations between the US and Latin America were 'at their lowest point since the end of the Cold War'. In a now familiar argument, he claims that after 9/11 Washington effectively lost interest in Latin America, as the region became peripheral to higher foreign policy priorities, such as the War on Terror and the invasion of Iraq. Latin America may still be the source of a number of issues that are perceived as damaging for the US, particularly illegal immigration and drug trafficking, but these problems do not constitute the same kind of systemic threat posed to US interests by the Soviet Union–Cuban alliance of the 1960s and 1970s or by terrorism and Islamic fundamentalism in the present.

Changes in the international political and economic environment have also contributed to the estrangement between the US and Latin America. The rise of China as a budding economic superpower seems to offer the Latin American countries an outlet for their commodity exports and a source of investment.[16] Russia and Iran have also trespassed in the US backyard, establishing close economic and political ties with Venezuela (Erikson 2008) and offering alternative sources of investment for oil and gas exploration and production. Russia has also become a major arms supplier to Venezuela.[17]

While international factors are important, regional issues have played a fundamental role in turning the mutual goodwill of the 1990s into a relationship that has been described as one of mutual disenchantment. For the US, Latin America's commitment to free trade and democracy has not lived up to expectations (Smith 1999). The common view in Washington is that Latin America has been reluctant to open its markets and fully and vigorously apply free trade principles (Shifter 2009). While Latin America remains a not insignificant economic partner for the US, its economic potential pales in comparison with that of China, India and other Asian countries.

In the late 1990s and early 2000s, many countries of Latin America abandoned the free market agenda of Miami. Furthermore, in spite of a region-wide upsurge in economic growth between 2003 and 2008, they have remained dependent on an export commodity model of development, which continues to be constrained by low educational levels, high inequality, lack of investment in research and development and low rates of savings. Democracy has largely survived in the region but liberal democracy has not taken root everywhere and, as seen in chapter 3, populism and nationalism, which in Latin America are always infused with a high dose of anti-Americanism, have raised their heads. As we have seen in previous chapters, mostly free and fair elections coexist with political instability, high levels of criminal violence, corruption, the non-rule of law and social polarization, as well as attempts to redefine democracy on different principles to those of liberal democracy (for example, the Venezuelan government's reservations to the Declaration of Quebec). Moreover, as US governments have found through history, democratic elections do not always result in the victory of friendly governments, as seen by the elections of the US's old foe, Daniel Ortega in Nicaragua, of Evo Morales in Bolivia, Rafael Correa in Ecuador and of course, of Hugo Chávez in Venezuela.

166

The Bush administration repeatedly stated that the US did not see the election of left-wing government as a problem, as long as these governments were democratic. It had good relations with a number of left-of-centre governments, particularly with those of President Lula da Silva in Brazil and President Tabaré Vázquez of Uruguay. But US officials raised concerns about the spread in Latin America of what they labelled as radical populism, which has since crystallized into a rather simplistic dichotomy between a 'good' (social democratic) left and a ('bad') populist one (Castañeda 2006).[18] The US government's uneasiness with the anti-American rhetoric of President Chávez, as well as with his high-handed treatment of the opposition, was compounded by disappointment at the refusal of 'friendly', democratic, left-of-centre Latin American governments to condemn President Chávez's alleged authoritarianism. This is exemplified by President Lula da Silva's claim in 2005 that Venezuela suffered from an excess, not a lack, of democracy (Hakim 2006: 44).

Perhaps the US optimism about the potential of the Miami Consensus to transform Latin American countries into free market, liberal democracies was always based on unrealistic assumptions. Writing shortly after the Mexican 1995–6 economic crisis damped the optimism of Miami, Howard Wiarda (1995: 65) argued that in Miami the US may have been swayed by its hopes for the region rather than by a hard-headed appraisal of reality. He noted that political, as well as economic, institutions were still fragile throughout Latin America. And writing with considerable foresight at a time in which neoliberalism appeared to be the only game in town, he argued that the struggle between statism and neoliberalism was not yet fully decided. Concerning democracy, he suggested that a more realistic expectation of the future evolution of the democratic order in Latin America was to recognize the existence of many halfway arrangements along the path to that end, such as: 'limited democracy, qualified democracy, Rousseauvian democracy, various transitional regimes between closed and open corporatism, and the ever present possibility (if not likelihood) of neo-corporatism as the end result rather than the liberal pluralism of John Locke'. He didn't, of course, envisage twenty-first century socialism.

Disenchantment has not been a one-sided feeling. The US has been perceived throughout Latin America as the driving force behind a failed neoliberal project that raised strong popular resistance (see chapter 2). Popular opposition to the FTAA and to bilateral trade agreements between the US and the countries of the region reflected this perception (Phillips 2008: 163). The shift in US foreign policy after 11 September towards a greater concern with security has resonated badly in Latin America. The Bush administration's assertion of the right to exercise unilateral and pre-emptive military power anywhere in the world to perceived threats against US security and its commitment to spread democracy at gunpoint looked to Latin Americans as the worldwide extension of the Monroe Doctrine.[19] The invasion of Iraq had parallels in the history of past military interventions within the region, reinforced by the presence in the first George W. Bush administration of many of the old hands of the Contras war against the Sandinista regime in the 1980s, such as Otto Reich, John Negroponte and Roger Noriega (Da Fonseca, manuscript). The strong rejection of the invasion throughout Latin America was evident in the refusal of Mexico and Chile, two governments friendly with the US, to support a US resolution in the Security Council in 2003 that would have given legitimacy to the operation.

The US commitment to human rights and the rule of law, the cornerstones of the conception of democracy of the Miami Consensus, appeared opportunist at best and hypocritical at worst. Revelations about the torture of prisoners in Abu Ghraib and Guantánamo Bay recalled similarly gross violations of human rights by US-trained police and military personnel in the Southern Cone military dictatorships of the 1970s. The US government's refusal to join the International Criminal Court was seen as yet another example of the US disregard for international institutions and a rule-based international order. Washington ambivalence for the short-lived coup in April 2002 against President Chávez (see chapter 1) raised questions about the Bush administration's commitment to democracy, as did Washington's pressure on President Jean-Bertrand Aristide to leave Haiti in 2004.

The end of the first decade of the twenty-first century, however, marks a new twist in US–Latin American relations. In the US, Barack Obama won the presidential election in November 2008 on a message of change. Change was also the theme of President Obama's speech in the Fifth Summit that took place in Trinidad and Tobago on 17–19 April 2009, less than four months after the US presidential inauguration. The political agenda prior to the Summit was dominated by the issue of Cuba which was the only country not represented at the Summit as it had been expelled from the Organization of American States (OAS) in 1962 during the Cold War (Malamud and García-Calvo 2009). While the Cuban question had barely registered in previous Summits, the overwhelming majority of the countries of Latin America were now demanding the readmission of Cuba to the Inter-American System. As 'the Cuban question' threatened to high-jack the summit in a pre-emptive move, in the weeks before the summit, President Obama said that the US was seeking 'a new begin-ning' with Cuba and an 'equal partnership with the nations of the Americas' in which the US government was willing to move from a policy of acting 'for' Latin America to one of acting 'with' it (Malamud and García-Calvo 2009). President Obama's overtures towards Cuba, the high levels of goodwill raised by his election and diplomatic interventions from some of the leading Latin American nations, par-ticularly Brazil and Mexico, avoided any mention of the Cuban ques-tion in the Summit's Declaration.[20]

In its 97 paragraphs, the document (titled 'Securing Our Citizens' Future by Promoting Human Prosperity, Energy Security and Environmental Sustainability') made only a passing mention of regional integration, the issue that had dominated the previous summits (Fifth Summit of the Americas 2009). In spite of taking place in the middle of the worst economic crisis since the 1930s, the Declaration contained no significant new economic initiatives and made no mention of models of economic development. Instead, it makes a long list of social commitments, including a commitment 'to reduce social disparities and inequality and to halve extreme poverty by the year 2015' and to 'identify and implement strategies to advance towards universal access to quality comprehensive health care'. It also commits the member countries to achieve universal primary educa-tion by 2015 (ibid.).

In all, the summit's Declaration was of relatively little practical significance. Instead, what defined the summit was a new warming in relations between the US and Latin America in a post-Bush, post-Washington Consensus era. The political climate of the summit could not be more different to that of Mar del Plata. As Kevin Casas-Zamora (2009) put it: 'The concrete results of the Summit were meager at best. Then again, this was never about results. For Latin America it was all about gauging Obama. The messenger was the message.' However, expectations that a new, progressive, US presi-dent will be able to close the fault lines between the US and Latin America may be premature, as important political differences remain among the countries of Latin America and between the US and Latin America as seen in the Honduras crisis of 2009 and the stalling dialogue between US and Cuba. Perhaps the enduring image of the summit was President Chávez's highly ambiguous gesture of gifting

169

Obama the book *Open Veins of Latin America: Five Centuries of the Pillage of a Continent*, by the Uruguayan writer Eduardo H. Galeano, a denunciation of the US history of intervention in Latin America.[21]

Conclusions

Economic and political integration has been a Latin American aspiration since independence. Two hundred years later the dream is still alive but, some advances notwithstanding, it remains largely unfulfilled. Behind the failures and limitations of a long history of incomplete integration initiatives are a number of political and economic fault lines that have prevented more rapid progress towards the goal of regional integration. Some of the fault lines have deep historical roots in colonial history and in the turbulent period of civil wars that followed the wars of independence; others are more contemporary and relate to the regional impact of the dual processes of democratization and free market reforms that dominated the region's political landscape in the 1990s and to the political backlash against neoliberalism that followed. The evolution of democracy in the region has also affected relations with the United States. As Peter Smith (1999: 183) put it, the greater the level of democratization in Latin America, the more complex and conflictual became the relationship with the United States.

This is not to deny that on many counts Latin America is today more integrated and interdependent than it ever has been, particularly in areas such as trade, investment, cultural exchanges and energy (Peña 2009). Economically, the countries of the region are engaged in an array of bilateral and multilateral agreements that include hemispheric, sub-regional, intra-regional and regional initiatives that operate on different principles and show different degrees of consolidation. But the proliferation of integration initiatives is itself a symptom of the underlying fragmentation of the region and of persistent political and economic differences between its countries that are driven as much by national interests as by ideological coincidences. As Carlos Malamud (2009) put it, there are too many integration processes and there is too little agreement on what kind of economic and political integration the region should strive for, whether hemispheric, Latin American, South American, sub-regional, bilateral, multilateral, market-led or state-led or a combination of all.

170

The oversupply of integration initiatives also creates coordination problems. The combination of highly politicized processes and weak institutional settings, which this book argues characterizes domestic politics in most Latin American countries, also affects the region's international relations. It reinforces Latin America's heavy reliance on presidential diplomacy as the key mechanism for integration initiatives and as the forum for the resolution of conflicts. Regional hyper-presidentialism promotes the personalization of processes of integration and makes more difficult the setting up of supranational institutions able to give stability and a rule-based framework to these processes (Serbin 2009). The natural problems of regional coordination in such a diverse area are compounded by nationalist conflicts and political differences and by the reluctance of the Latin American nations to cede or share sovereignty and to agree to be bound by legally enforceable decisions, a reality often masked by empty appeals to Latin American unity and the setting up of toothless regional and sub-regional parliaments. As Passini and Ramanzini Jr (2009) put it, the fault lines of Latin American integration are the result of the increasing interdependency of the countries of the region, combined with the lack of institutions capable of managing politically driven processes.

The nature of integration during the present (post-Miami Consensus) phase suggests that there are different political options open to a region in which Brazil and Venezuela are leading alternative projects of integration (Kellogg 2007; Pérez Flórez 2009; Serbin 2009; Shifter and Joyce 2009).[22] Whichever course is adopted – and, as argued in this chapter, there is no reason to assume that only one option is available, given the increasingly plural nature of international relations since the end of the Cold War – the region will continue to face several key challenges, both internal and external. While MERCOSUR remains mired in its own crisis of identity, UNASUR and to a lesser extent ALBA have emerged in the twenty-first century as forums for political coordination and the resolution of conflicts in the region, marking the growing autonomy of the region from the United States. As seen in this chapter, Brazil and Venezuela have been the driving forces behind these integration initiatives. But, for different reasons, the leadership of the two countries has not provided solid foundations for overcoming political and institutional obstacles for more solid processes of integration. Brazil has been the key strategic actor in two of the main processes of South American integration, MERCOSUR and UNASUR, as well as a one of the main actors,

171

together with the US, in the frustrated negotiations of the FTAA. Current regional integration initiatives reflect Brazil's preference for shallow processes of integration. This is so that they do not place a heavy financial burden on its regional and global leadership ambitions and do not constrain its autonomy to pursue domestic developmentalist policies. On these terms, Brazil can use South America as a geo-strategic power base for the pursuit of its interests in world politics without having to bind itself to the region's turbulent politics or seek a difficult-to-achieve consensus to represent regional interests at the global level (Flemes 2009).

Meanwhile, Chávez's protagonist role in regional politics is based on more than just oil money and the Venezuelan president's charisma and leadership. It also encapsulates the widely perceived failures of both the political and the economic dimensions of the Miami Consensus (Hurrell 2008). As a space for the projection of Chávez's ambitions of regional leadership, ALBA competes with UNASUR on political, ideological and economic terms and Venezuela competes with Brazil for regional leadership. The potential for conflict between the two entities is, however, more limited than suggested by a simplistic view of the varieties of the left in the region. ALBA has a greater presence in the Caribbean and Central America, which are outside the geographical boundaries of UNASUR. Moreover, Chávez remains a highly divisive figure in Latin America and his leadership is not accepted by a majority of governments in the region.

While a majority of Latin American countries welcome the setting up of regional institutions autonomous of the US, very few, including only some of those who are members of ALBA, share Chávez's anti-imperialist drive. Whatever their differences with the US administrations, most Latin Americans have vested interests in maintaining good political and economic relations with the United States. Heavily dependent on the use of oil money as an instrument of international diplomacy, Chávez is vulnerable to fluctuations in energy prices and to domestic economic problems. As a result of these limitations, and despite Venezuela's strong presence in the region, Brazilian diplomacy has largely had the upper hand in the struggle for regional leadership. However, despite Brazil's apparently benign preponderance, enthusiasm for its role as regional hegemon is not universal. For those of a more radical political disposition, its regional objectives remain too linked to the neoliberal model and sub-imperial ambitions (either as the local policeman for the US or to assert the capitalist impulses of its ruling classes) and President Chávez's Venezuela offers a more attractive alternative (Kellogg 2007).

Finally, it is necessary to conclude by addressing the question of whether the United States has effectively 'lost' Latin America and whether President Obama can establish a new pattern of collaborative relations between the US and Latin America. Our analysis of the presidential summits since 1994 showed the growing political divergence between the countries of Latin America and the United States. Yet, political divergences and the search for autonomy have been as integral to the history of US–Latin American relations as political and economic interdependence (Rivarola Puntigliano 2008). The pattern continues. It should not be overlooked that, during the administration of George W. Bush, possibly the most unpopular ever US president in Latin America, the US signed free trade agreements with a majority of the countries of the region. The extent to which President Obama will be able to restore US–Latin American relations to the golden era of the Miami Summit is open to question. The world has changed since Miami and so have the United States and Latin America. President Obama appears to be highly conscious of the increasingly limited economic and political resources of the US to assert its interests worldwide. There is no reason to believe that he will divert scarce resources to a region that, for all its nationalist rhetoric and its quest for autonomy, does not impose a strategic threat to the US. Instead, President Obama is likely to offer the countries of the region a mixture of soft power and a promise to strengthen multilateral mechanisms for political dialogue and coordination. However, soft power and multilateralism will still be at the service of US interests in the region that are yet to be redefined by the current administration.

CONCLUSION

We are now in a position to better examine what was meant in this book about the triumph of politics. What is referred to in the introduction as 'the Miami Consensus' represented a critical juncture in Latin American history in which the region appeared to be going through a radical transformation of its politics and economy, away from populism, political instability, economic statism and nationalism towards liberal democracy, technocratic politics, a centrist consensus, market reform and free trade cosmopolitanism. The main practical commitment of the Miami Summit, the Free Trade Area of the Americas, was meant to crystallize at hemispheric level both the hegemony of market relations and the shared political vision and liberal democratic values of the US and Latin America. Much has been written about the reasons for the failures of the Miami Consensus (or, rather, of the more narrowly defined Washington Consensus) and this book did not intend to re-examine the issue. Rather than discussing why politics has 'returned' to the region, it has sought to analyse one of *the different forms* this new politicization has adopted.

The model of democratic politics that dominated the political landscape of the mid-1990s placed a heavy emphasis on the institutional and procedural elements of liberal democracy. Still haunted by the memories of the polarized politics that contributed to the democratic breakdowns of the 1970s, the Miami Consensus sought the underpinning of political stability by a predominantly centrist consensus. Technocratic elites that had gained considerable political leverage in the wake of the 1980s debt crisis and subsequent free market reformation emphasized the importance of good governance as a condition for economic development. Civil society was no longer perceived as an arena for the mobilization of subordinate social

174

sectors against elitist political orders or a locus of resistance to tyrannical governments. Instead, it was redefined as the realm of voluntary associations engaged in building up citizens' mutual relations of trust that was being 'empowered' to perform the social development role states were no longer fit to undertake. However, governability, centrist politics, technocratic good governance and a depoliticized civil society were not recipes for stasis. Rather, as is well known, the 1990s was a decade of radical social, political and economic change in Latin America which was dominated by the expansion of market relations at domestic and international level.

If the Miami Consensus does not hold any more, what is it that is taking its place? There is no single answer to this question. One thing that is clear is that politics in the region have become much more heterogeneous. Rather than try to sum up political change in the region as a whole, this book looked at an important strand of politics, a strand associated with radical opposition to the values of the Miami Consensus. In this version of the new politics, centrist consensus has given way to political polarization, participation and mobilization are assigned a higher democratic value than governability and good governance, new institutional orders crystallize rather than erase the dividing lines between conflicting political actors, twenty-first century socialism is being built as an alternative to the Washington Consensus and politics rather than markets is the driving force for regional integration.

There is much here that looks like a trip to the past. This, in itself, need not be surprising. While much has been written about the long history of authoritarianism in the region, relatively less attention has been given to an equally long history of contestation and social mobilization. After all, four of the successful revolutions of the twentieth century took place in Latin America: Mexico 1917, Bolivia 1952, Cuba 1959 and Nicaragua 1979. The history of Latin America is marked by charismatic leaders who challenged the existing political order in the name of those who didn't feel represented by traditional political elites. While Latin America traditionally has been 'the US backyard', it also has a long history of anti-imperialism and economic nationalism. Thus, a certain reading of contemporary Latin American history may conclude that twenty-first century socialism very much resembles aspects of politics in the not-so-distant past, an era also of populism, military involvement in politics, social polarization and economic nationalism that the dual process of re-democratization and economic reforms of the 1980s and 1990 appeared to have left behind.

It is easy to see the parallels between Chávez and Perón and the chapter on populism looks at the enduring influence of Velasco Ibarra's style of politics in Ecuador. Chávez started out as a military nationalist as much as a socialist or a populist. The people in the streets have effected regime change in Bolivia and elsewhere many times before. As the chapter on personalism, plebiscites and institutions reminds us, plebiscites have also been used in the past, not least by conservatives such as Pinochet and Fujimori. Demands for the nationalization of oil were part of the national popular wave of the mid-twentieth century. And the new patterns of regional integration described in chapter 6 have many elements in common with early attempts at regional integration characteristic of the Import-Substitution-Industrialization (ISI) period. There is some truth in the perception that, when the 'smiling mask' (Lagos 1997) of the Miami Consensus is peeled away, one face of Latin America looks back to the future: political culture trumps institutions and popular resistance beats top-down attempts at implanting political and economic liberalism. Yet that is not the whole story. Even on the left, what is notable is as much what is different in today's Latin America from its pre-Miami Consensus past as it is about its political differences with the Miami Consensus.

Latin America as a whole in the twenty-first century looks very different from the political and economic model envisaged in Miami. It has not been the purpose of this book to map the nature and scope of the changes of the 1990s, less so their social costs and benefits, an undertaking that has been extensively done elsewhere (Epstein 2000; Korzeniewicz and Smith 2000; Roberts 2002; Weyland, Madrid and Hunter 2010). It claims only that significant countries in Latin America have experienced deep political, social and economic dislocations from which new forms of politicization have taken shape. As part of this process, political systems have been renewed, government elites have been replaced and the predominance of politics over institutions and of politicians over technocrats has been reasserted (Fernández 2010). The FTAA never saw the light of the day and new, more politically driven projects of regional integration have taken its place. In parallel, the dividing lines between politics and economics and between states and markets are being redrawn yet again.

While new forms of politicization have been a common trend in much of the region, there are significant national variations in the ways that the new politics have been shaped. These can be accounted for by the weight of national histories in a region that shares many common legacies, by the common impact of the free market reforma-

176

tion on societies with very different socio-economic structures and levels of economic development and by both regional and national institutional contexts. Broadly and in general, in a process of political change that started with the election of Hugo Chávez in Venezuela in 1998, the region's political centre of gravity has shifted – to varying degrees – to the left. But again, the so-called pink tide has not reached all countries in the region and differences between left and left-of-centre governments are as significant as their similarities (Shifter and Jawahar 2005). Rather than attempting to encapsulate the changes in detail or making claims of exceptionalism, the focus of this book has been to try to understand better the specific forms of politicization that have characterized the rise to office of a distinctive group of left-wing leaders, namely Chávez, Correa and Morales, and in the process throw new light on some themes familiar to scholars of Latin America.

An underlying theme that cuts across the book's different chapters is the relations between politics, institutions and democracy. Historically, and with some notable exceptions, democracy in Latin America has not fitted the traditional liberal democratic pattern of strong institutions, rule of law, checks and balances and market-oriented economies. Rather, it has been weakly institutionalized, populist, personalist, majoritarian and economically statist rather than market oriented. In the current century, the gap between countries with strong and those with fragile political institutions remains as apparent as ever. Institution building, however, is not a one-directional process, and the rise to office of left-of-centre administrations has had contrasting impacts upon national institutions. In some cases, most notably in Chile and Uruguay, institutional strength has an in-built historical legacy that has, if anything, become greater under left-of-centre administrations. In others, such as Brazil, it has been a more recent and incomplete process to which the Partido dos Trabalhadores (PT) has also made a significant contribution. In contrast, in the late 1990s and early 2000s Bolivia, Ecuador and Venezuela experienced a breakdown of the mechanisms for the aggregation of demands and conflict resolution and saw elections running alongside anti-institutional forms of politics. As is made apparent in this book, while the three countries broadly shared the same direction of travel in their political journeys, their starting points were significantly different. While Ecuador has historically been characterized by weak political institutions, Venezuela was regarded recently as one of the most strongly institutionalized democracies in the region and, after being historically the most unstable country in South America, Bolivia was considered in the 1990s as a successful case of political institutionalization. Yet, in the late 1990s and early twenty-first century, the three countries went through serious institutional crises manifested in extreme political polarization, failed *coups d'état*, the forced resignation of presidents and mass civil protests followed by foundational projects that have redrawn the institutional bases of their respective political orders.

Chapters 1 and 2 analysed two key actors in processes of political deinstitutionalization in which democracy coexisted with para-constitutional or anti-constitutional forms of politics (presidential removals, mass popular protests, civil disobedience, illegal removal of members of Congress, failed *coups d'état*) – namely, the military and mass popular movements. Appropriately, Huntington's work provides the analytical tools that link the two actors together as well as allowing comparison and contrast between current developments in Latin America and the historical episodes that informed Huntington's writing. Huntington's analysis of mass praetorianism resonates with our account of the politics of mass protest, as it appears more relevant for the understanding of the crises of representation in the three countries than the depoliticized notion of civil society of the Miami Consensus. If the latter expressed a vision of civil society strangely void of politics, the politics of mass protest crystallizes the reality of a hyper-politicized civil society confronting the state, acting outside institutions and often on the fringes of legality. The radical social mobilizations that effectively brought down the constitutional orders of Bolivia and Ecuador recall Huntington's argument about mass praetorianism and its potential to trigger authoritarian backlashes, as exemplified by the military dictatorships of the 1970s. In contrast, however, in the 2000s, democracy, if not political institutions, survived mass praetorianism and, with the partial but significant exception of Honduras, the democratic breakdowns predicted by Huntington have not materialized. Explanations for the absence of military dictatorships can only be speculative and some of the more relevant ones are discussed in detail in chapter 1. There is no doubt that the end of the Cold War has taken away the US government's rationale to support military coups. The links between military interests and those of the economic and political elites that appeared to overlap in the 1970s are more contingent than was assumed by some scholars of the period. The legacy of the right-wing military regimes of the 1970s has overshadowed the importance of progressive military nationalism in the region, which manifested itself in many forms from the *revolta dos tenentes* (the Lieutenants' Revolt) in Brazil in the 1920s to the government of General Juan Velasco Alvarado in Peru between 1968 and 1975 and has been reincarnated in the figure of Hugo Chávez and briefly in that of Colonel Lucio Gutiérrez.

As the same chapter makes clear, however, lack of military dictatorship is not the same as lack of military intervention in politics. But while the military's actions and inactions at times of crises are still crucial for their outcome, the military are reluctant to defend constitutionally elected presidents at any cost in terms of the use of force or to take the sole responsibility of ruling the country as a dictatorship as they did in the 1970s. Both the failed civic-military coups in Ecuador in January 2000 and in Venezuela in April 2002, as well as the most recent successful one in Honduras in June 2009, illustrate these points. A combination of the goals of self-preservation of the military officers and of the preservation of the unity of the armed forces, together with a much higher risk of regional and international political and financial isolation for an outright military dictatorship, poses much higher constraints on military intervention than those of the 1970s. Conversely, the limits on military intervention have increased the political impact of mass protests. As argued in chapter 2, in times of institutional crises the political decisions of both the military and Congress have been strongly influenced by the size and strength of mass protests and particularly by considerations about which course of action would be more in line with the run of popular feelings as expressed by the protests. As suggested in chapter 2, the importance of mass mobilizations in both triggering institutional crises and in shaping their outcome has made civil society movements the new moderating power in weakly institutionalized political orders within the region.

The analysis of the relations between politics, institutions and democracy continues to be developed in chapters 3 and 4 from a wider angle. As chapter 3 reminds us, if antagonism is the essence of populism, it is also the essence of politics, at least if we accept Carl Schmitt's (1996) definition of the political as based on the distinction between friend and enemy. As shown in the same chapters, political polarization was not an automatic outcome of the social polarization that characterized the three countries' social make-up. Rather, it was a deliberate political strategy used by Chávez, Correa and Morales to consolidate new political identities, re-politicize economic policy, promote new forms of state intervention and mobilize the popular sectors against both the political elite and the neoliberal economic order. But only failed states can remain for a long period

179

of time in an institutional vacuum. In chapters 3 and 4, we looked at how the politics of deinstitutionalization was followed by political strategies to legitimate a new political order in the three countries. By its very nature, populism combines elements of deinstitutionalization when in opposition with attempts at constructing a new political regime with its own distinctive institutions and sources of legitimacy once in office. Populism has characterized political regimes, such as Peronismo and Varguismo, which spent many years in office in Argentina and Brazil. Both in the streets and in office, the figure of the leader is crucial for the characterization of populism but his/her role is significantly different in opposition and in government. As seen in chapter 3, as the unifying figure of the people marching in the streets, the populist leader became the nodal point of disparate demands and of different popular identities. But, as shown in chapter 4, as the heads of new political regimes, presidents need to legitimize their rule as well as the new institutional arrangements that underpin the new order. To this purpose, Correa, Chávez and Morales relied on a combination of majoritarian and participatory forms of democratic legitimation that mobilized their supporters and crystallized the divide between their followers and their political enemies. If political polarization was a successful strategy deployed by these leaders to gain power, polarization has also contributed to consolidating their power once in office, as seen by Presidents Chávez, Morales and Correa's use of plebiscites to de-legitimize opposition-dominated parliaments, redraw constitutions and allow their re-elections.

While this strategy has much in common with the one followed by the *classical populists* of the 1940s and 1950s against liberal oligarchies, it can be argued that there are significant differences between the two waves. These are mainly related to the stronger hold of democracy on contemporary Latin America compared to earlier populist waves, which limits the ability of personalist leaders to use the authoritarian top-down strategies of social activation and control characteristic of past populist relations. The social bases of support of contemporary personalist leaders are also more fragmented and autonomous than the new industrial working class of the populism of the ISI era. As chapter 3 points out, to different degrees and through different mechanisms, Morales, Correa and Chávez have to listen to their supporters and account for their decisions to their followers. Significantly, the new constitutional order in the three countries combines elements of participatory democracy and hyper-

180

presidentialism in an uneven and potentially unstable relationship. A detailed empirical study of the three governments would be required to find out how the balance between the presidentialist and participatory elements of the new institutional orders differs within the three countries.

Strategies of political polarization also allow us to distinguish Chávez, Correa and Morales from other popular left-of-centre presidents, particularly Presidents Luiz Inácio Lula da Silva of Brazil and José Pepe Mujica of Uruguay with whom they may have some elements in common. As is the case with Morales, the social origins of both Lula da Silva and Mujica mark the two presidents as outsiders to their countries' traditional political elites: the former is a metal worker and trade union leader, the latter a small farmer and former Tupamaro guerrilla leader. Their life stories embody the traditional populist narrative of the man of plebeian origins who, through his charisma and political struggles, has achieved the highest office without betraying his roots. They both have a strong following among the rural and urban poor who feel represented by them as 'one of us' and have been rewarded by relatively generous social programmes. But if Lula da Silva and Mujica's personal narratives are similar to those of many populist politicians, their political strategies are significantly different. Chávez, Correa and Morales have been trench-diggers: anti-systemic politicians that sought to de-legitimize traditional parties as self-serving partycracies and opposition leaders as corrupt defenders of oligarchic interests. For them, the incorporation of excluded popular sectors into a truly inclusive demos requires the foundation of a new political order. In contrast, Lula da Silva and Mujica have been bridge-builders: they have sought to construct broad political alliances and promote more inclusive politics by working within the system rather than against it and have maintained fluid relations with the opposition and the business sector. If Chávez, Correa and Morales's political strategies are based on the construction of antagonisms, those of Lula da Silva and Mujica are based on the bridging of differences.

While political leadership and political strategies are important elements in explaining the differences between left-of-centre administrations, these should be placed within the institutional contexts in which they operate. As noted in the introduction to this book, it is possible to argue that the administrations of the late Néstor Kirchner (2003–7) and Cristina Fernández de Kirchner (2007–11) in Argentina share many elements with our case studies. As happened at different times in the early twenty-first century in Ecuador and Bolivia, Argentina experienced intense street protest that led to the country having five different presidents between December 2001 and January 2002. Both Néstor Kirchner and Cristina Fernández de Kirchner sought to centralize power in the presidency and have repeatedly used and, arguably, abused their constitutional powers to legislate by presidential decree. They have both clashed repeatedly with Congress and the judiciary and divided Argentine society, as exemplified by Cristina Fernández de Kirchner's confrontation with the farmers in 2008. And yet Argentina's institutional order has been preserved throughout this often turbulent political and economic period. Neither administration has changed the nature of Argentina's political system, and they have both ultimately submitted to the rules of the game.

As noted above, the promotion of free market economics (including openness to foreign investment) and hemispheric integration were at the heart of the Miami Consensus. Chapters 5 and 6 showed how the politics of oil and of regional integration break from the principles of Miami and are tied instead to the triumph of politics. More than any other elements of economic policy, oil and gas politics and diplomacy in Venezuela and Bolivia have illustrated the new emphasis on redistribution and the determination to reassert the power of government over market forces and autonomous state enterprise.

There is an evident relationship between an economic policy aimed at short-term resource-rent maximization and a politics of using oil rents to consolidate support among the popular sectors, which, as noted in chapter 3, demanded both recognition and redistribution. There is also a foreign policy dimension involved in that Chávez has used oil revenues to finance an anti-US version of economic diplomacy. By adopting an aggressive policy of redistribution and enjoying the benefit of high oil and gas prices, Chávez and Morales successfully accrued political capital and state revenue in the short run. The flipside of this strategy, however, is the long-term cost of confrontational policy making in terms of attracting the investment and technology necessary to increase or even maintain current levels of production. Finally, by mapping Latin America's political journey from Miami to Mar del Plata, chapter 6 adds a broader regional dimension to our analysis than in the rest of the book which is limited to a select group of countries. The contrast between the two summits shows the extent of the region's political change and its growing autonomy from the host of the Miami Summit, the US. It highlights the extraordinary influence of President Chávez in shaping the new regional landscape but also the limits to his petro-diplomacy and the rise of Brazil as the region's leader in a relation of competition and collaboration with the Venezuelan government. Never before have there been so many projects of regional and sub-regional integration. But in consonance with our analysis of domestic policies, we argue that politics without institutions – that is, an over-reliance on presidentialist diplomacy and the failure to strengthen regional institutions and abide by them – has exacerbated rather than bridged the fault lines that prevent the deepening of integration in the region.

Arguments about polarization, confrontation and antagonism cut across most chapters of the book. They raise questions about the nature of the contemporary democratic order in the region and highlight differences between past and contemporary forms of politicization. Let us conclude by looking again at the question of democracy in the region, as addressed in this book. In the introduction, we argued that Chávez, Morales and Correa's claims to be re-founding and deepening democracy in their countries should not be taken at face value but should be taken seriously. We have further argued that fears that the polarization brought by processes of radical change as expressed in 'twenty-first century socialism' may lead to an authoritarian backlash have become less clear and present, although the events in Honduras in 2009 should serve as a reminder that powerful political and economic forces could still resort to military intervention if conflicts cannot be solved within existing institutions. Democratic socialism (so long as it remains democratic) should be considered a legitimate option, as long as it is supported by a majority of the people. But the objections of the critics of twenty-first century socialism must also be taken seriously and the new forms of politicization in Latin American democracy also raise legitimate concerns. Polarization may not endanger democracy, at least as directly as it did in the past. Indeed, polarization may be a necessary price to pay for radical change but it can affect the quality of democracy, as it makes it more difficult to promote the social relations of trust and reciprocity that are a condition for a deliberative democracy. Concentration of power in the Executive and rule by public opinion are poor second-best options to negotiation and political learning for solving conflicts of power. Those who promote a return to economic nationalism and state control over the economy should at least explain why and how this should work better in the twenty-first century than it did in the past. How the balance between politics and institutions and between the majoritarian and pluralist elements of democracy will play in the future remains an open question. The ways it is answered will define the future of democracy in the region, particularly in the countries that, as seen in this book, epitomize the triumph of politics.

NOTES

1   In Venezuela, the 1989 riots known as the *Caracazo* aborted President Carlos Andrés Pérez's attempt to impose top-down free market reforms and effectively drained his political capital. The *Caracazo* was followed by two failed military coups in 1992 (neither of which involved significant mass demonstrations), the impeachment of President Pérez in 1993 and by the electoral victory of the failed coup leader, Hugo Chávez, in 1998. Chávez was himself the victim of a failed civic-military coup in April 2002 and his years in office have been characterized by intense street mobilization of both his supporters and his opponents.

2   Zakaria was a student of Huntington.

3   There are several definitions of social capital but it is generally understood as referring to the collective value of social networks and the inclinations that arise from these networks to promote social cooperation based on relations of mutual trust and reciprocity (Putnam 2000). For a discussion about the applicability of social capital for analysing social movements in Latin America, see Muse Sinek 2006.

4   Foley and Edwards acknowledge there is no reason in principle why the counterweight of civil society should not become a burden to a democratic as well as to an authoritarian state but this was not the their main concern.

5   For a discussion of the figures and a much lower estimate, see Laserna (2007).

6   The 1979 constitution eliminated literacy requirements that had excluded most Indians from the vote. President Roldós

(1979–81) promoted the participation of Indian organizations in rural development, see www.llacta.org/notice/2009/not0127a.htm, accessed 6 August 2009.

7 CONAIE emerged out of the amalgamation of two smaller indigenous organizations, the Confederación de Nacionalidades Indígenas de la Amazonía Ecuatoriana, CONFENAIE, that represented the western Oriente indigenous people, and ECUARUNARI, that represented the indigenous populations of the highlands (Beck and Mijeski 2006).

8 In early 1995, CONAIE had been at the forefront of a succesful campaign for a 'No' vote on a referendum that would have allowed the privatization of state enterprises and strengthen the power of the Executive. CONAIE leaders saw the victory of the 'No' campaign as confirmation of the movement's electoral appeal and mobilizing power.

9 In the 1998 election that followed the impeachment of President Abdalá Bucaram, Pachakutik candidates won eight seats but, because of congressional reforms that increased the number of seats in Congress, this represented only 6 per cent of the seats (Beck and Mijeski 2006).

10 Paradoxically, by creating more than three hundred new municipalities, the laws of political and administrative decentralization passed by President Sánchez de Lozada in 1994 and 1995 undermined the political influence of regional elites. The law introduced automatic transfers from the central government to the municipalities that bypassed departmental (regional) political authorities. It also set up new mechanisms for the participation of indigenous organizations in public life. It was at municipal level that MAS and Pachakuti made their first political gains (Eaton 2007).

11 These demands provoked a strong response from the military, with a warning by Armed Forces Commander Marco Antonio Justiniano in June 2005 that any unilateral declaration of autonomy would be considered a breach of the constitution.

12 The key business organizations that supported the January Agenda included the Cámara Agropecuaria del Oriente (Agricultural Chamber of Eastern Bolivia), the Federación de Ganaderos de Santa Cruz (Federation of Ranchers of Santa Cruz), and, most important, the Cámara de Industria, Comercio, Servicios y Turismo de Santa Cruz (Chamber of Commerce, Industry, Service and Tourism of Santa Cruz – CAINCO). The

Spanish oil giant Repsol-YPF, Brazilian state-owned Petrobras, and Enron are members of CAINCO's board of directors (Spronk and Webber 2008: 84).
13 http://news.bbc.co.uk/1/hi/world/americas/7607158.stm.

CHAPTER 3   POPULISM AND THE RETURN OF THE POLITICAL

1   Throughout Latin America, social pacts (*concertación*) between business, labour and political parties were seen as a strategy for dealing with the challenge of securing democratic transitions in the context of the economic crises characteristic of the 1980s. Nowhere was this more evident than in Chile, where the political successors of Salvador Allende in the Socialist Party went out of their way to distance themselves from the Communist Party, forged an alliance with their former centrist Christian Democratic adversaries and reassured both the economic elite and the military that they had little to fear if they were to return to office. While the left's strategy was successful in achieving the goal of bringing an end to the military dictatorship, the return to democracy was overshadowed by General Pinochet's proclamation at the time of leaving office of 'mission accomplished' and by the constraints to democracy imposed by the *leyes de atado* that limited the new democratic government scope for political and economic reform.

2   As the minister for planning of Paz Estenssoro's government, Sánchez de Lozada was the architect and overseer of the NEP.

3   This perception is neatly captured by the following excerpt from Morales's inaugural address:

> Permanentemente antes se hablaba de democracia, se lucha por la democracia, se hablaba de pacto por la democracia, pacto por la gobernabilidad. El año 1997 cuando llegué a este Parlamento que he visto personalmente, ningún pacto por la democracia ni por la gobernabilidad, sino los pactos por la corrupción, pacto de cómo sacar plata de donde y cómo, felizmente había tenido límite y se acabó gracias a la conciencia del pueblo boliviano.

4   As a former mine union leader, Filemon Escobar, eloquently put it:

With our vote, we have condemned ourselves to our present misery. With our vote, we have facilitated the forceful eradication of the coca leaf. With our vote, we have facilitated unemployment and the destruction of national firms. With our vote, 90 per cent of the population lives in extreme poverty... With our vote, we have helped the Bolivian economy pass to foreign hands. With our vote, we have taken the path toward our own suicide. (Cited in Durand 2010)

5 In 1993, President Sánchez de Lozada appointed the aymara intellectual Víctor Hugo Cárdenas as vice-president, who became the first indigenous man in Bolivian history to occupy the position.
6 As John-Andrew McNeish (2007: 890) put it, neoliberal multiculturalism's new language of citizenship and formation of new aspirations had unexpected consequences. Rather than accepting the limited gains of multicultural citizenship, the indigenous groups' struggle for survival and representation played into a much larger movement of the excluded that recast the country's history of identity politics, aiming to transform fundamental ideas about the basis of the nation-state and the extent of existing discourses on rights and democracy.
7 'En general, se conoce a Bolivia como un país fundamentalmente andino, encerrado en sus montañas, una especie de Tibet Sudamericano constituido mayoritariamente por las etnias aymará-queschua, atrasado y miserable, donde prevalece la cultura del conflicto, comunalista, pre-republicana, iliberal, sindicalista, conservadora, y cuyo centro burocrático (La Paz) practica un execrable centralismo colonial de Estado que explota a sus "colonias internas", se apropia de nuestros excedentes económicos y nos impone la cultura del subdesarrollo, su cultura. Pero también existe otra "Nación" no oficial y que representa más del 30% de la población y se asienta sobre un territorio predominantemente constituido por selvas y llanuras ubicadas en el corazón de América del sur y que constituye mas del 70% del territorio nacional -unos 700 mil kilómetros cuadrados, cuya cultura mestiza proviene del cruzamiento de hispanos y guaraníes. Su Índice de Desarrollo Humano (IDH) es el más alto de Bolivia y se halla por encima del promedio de América Latina. Su analfabetismo no excede el 7%, y desde el punto de vista productivo, es el quinto productor mundial de soja. En la ciudad

de Santa Cruz de la Sierra (1.2 millones de habitantes), se realizan al año más de 600 eventos internacionales al año, lo que demuestra su amplia e indiscutible inserción en el mundo globalizado. Constituye "la otra versión" de Bolivia y cuyo Movimiento aspira a lograr la autonomía radical de esta nación oprimidà': www.nacioncamba.net/quienesomos.htm (last accessed 22 May 2009).

8 Evo Morales's inaugural speech is typical of this discourse: 'Estamos acá para decir, basta a la resistencia. De la resistencia de 500 años a la toma del poder para 500 años, indígenas, obreros, todos los sectores para acabar con esa injusticia, para acabar con esa desigualdad, para acabar con la discriminación, opresión donde hemos sido sometidos como aymarás, quechuas, guaraníes.' http://discursasparalahistoria.wordpress.com/2010/03/16evo-morales-discurso-de-investidura, last accessed 30 May 2010.

9 Although it only took its current name in 1997, its political origins can be traced back to the decision of the VIth Congress of the Confederación Sindical Única de Trabajadores Campesinos de Bolivia (CSUTCB) in 1994 to set up a so-called 'political instrument' of the peasant-indigenous organizations. The resolution materialized in March 1995 in the decision by an alliance of peasant movements in the Congreso Tierra, Territorio e Instrumento Político to set up a political movement originally named Asamblea por la Soberanía de los Pueblos (ASP), which later became MAS.

10 Opposition to the export of liquid gas to the US through Chilean ports was a central element of the so-called gas war. It was rooted in Bolivia's historical grievance about the loss of the Pacific port of Antofagasta to Chile as a result of the 1879 war and the redemptive vindication of a *salida al mar* as the reparation of an historical humiliation that should not be traded for the commercial gains of using Chilean ports. It also incorporated the economic nationalist demand that natural resources, such as gas and oil, should be used to industrialize the country rather than be exported as raw materials.

11 http://news.bbc.co.uk/1/hi/world/americas/7849666.stm.

12 This paragraph was taken from Panizza and Miorelli (2009).

13 The new constitution establishes state control over key economic sectors and grants fundamental new social, political and economic rights to Bolivia's indigenous groups but the new

constitutional text leaves some fundamental questions unsolved. Where the previous constitution defined Bolivia as a pluri-ethnic state, the new one defines the country as a *pluri-national communitarian* state. The new formulation represents a major political change because of the implication of the recognition of multiple nationalities for state policies and claims to control natural resources. The constitution has strong participative components. It decentralizes power along four levels of autonomy: departmental, regional, municipal and indigenous. It awards significant levels of autonomy to indigenous groups (Pueblos Indígenas Originarios), including control over renewable natural resources and shared control with the state over non-renewable ones, with the potential implication of different sovereign holders transecting at ethnic, departmental and national levels.

14 Morales was first elected to Congress in 1998. He was expelled from Congress in 2002, after leading violent protests against coca eradication (Barr 2005: 69–72; Hochstetler and Friedman 2008: 9).

15 Carlos de la Torre's (2004: 690) description of the 1939–40 presidential campaign highlights the patterns of recognition and inclusion that were at the heart of Velasco's populism and have resonances in more contemporary developments.

> Starting with the 1939–40 presidential campaign, Velasco Ibarra's followers felt themselves to be participants in the political struggle and asserted their rights by symbolically occupying public spaces and demonstrating for their leader. The occupation of public spaces was in itself an act of self-recognition and affirmation of the political rights of people excluded by the lack of honesty at the polls and by a restricted franchise from the political decision-making apparatus.

16 These were Abdalá Bucaram (1996–7), Jamil Mahuad (1998–2000) and Lucio Gutiérrez (2003–5).

17 During the April 2002 general strike called by the opposition, Chávez declared 'this is not about the pro-Chávez against the anti-Chávez...but...the patriots against the enemies of the homeland' (quoted in Zuquete 2008: 105). Similarly, during the 2006 electoral campaign, he claimed that a vote for the opposition was a vote for President Bush.

CHAPTER 6 THE FAULT LINES OF LATIN AMERICAN INTEGRATION

1 ALBA is not solely a South American organization as it comprises the nations of Central America and the Caribbean. However, we include it in this chapter because of the importance of Venezuela's leadership and because it helps a better understanding of alternative projects of regional integration.

2 In the Declaration of Quebec City, the leaders of the Americas committed to a democratic clause which led to the creation of the Inter-American Democratic Charter in September 2001.

3 'Sem acordo, texto final contempla posição do Mercosul e da Venezuela, de um lado, e a dos Estados Unidos do outro.' *Folha de São Paulo*, 6 November 2005.

4 MERCOSUR is the most ambitious integration project of the western hemisphere, as its final goal is the constitution of a common market rather than just a free trade agreement, as is the case with the North American Free Trade Agreement (NAFTA) between Canada, Mexico and the US, and other trade agreements in Central America, the Caribbean and the Andean Region.

5 In 2006, Venezuela abandoned the CAN because two of its members, Colombia and Peru, had signed free trade agreements with the United States. Chávez then applied to join MERCOSUR. At the time of writing this book, Venezuela's full incorporation to MERCOSUR is pending the approval of the Paraguayan parliament.

6 As noted above, full membership is pending Paraguay's parliamentary ratification of the accession agreement.

7 BBC News, 'Venezuela Signs Up to Trade Group', available at http://news.bbc.co.uk/go/pr/fr/-/1/hi/business/5148660.stm, published 5 July 2006, and FoxNews.com, 'Venezuela Formally Joins Mercosur Trade Bloc', available at www.foxnews.com/printer_friendly_story/0,3566,205073,00.html (both accessed 19 November 2009).

8 See, for instance, 'Vázquez elogia a Bush e pressiona Brasil', *Folha de São Paulo*, 11 March 2007.

9 Moreover, political affinities have not prevented new conflicts between member countries, as exemplified in the conflict between Argentina and Uruguay over the building of a paper mill on the Uruguayan bank of the river that forms the border between the two countries (Serbin 2009).

10 UNASUR is the continuation of the Comunidad Sudamericana de Naciones (CSN, the South American Community of Nations) that had its origins in the Third Summit of South American Presidents in Ayacucho, Peru, in December 2004.

11 www.comunidadandina.org/ingles/csn/treaty.htm.

12 Honduras joined ALBA on October 9 2008 but, following the deposition of President Manuel Zelaya and the subsequent election of President Porfirio Lobo in November 2009, it withdrew on 13 January 2010.

13 In January 2007, prior to Morales's formal adherence to ALBA, Venezuela signed a number of agreements with Bolivia to exchange Bolivian agricultural goods for Venezuelan oil products. Venezuela also committed itself to purchase an extra 200,000 tons of soy and 20,000 tons of poultry a year and to assist Bolivia with energy development (Kellogg 2007: 203).

14 For a full text of the treaty, see http://alainet.org/active/33791&lang=es (accessed 9 December 2009).

15 www.pdvsa.com/index.php?tpl=interface.sp/design/readmenuprinc.tpl.html&newsid_temas=47, last accessed 18 April 2011.

16 For instance, in September 2009 Venezuela announced a $16bn investment deal with China for oil exploration in the Orinoco basin (http://news.bbc.co.uk/go/pr/fr/-/1/hi/world/americas/8260200.stm, published 17 September 2009. In the first semester of 2009, China became Brazil's biggest single export market for the first time and in May 2009 an agreement was signed between the two countries under which the China Development Bank and Sinopec, a Chinese oil company, will lend Petrobras US$10bn in return for up to 200,000 barrels a day of crude oil for ten years from the country's new deep-sea fields, *The Economist*, 17 September 2009.

17 'Venezuela's Foreign Policy: Dreams of a Different World', *The Economist*, 17 September 2009. Available at www.economist.com/world/americas/displaystory.cfm?story_id=14460201, last accessed 27 April 2011.

18 Addressing Congress in March 2004, the former Commander of US Southern Command stated that the major security threat in the region was 'radical populism'; he maintained that 'some leaders are tapping into deep seated frustrations...to reinforce their radical positions by inflaming anti-US sentiment' (Lievesley and Ludlam 2009: 218).

19 The parallels between the Bush and the Monroe Doctrines were not lost on several international analysts. The foreign affairs

editor of the British newspaper *The Observer* wrote that the Bush Doctrine recalled the Monroe Doctrine, except that 'in the following 180 years, America has moved from local to regional and then to global superpower...' (cited in Erikson 2008: 59).

20 However, in a new manifestation of divisions within the Latin American countries, the nation members of ALBA refused to sign the declaration, which was signed only by the Summit's host, the prime minister of Trinidad and Tobago, Patrick Manning, 'on behalf of the Heads of State and Government' attending the Summit.

21 Former Vice-President Dick Cheney admonished Obama for 'cosying up' up to Chávez and for not defending remarks he considered disparaging towards the United States. A column by Mary O'Grady in the *Wall Street Journal* noted that 'if President Barack Obama's goal at the fifth Summit... was to be better liked by the region's dictators and left-wing populists than his predecessor, George W. Bush, the White House can chalk up a win' (Newman 2009).

22 We are grateful to Guy Burton for his contribution to the formulation of this argument.

REFERENCES

Aboy Carlés, G. (2003) 'Repensando el populismo'. *Política y gestión* 4.

Acuña, C. and Smulovitz, C. (1997) 'Guarding the Guardians in Argentina; Some Lessons about the Risks and Benefits of Empowering the Courts', in A. J. McAdams (ed.), *Transitional Justice and the Rule of Law in New Democracies*. Notre Dame: University of Notre Dame. 93–122.

Adrianzén, A. and Ballón, E. (eds) (1992) *Lo Popular en América Latina: Una Visión en Crísis?* Lima: Desco.

Alberts, S. (2008) 'Why Play by the Rules? Constitutionalism and Democratic Institutionalization in Ecuador and Uruguay'. *Democratization* 15(5): 849–69.

Altman Borbón, J. (2009) 'El ALBA, Petrocaribe y Centroamérica: ¿Intereses comunes?' *Nueva Sociedad* 219 (enero–febrero): 127–44.

Álvarez Valdés, R. (2009) 'UNASUR: desde la perspectiva subregional a la regional,' Serie Documentos Electrónicos No 6, octubre Programa Seguridad y Ciudadanía, FLACSO Chile.

Andolina, R. (2003) 'The Sovereign and Its Shadow: Constituent Assembly and Indigenous Movement in Ecuador'. *Journal of Latin American Studies* 35(4): 721–51.

Arce, M. and Rice, R. (2009) 'Social Protest in Post-Stabilization Bolivia'. *Latin American Research Review* 44(1): 88–101.

Arditi, B. (2004) 'Populism as a Spectre of Democracy: A Response to Canovan'. *Political Studies* 52: 135–43.

Arditi, B. (2008) 'Arguments about the Left Turns in Latin America: A Post-Liberal Politics?' *Latin American Research Review* 43(3): 59–81.

Arriagada, G. (2006) 'Petropolitics in Latin America; a review of energy policy and regional relations'. Inter-American Dialogue, Andean Working Paper.

Assies, W. (2003) 'David versus Goliath in Cochabamba: Water Rights, Neoliberalism, and the Revival of Social Protest in Bolivia'. *Latin American Perspectives* 30(3) (Popular Participation against Neoliberalism): 14–36.

REFERENCES

Assies, W. and Salman, T. (2003) 'Bolivian Democracy: Consolidating or Disintegrating?' *Focal: European Journal of Anthropology* 42: 141–60.
Auty, R. B. (1990) *Resource-Based Industrialisation: Sowing the Oil in Eight Developing Countries.* Oxford: Clarendon Press.
Baena, C. (1999) *The Policy Process in a Petro-State: An Analysis of PdVSA's Internationalisation Strategy.* Basingstoke: Ashgate.
Barr, R. (2005) 'Bolivia: Another Uncompleted Revolution'. *Latin American Politics and Society* 47(3): 69–70.
Barros, S. (2005) 'Espectrabilidad e inestabilidad institucional. Acerca de la ruptura populista'. Trabajo presentado en el VII Congreso Nacional de Ciencia Política de la Sociedad Argentina de Análisis Político, 15–18 November 2005.
BBC News (2009) Obama offers Cuba 'new beginning', available at http://news.bbc.co.uk/go/pr/fr/-1/hi/world/americas/8004798.stm, Published 18 April 2009 (last accessed 4 December 2009).
Beck, S. and Mijeski, K. J. (2006) 'The Indigenous Vote in Ecuador's 2002 Presidential Election'. *Latin American and Caribbean Ethnic Studies* 1 (September): 165–84.
Becker, M. (2008a) 'Pachakutik and Indigenous Political Party Politics in Ecuador', in R. Stahler-Sholk, H. E. Vanden and G. D. Kuecker (eds), *Latin American Social Movements in the Twenty-First Century: Resistance, Power and Democracy.* Lanham, MD: Rowman and Littlefield, pp. 165–80.
Becker, M. (2008b) 'Ecuador, Indigenous Uprisings', in P. N. Stearns (ed.), *Oxford Encyclopedia of the Modern World.* Oxford: Oxford University Press.
Becker, M. (2011) 'Correa, Indigenous Movements and the Writing of the New Constitution in Ecuador'. *Latin American Perspectives* 38(1): 47–62.
Beissinger, M. (2007) 'Structure and Example in Modular Political Phenomenon: The Diffusion of Bulldozer/Rose/Orange/Tulip Revolutions'. *Perspectives on Politics* 5(2): 259–76.
Benford, R. and Snow, D. A. (2000) 'Framing Processes and Social Movements: An Overview and Assessment'. *Annual Review of Sociology* 26: 611–39.
Blanco Munoz, A. (ed.) (1998) *Habla el Comandante: Hugo Chávez Frias (Testimonios Violentos).* Caracas: Pablo Neruda.
Bonifaz, G. (2008) 'De la exclusión a la segmentación? Institucionalidad democrática y relaciones interétnicas en la coyuntura sociopolítica boliviana', in G. Bonifaz and D. Ayo Saucedo (eds), *Asamblea Constituyente ¿Hegemonía indígena o interculturalidad?* La Paz: FES-ILDIS.
Botelho, J. C. A. (2008) 'La creación y la evolución de Unasur'. *Revista Debates* 2(2): 299–324.
Bouzas, R. and Soltz, H. (2001) 'Institutions and Regional Integration,' in V. Bulmer-Thomas (ed.), *Regional Integration in Latin America and the Caribbean: The Political Economy of Open Regionalism.* London: Institute of Latin American Studies.

Bowman, G. (2005) 'Constitutive Violence and the Nationalist Imaginary: The Making of "The People" in Palestine and "Former Yugoslavia"', in F. Panizza (ed.), *Populism and the Mirror of Democracy*. London: Verso, pp. 118–43.

Branford, S. and Rocha, J. (2002) *Cutting the Wire: The Story of the Landless Movement in Brazil*. London: Latin American Bureau.

Breuer, A. (2007) 'Institutions of Direct Democracy and Accountability in Latin America's Presidential Democracies'. *Democratization* 14(4): 554–79.

Breuer, A. (2008) 'The Problematic Relation between Direct Democracy and Accountability in Latin America: Evidence from the Bolivian Case'. *Bulletin of Latin American Research* 27(1): 1–23.

British Petroleum (various years) *Statistical Review of the World Oil Industry*.

Brun, E. (2010) 'Iran's Place in Venezuelan Foreign Policy', in C. Arnson, H. Esfandiari and A. Stubits (eds), *Iran in Latin America: Threat or Axis of Annoyance?* Woodrow Wilson Center Reports on the Americas 23, pp. 35–49.

Brysk, A. (1994) *The Politics of Human Rights in Argentina: Protest Change and Democratization*. Stanford, CA: Stanford University Press.

Burges, S. W (2006) 'Without Sticks or Carrots: Brazilian Leadership in South America during the Cardoso Era, 1992–2003'. *Bulletin of Latin American Research* 25(1): 23–42.

Burggraaff, W. and Millet, R. (1995) 'More than Failed Coups: The Crisis in Venezuelan Civil–Military Relations', in L. Goodman et al. (eds), *Lessons of the Venezuelan Experience*. Baltimore: Johns Hopkins University Press, pp. 54–79.

Burnell, P. and Calvert, P. (eds) (2004) *Civil Society in Democratization*. London: Frank Cass.

Butler, D. and Rannay, A. (1994) *Referendums around the World*. London: Macmillan.

Buxton, J. (2001) *The Failure of Political Reform in Venezuela*. Basingstoke: Ashgate.

Buxton, J. (2005) 'Venezuela's Contemporary Political Crisis in Historcal Context'. *Bulletin of Latin Amercan Research* 24(4): 328–47.

Buxton, J. (2009a) 'The Bolivarian Revolution as Venezuela's Post-Crisis Alternative', in J. Grugel and P. Riggirozzi (eds), *Governance After Neoliberalism in Latin America*. New York: Palgrave Macmillan, pp. 147–73.

Buxton, J. (2009b) 'Venezuela: It's Not the Economy Stupid'. Paper submitted to the conference on Latin American and the Caribbean in the Global Financial Crisis, Institute for the Study of the Americas and Foreign and Commonwealth Office, London, 21–22 April 2009.

Cammack, P. (2000) 'The resurgence of populism in Latin America'. *Bulletin of Latin American Research* 19(2): 149–61.

Cannon, B. (2004) 'Venezuela, April 2002: Coup or Popular Rebellion? The Myth of a United Venezuela'. *Bulletin of Latin American Research* 23(3): 285–302.

Canovan, M. (1999) 'Trust the People! Populism and the Two Faces of Democracy'. *Political Studies* 47(1): 2–16.

Capriles, C. (2008) 'The Politics of Identity. Bolívar and Beyond'. *Harvard Review of Latin America* (Fall): 8–10.

Carrion, J. (1996) 'La Opinión Pública bajo el primer gobierno de Fujimori; de identidades a intereses?' in F. Tuesta Soldevilla (ed.), *Los Enigmas del Poder: Fujimori 1990–1996*. Lima: Friedrich Ebert.

Casas-Zamora, K. (2009) 'Obama at the Summit of the Americas', The Brookings Institution, 24 April 2009, available at www.brookings.edu/opinions/2009/0424_summit_of_the_americas_casaszamora.aspx (last accessed 5 December 2009).

Castañeda, J. (2006) 'Is Evo Morales an Indigenous Che?'. *New Perspectives Quarterly* 23(2) (Spring): 58–60.

Cason, J. (2000) 'Democracy Looks South. Mercosur and the Politics of Brazilian Trade Strategy', in P. R. Kingston and T. J. Power (eds), *Democratic Brazil. Actors, Institutions and Processes*. Pittsburgh, PA: The Pittsburgh University Press, pp. 204–16.

Castañeda, C. (2006) 'Latin America's Left Turn'. *Foreign Affairs* 85(3) (May–June): 28–43.

Céspedes, A. (1956) *El Dictador Suicida*. Santiago de Chile. Editorial Universitaria.

CIA World Factbook (2009) available at https://www.cia.gov/library/publications/the-world-factbook/ (last accessed 21 April 2011).

Comunidad Andina, Secretaria General (2008) Presidentes aprobaron Consejos de Defensa y de Salud Sudamericanos, available at www.comunidadandina.org/prensa/articulos/chile16-12-08.htm (last accessed 22 October 2009).

Comunidad Andina (2009) Política Exterior Común, CAN-Mercosur, available at www.comunidadandina.org/exterior/can_mercosur.htm (last accessed 18 April 2010)

Conaghan, C. (2005) *Fujimori's Peru: Deception in the Public Sphere*. Pittsburgh: University of Pittsburgh.

Conaghan, C. (2008) 'Ecuador; Correa's Plebiscitary Presidency', in L. Diamond, M. Plattner and D. A. Brun (eds), *Latin America's Struggle for Democracy*. Baltimore: Johns Hopkins University Press, pp. 199–214.

Conaghan, C. and de la Torre, C. (2008) 'The Permanent Campaign of Rafael Correa: Making Ecuador's Plebiscitarian Presidency'. *The International Journal of Press/Politics* 13: 267–84.

Coronel, G. (1983) *The Nationalization of the Venezuelan Oil Industry: From Technocratic Success to Political Failure*. Lexington: Lexington Books.

Coronil, F. (2008a) 'Chávez's Venezuela: A New Magical State?' *Harvard Review of Latin America* (Fall): 3–4.

Coronil, F. (2008b) 'It's the Oil, Stupid: An Overview'. *Harvard Review of Latin America* (Fall): 19–20.

Corporación Latinobarómetro (2004) *Summary Report. Latinobarómetro 2004. A Decade of Measurements*, available at www.latinobarometro.org (last accessed 22 May 2009).

Corporación Latinobarómetro (2008) *Informe 2008*, available at www.latinobarometro.org (last accessed 22 May 2009).

Costa, F. (1993) 'Peru's Presidential Coup'. *Journal of Democracy* 4: 28–40.

Costa Benavides, J. (2005) 'La Guerra del Gas en Bolivia. Representaciones sobre el neoliberalismo y el rol del Estado en la defensa de los recursos naturales en la crisis de octubre de 2003', in D. Matto (ed.), *Políticas de economía, ambiente y sociedad en tiempos de globalización*. Facultad de Ciencias Económicas y Sociales, Caracas: Universidad Católica de Venezuela, pp. 233–51.

Cotler, P. (1995) 'Political parties and the problems of democratic consolidation in Peru', in S. Mainwaring and T. Scully (eds) *Building Democratic Institutions; Party Systems in Latin America*. Stanford, CA: Stanford University Press, pp. 323–53.

Council on Foreign Relations (2009) Mercosur: South America's Fractious Trading Bloc www.cfr.org/publication/12762/ (last accessed 4 December 2009).

Council on Hemispheric Affairs (2003) 'Bolivia's gas war becomes explosive'. Washington: COHA.

Cox, G. and Morgenstern, S. (2001) 'Latin America's Reactive Assemblies and Proactive Presidents'. *Comparative Politics* 33(2): 172–88.

Crabtree, J. (2005) *Patterns of Protest: Politics and Social Movements in Bolivia*. London: Latin America Bureau.

Da Fonseca, C. (n/d) O Governo George W. Bush e o Relacionamento EUA-América Latina (manuscript).

de la Torre, C. (2004) 'Velasco Ibarra and "La Revolución Gloriosa": The Social Production of a Populist Leader in Ecuador in the 1940s'. *Journal of Latin American Studies* 26: 683–711.

de la Torre, C. (2006) *Populismo, democracia, protestas y crisis recurrentes en Ecuador*. Rio de Janeiro: Fundación Konrad Adenauer.

de la Torre, C. (2007) 'The Resurgence of Radical Populism in Latin America'. *Constellations* 14(3): 384–97.

de la Torre, C. (2008) 'Populismo, ciudadanía y estado de derecho', in C. de la Torre and E. Peruzzotti (eds), *El Retorno del Pueblo. Populismo y nuevas democracia en América Latina*. Quito: Flacso Ecuador/Ministerio de Cultura, 23–53.

de la Torre, C. (2009) 'Populismo Radical y Democracia en los Andes'. *Journal of Democracy en Español* 1 (July): 24–37.

de la Torre, C. (2010) 'El Tecnopopulismo de Rafael Correa' (manuscript).

De Sousa Santos, B. (2008) 'The World Social Forum and the Global Left'. *Politics and Society* 36(2) (June): 247–70.

Della Porta, D. and Diani, M. (1999) *Social Movements: An Introduction*. Oxford: Blackwell.

Diamond, L. (1996) 'Toward Democratic Consolidation,' in Larry Diamond and Marc F. Plattner (eds), *The Global Resurgence of Democracy*, 2nd edn. Baltimore: Johns Hopkins University Press, pp. 227–40.

Diamond, L. (1999) *Deepening Democracy: Towards Consolidation*. Baltimore: Johns Hopkins University Press.

Diamond, L. (2008) 'Latin America's Indigenous Peoples', in L. Diamond, M. Plattner and D. A. Brun (eds), *Latin America's Struggle for Democracy*. Baltimore: Johns Hopkins University Press.

Dornbusch, R. and Edwards, S. (eds) (1991) *The Macroeconomics of Populism in Latin America*. Chicago: University of Chicago Press.

Drake, P. W. and Hershberg, E. (eds) (2006) *State and Society in Conflict: Comparative Perspectives on Andean Crises*. Pittsburgh: University of Pittsburgh Press.

Dunkerley, J. (1984) *Rebellion in the Veins: Political Struggle in Bolivia, 1952–1982*. London: Verso Books.

Dunkerley, J. (2007) 'Evo Morales, the "Two Bolivias" and the Third Bolivian Revolution'. *Journal of Latin American Studies* 39: 133–66.

Dunning, T. (2008) *Crude Democracy: Natural Resource Wealth and Political Regimes*. Cambridge: Cambridge University Press.

Durand, U. (2008) *Coca o Muerte: La Radicalizacion del Movimiento Cocalero*. Lima: Desco.

Durand, U. (2010) 'The Defense of Coca as a Source of Political Empowerment'. Paper given at the Political Studies Association, Edinburgh.

Eaton, K. (2007) 'Backlash in Bolivia: Regional Autonomy as a Reaction Against Indigenous Mobilization'. *Politics and Society* 35(1) (March): 71–102.

Eckstein, S. (ed.) (1989) *Power and Popular Protest: Latin American Social Movements*. Berkeley, CA: University of California Press.

Economist, The (2009) 'Correa and the golden ponchos: A popular leader faces mounting opposition on both left and right' (1 October).

Edwards, B., Foley, M. W., and Diani, M. (eds) (2001) *Beyond Tocqueville: Civil Society and the Social Capital Debate in Comparative Perspective*. Hanover, NH: University Press of New England.

Ellner, S. (2007) *Rethinking Venezuelan Politics: Class Conflict and the Chávez Phenomenon*. Boulder, CO: Lynne Rienner.

Ellner, S. (2008) 'A "Revolutionary Process" Unfolds in the Absence of a Well-Defined Plan'. *Harvard Review of Latin America* (Fall): 14–16.

Ellner, S. (2010) 'Hugo Chávez's First Decade in Office: Breakthroughs and Shortcomings'. *Latin American Perspectives* 37(1): 77–96.

Ellner, S. and Hellinger, D. (eds) (2004) *Venezuelan Politics in the Chávez Era: Class, Polarization and Conflict*. London: Lynne Rienner.

Ellner, S. and Tinker Salas, M. (eds) (2007) *Venezuela: Hugo Chavez and the Decline of an 'Exceptional Democracy'*. Boulder, CO: Rowman and Littlefield.

Encarnación, O. G. (2002) 'Venezuela's Civil Society Coup'. *World Policy Journal* 19(2) (Summer): 38–42.

Epstein, E. (2000) 'Changing Latin American Labor Relations Amidst Economic and Political Liberalization'. *Latin American Research Review* 35(1): 208–19.

Erikson, D. (2008) 'Requiem for the Monroe Doctrine'. *Current History* (February): 58–64.

Espinasa, R. (2009) 'The Performance of the Venezuelan Oil Sector 1997–2008: Official vs Estimated Figures', in *Energy Co-operation and Security in the Hemisphere Task Force*. Houston, TX: Council of the Americas.

European Commission External Relations (2009) Mercosur (Common Market of the South), available at http://ec.europa.eu/external_relations/mercosur/index_en.htm (last accessed 4 December 2009)

Evans, P. (1979) *Dependent Development; an Alliance of Multinational, State and Local Capital in Latin America*. Princeton NJ: Princeton University Press.

Evans, P. (1985) *Embedded Autonomy: States and Industrial Transfomation*. Princeton, NJ: Princeton University Press.

Feinberg, R. E. (1997) *Summitry in the Americas: A Progress Report*. Washington, DC: Institute for International Economics.

Fernández, G. (2010) 'Bolivian Foreign Policy: Observations on the Bolivian–Iran Relationship', in C. Arnson, H. Esfandiari and A. Stubits (eds), *Iran in Latin America: Threat or Axis of Annoyance?* Woodrow Wilson Center Reports on the Americas 23: 83–99.

Fifth Summit of the Americas (2009) Declaration of Commitment of Port of Spain, Port of Spain, Trinidad and Tobago, 19 April 2009, available at www.summitamericas.org/V_Summit/decl_comm_pos_en.pdf (last accessed 6 December 2009).

First Summit of the Americas (1994) 'Declaration of Principles', Miami, FL, 9–11 December, available at www.summit-americas.org/miamidec.htm (last accessed 3 December 2009).

Fishlow, A. (1999) 'The Western Hemisphere Relation: Quo Vadis?' in A. Fishlow and J. Jones (eds), *The United States and Latin America: A Twenty-First Century View*. New York and London: W. W. Norton, pp. 15–35.

Fitch, J. (1978) *The Military Coup d'Etat as a Political Process: Ecuador 1943–66*. Baltimore: Johns Hopkins University Press.

Fitch, J. (1998) *The Armed Forces and Democracy in Latin America*. Baltimore: Johns Hopkins University Press.

Flemes, D. (2009) 'Brazil's Vision of the Future Global Order'. Paper prepared for delivery at the 28th International Congress of the Latin American Studies Association, Rio de Janeiro, Brazil, 11–14 June 2009.

Foley, M. and Edwards, B. (1996) 'The Paradox of Civil Society'. *Journal of Democracy* 7(3): 38–52.

Fourth Summit of the Americas (2005) Declaration of Mar del Plata, Mar del Plata, Argentina, November 5, 2005, available at www.summit-americas.org/iv_summit/iv_summit_dec_en.pdf (last accessed 3 December 2009).

Foweraker, J. (1998) 'Institutional Designs, Party Systems and Governability; Differentiating the Presidential Regimes of Latin America'. *British Journal of Political Science* 28(4): 651–76.

Freidenberg, F. (2008) 'El flautista de Hammelin. Liderazgo y populismo en la democracia ecuatoriana', in C. de la Torre and E. Peruzzotti (eds), *El Retorno del Pueblo: Populismo y nuevas democracias en América Latina*. Quito: Flacso Ecuador/Ministerio de Cultura, pp. 189–237.

Fundación UNIR Bolivia (2010) 'Informe de seguimiento y análisis de la conflictividad en Bolivia (junio a diciembre de 2009), Elaborado por la Unidad de Análisis de Conflictos de la Fundación UNIR Bolivia, available at. www.unirbolivia.org (last accessed 28 June 2010).

Galeano, E. (1973) *Open Veins of Latin America: Five Centuries in the Pillage of a Continent*. New York: Monthly Review Press.

Garrido, A. (ed.) (2000) *La Historia Secreta de la Revolución Bolivariana*. Mérida: Editorial Venezolana.

Gerlach, A. (2003) *Indians, Oil and Politics; A Recent History of Ecuador*. Wilmington: Scholarly Resources.

Germani, G. (1979) *Política y Sociedad en una Época de Transición*. Buenos Aires: Paidós.

Gill, G. (2000) *The Dynamics of Democratization: Elites, Civil Society and the Transition Process*. Basingstoke: Palgrave Macmillan.

Gills, B. and Rocamora, J. (1992) 'Low Intensity Democracy'. *Third World Quarterly* 13(3): 501–23.

González Urrutia, E. (2006) 'Las dos etapas de la política exterior de Chávez'. *Nueva Sociedad* 205 (septiembre–octubre): 159–71.

Gott, R. (2000) *In the Shadow of the Liberator: Hugo Chavez and the Transformation of Venezuela*. London: Verso.

Grindle, M. (1989) 'The New Political Economy: Positive Economics and Negative Politics'. The World Bank, Policy Planning and Research, Working Papers, Macroeconomic Adjustment and Growth, WPS 304 (December).

Grugel, J. (ed.) (1999) *Democracy without Borders: Transnationalization and Conditionality in New Democracies*. London: Routledge.

Grugel, J. and Riggirozzi, P. (eds) (2009) *Governance After Neoliberalism in Latin America*. New York: Palgrave Macmillan.

Guedes de Oliveira, M. A. (2001) *Mercosul e Política*. São Paulo: Editora LTR.

Haggard, S. and McCubbins, M. (eds) (2001) *Presidents, Parliaments and Policy*. Cambridge: Cambridge University Press.

Hakim, P. (2006) 'Is Washington Losing Latin America?' *Foreign Affairs* 85(1): 39–53.

Hakim, P. (2008) 'Why We Are Together', Focal Point. *Canada's Spotlight on the Americas* 7(6) (July–August): 4–6.

Hammond, J. L. (2005) 'The World Social Forum and the Emergence of Global Grassroots Politics'. Paper prepared for delivery at the 2006

Meeting of the Latin American Studies Association, San Juan, Puerto Rico, 15–18 March 2006.

Hart-Landsberg, M. (2009) 'Challenges and Possibilities: Learning from ALBA and the Bank of the South,' International Debt Observatory (22 May), available at www.oid-ido.org/article.php3?id_article=947 (last accessed 4 June 2009).

Harten, S. (2008) 'Analysis of the Dialectic of Democratic Consolidation, De-Institutionalization and Re-Institutionalization in Bolivia, 2002–2005', PhD thesis, Department of Government, London School of Economics and Political Science, London.

Hawkins, K. A. and Hansen, D. R. (2006) 'Dependent Civil Society: The Círculos Bolivarianos in Venezuela'. *Latin American Research Review* 41(1): 102–32.

Healy, K. (1988) 'Coca, the State, and the Peasantry in Bolivia: 1982–1988'. Journal of Interamerican Studies and World Affairs 30(2/3), Special Issue: *Assessing the Americas' War on Drugs*: 105–26.

Hellinger, D. (2000) 'Nationalism, Oil Policy and the Party System in Venezuela'. Unpublished paper given at LASA conference in Miami.

Hellinger, D. (2007) 'When "No" Means "Yes to Revolution": Electoral Politics in Bolivarian Venezuela', in S. Ellner and M. Tinker Salas (eds), *Venezuela: Hugo Chávez and the Decline of an Exceptional Democracy*. Plymouth: Rowman and Littlefield, pp. 157–84.

Henk, N. (2007) *Subcomandante Marcos: The Man and the Mask*. London: Duke University Press.

Hernández, J. A. (2004) 'Against the Comedy of Civil Society: Posthegemony, Media and the 2002 Coup d'Etat in Venezuela'. *Journal of Latin American Cultural Studies* 13(1): 137–45.

Herrera Aráuz, F. (2001) 'Los golpes del poder al aire. El 21 de enero a traves de la radio'. Quito: Abya Yala.

Herrera Salas, J. M. (2007) 'Ethnicity and Revolution: The Political Economy of Racism in Venezuela', in S. Ellner and M. Tinker Salas (eds), *Venezuela: Hugo Chávez and the Decline of an Exceptional Democracy*. Plymouth: Rowman and Littlefield, pp. 99–117.

Hidalgo, M. (2009) 'Hugo Chávez's Petro-Socialism'. *Journal of Democracy* 20(2): 78–92.

Hochstetler, K. (2008) 'Repensando el Presidencialismo: Desafíos y Caídas Presidenciales en el Cono Sur'. *América Latina Hoy* 49 (August): 51–72.

Hochstetler, K. and Friedman, E. Jay (2008) 'Can Civil Society Organizations Solve the Crisis of Partisan Representation in Latin America?' *Latin American Politics and Society* 50(2): 1–32.

Hooghe, M. and Stolle, D. (2003) *Generating Social Capital: Civil Society and Institutions in Comparative Perspective*. Basingstoke: Palgrave Macmillan.

Huber, E., Rueschemeyer, D. and Stephens, J. D. (1997) 'The Paradoxes of Contemporary Democracy: Formal, Participatory and Social Dimensions'. *Comparative Politics* 29(3): 323–42.

Huntington, S. (2006) *Political Order in Changing Societies*. London: Yale University Press.

Hurrell, A. (2008) 'Lula's Brazil: A Rising Power, but Going Where? *Current History* (February): 51–7.

Ianni, O. (1975) *La Formación del Estado Populista en América Latina*. México: Era.

Ibañez Rojo, E. (2000) 'The UDP Government and the Crisis of the Bolivian Left (1982–1985)'. *Journal of Latin American Studies* 32(1), Andean Issues (Feb. 2000): 175–205.

IDB (Inter-American Development Bank) (1997) *Latin America after a Decade of Reforms; Economic and Social Progress*. 1997 Report. Washington, DC.

Imaz, J. (1964) *Los que Mandan*. Buenos Aires: Editorial Universitaria.

Jobert, B. (1989) 'The Normative Frameworks of Public Policy'. *Political Studies* 37: 376–86.

Jones, B. (2008) *Hugo: The Hugo Chávez Story: From Mud Hut to Perpetual Revolution*. London: Bodley Head.

Karl, T. (1997) *The Paradox of Plenty: Oil Booms and Petro States*. Berkeley: University of California.

Kazin, M. (1998) *The Populist Persuasion: An American History*. Ithaca and London: Cornell University Press.

Kellogg, P. (2007) 'Regional Integration in Latin America: Dawn of an Alternative to Neoliberalism?' *New Political Science* 29(2): 187–209.

Kenney, C. (2004) *Fujimori's Coup and the Breakdown of Democracy in Latin America*. Notre Dame: University of Notre Dame.

Knight, A. (1998) 'Populism and Neopopulism in Latin America, Especially in Mexico'. *Journal of Latin American Studies* 30: 223–48.

Korzeniewicz, R. P. and Smith, C. (2000) 'Poverty, Inequality, and Growth in Latin America: Searching for the High Road to Globalization'. *Latin American Research Review* 35(3): 7–54.

Kurtz, M. (2004) 'The Dilemmas of Democracy in the Open Economy: Lessons from Latin America'. *World Politics* 56(2): 262–302.

Laclau, E. (1977) *Politics and Ideology in Marxist Theory*. London: Verso.

Laclau, E. (2006) 'La Deriva Populista y la Centro Izquierda Latinoamericana'. *Nueva Sociedad* 205 (Sept.–Oct.): 56–61.

Lagos, M. (1997) 'Latin America's Smiling Mask'. *Journal of Democracy* 8(3): 125–38.

Lalander, R. (2004) *Suicide of the Elephants? Venezuela Decentralisation beween Partyarchy and Chavismo*. Helsinki: University of Stockholm.

Larrea, A. M. (2005) *Forajido Ecuador: Crónica de una rebelión*. Quito: Adital, available at http://llacta.org/notic/2005/not0505b.htm (last accessed 14 April 2009).

Laserna, R. (2007) 'Etnicidad, Libertad y Democracia: Buscando Ciudadanía en Bolivia'. Paper prepared for delivery at the 2007 Congress of the Latin American Studies Association, Montreal, Canada, 5–8 September, 2007.

Lazar, S. (2006) 'El Alto, Ciudad rebelde; Oganisational Bases for Revolt'. *Bulletin of Latin American Reseach* 25(2) (April): 183–99.

Lechner, S. (2006) 'Presidents and economic policy-making; the politics of tax reform in Bolivia and Ecuador'. PhD thesis, London School of Economics.

Leftwich, A. (2000) *States of Development: On the Primacy of Politics in Development*. Cambridge: Polity.

Leogrande, W. M. (2007) Book Review, David Scott Palmer, 'US Relation with Latin America During the Clinton Years: Opportunities Lost or Opportunities Squandered?' *Journal of Latin American Studies* 39(3): 196–8.

Leon, L. (2002) 'Y los encuestas, que dicen', in A. Frances and C. Allison (eds), *Venezuela: la crisis de abril*. Caracas: IESA.

Lettieri, M. (2005) 'The Summit that Lost Its Way'. Council on Hemispheric Affairs (COHA), available at www.coha.org/the-summit-that-lost-its-way/ (last accessed 3 November 2005)

Levitsky, S. (2003) 'From Labor Politics to Machine Politics: The Transformation of Party-Union Linkages in Argentine Peronism, 1983–1999'. *Latin American Research Review* 38(3) (October): 4–36.

Levitsky, S. and Murillo, M. (2005) *Argentina's Democracy: The Politics of Institutional Weakness*. University Park: Pennsylvania State University Press.

Levitsky, S. and Murillo, M. (2008) 'Argentina, from Kirchner to Kirchner', in L. Diamond, M. Plattner and D. A. Brun (eds), *Latin America's Struggle for Democracy*. Baltimore: Johns Hopkins University Press.

Levitt, B. (2007) 'Ecuador 2004–5; Democratic Crisis Redux', in T. Legler, S. Lean and D. Boniface (eds), *Promoting Democracy in the Americas*. Baltimore: Johns Hopkins University Press.

Lievesley, G. and Ludlam, S. (2009) 'Conclusions: Nuestra América – the Spectre Haunting Washington', in G. Lievesley and S. Ludlam (eds), *Reclaiming Latin America: Experiments in Radical Social Democracy*. London: Zed Books, pp. 217–29.

Linz, J. (1994) 'Presidential or Parliamentary Government: Does it make a Difference?' in J. Linz and A Valenzuela (eds), *The Failure of Presidential Democracy: The Case of Latin America*. Baltimore: Johns Hopkins University Press.

Linz, J. and Stepan, A. (1996) *Problems of Democatic Transition and Consolidation*. Baltimore and London: Johns Hopkins University Press.

Lowenthal, A (ed.) (1976) *Armies and Politics in Latin America*. New York: Holmes and Meier.

Madrid, R. (2008) 'The Rise of Ethnopopulism in Latin America'. *World Politics* 60(3) (April): 475–508.

Mainwaring, S. (2008) 'The Crisis of Representation in the Andes', in L. Diamond, M. F. Plattner and D. Abente Brun (eds), *Latin America's Struggle for Democracy*. Baltimore: Johns Hopkins University Press, pp. 18–32.

Mainwaring, S., Bejarano, A. M. and Pizarro Leongómez, E. (eds) (2006) *The Crisis of Democratic Representation in the Andes*. Stanford, CA: Stanford University Press.

Mainwaring, S. and Scully, T. (1995) 'Party Systems in Latin America', in S. Mainwaring and T. Scully (eds), *Building Democratic Institutions: Party Systems in Latin America*. Stanford, CA: Stanford University Press, pp. 1–36.

Malamud, C. (2009) 'La crisis de la integración se juega en casa'. *Nueva Sociedad* 219 (enero–febrero): 97–112.

Malamud, C. and García-Calvo, C. (2009) 'The Fifth Summit of the Americas: Relations with the US are Played Out in Cuba (ARI)', Real Instituto Elcano ARI 74/2009, 28 May 2009, available at http://realinstitutoelcano.org (last accessed 28 September 2009).

Manzetti, L. (1994) 'The Political Economy of Mercosur'. *Journal of Interamerican Studies and World Affairs* 35: 101–41.

Mattiace, S. (2005) 'Representation and Rights. Recent Scholarship on Social Movements in Latin America'. *Latin American Research Review* 40(1): 237–50.

Mayorga, F. (2009) 'Prólogo' in M. Zuazo, *Como nació el MAS? La ruralización de la política en Bolivia*. La Paz: Friedrich Ebert Stiftung, pp. 15–19.

McAdam, D., Tarrow, S. and Tilly, C. (2001) *Dynamics of Contention*. New York: Cambridge University Press.

McAdams, A. J. (1997) *Transitional Justice and the Rule of Law in New Democracies*. Notre Dame: University of Notre Dame Press.

McBeth, B. (2005) 'Venezuelan Oil Policy: A Historical Perspective'. Paper presented at St Antony's College, Oxford.

McFaul, M. (2005) 'Transitions from Postcommunism'. *Journal of Democracy* 16(3): 5–19.

McNeish, J. A. (2007) Review of N. Grey Postero, *Now We Are Citizens: Indigenous Politics in Postmulticultural Bolivia. Journal of Latin American Studies* 39: 889–91.

Mecham, M. (2003) 'Mercosur: a failing development project?' *International Affairs* 79(2): 369–87.

Meyer, P. J. (2008) 'Fifth Summit of the Americas, Port of Spain, Trinidad and Tobago, April 2009: Background, Agenda, and Expectations'. Congressional Research Service, Report R 40074, 17 December 2008, www.crs.gov

Miorelli, R. (2009) 'The Discourse on Civil Society in Poverty Reduction Policy in the Argentina of the 1990s: The Neoliberal and Populist Project's Struggles for Hegemony'. PhD thesis, London School of Economics and Political Science (manuscript).

Molina, J. and Pérez, C. (2002) 'Radical Change at the Ballot Box: Causes and Consequences of Electoral Behaviour in Venezuela's 2000 Elections'. *Latin American Politics and Society* 46(1): 103–34.

Montenegro, C. (1990) *Nacionalismo y Coloniaje*. La Paz: Juventud.

REFERENCES

Montúfar, C. (2008) 'El populismo intermitente de Lucio Gutiérrez', in C. de la Torre and E. Peruzzotti (eds), *El Retorno del Pueblo. Populismo y nuevas democracias en América Latina*. Quito: Flacso Ecuador – Ministerio de Cultura, pp. 267–98.

Morales, E. (2006) 'Discurso de posesión del Presidente Constitucional de la República, Evo Morales Aima pronunciado el 22 de enero de 2006'. Portal de la Presidencia de Bolivia, available at www.presidencia.gov.bo (last accessed 8 June 2009).

Motta, S. C. (2007) 'The Reinvention of the Political in Venezuela: The Case of the Urban Land Movement (CTU)'. Paper presented at the Everyday Life in World Politics and Economics International Conference organized by the LSE Centre for International Studies, London, England, 11 May.

Motta, S. C. (2011) 'Populism's Achilles Heel: Popular Democracy Beyond the Liberal State and Market Economy in Venezuela'. *Latin American Perspectives* 38(1) (January): 28–46.

Munck, R. (1993) 'After the Transition. Democratic Disenchantment in Latin America'. *European Review of Latin American and Caribbean Studies* 55: 7–19.

Muse Sinek, W. (2006) 'Caminos to Conceptualizing Social Capital: Some Dimensions for Analyzing Latin American Social Movements'. Paper prepared for delivery at the 2006 Meeting of the Latin American Studies Association, San Juan, Puerto Rico, 15–18 March.

Myers, D. and O'Connor, R. (1998) 'Support for Coups in Democratic Political Culture: A Venezuelan Exploration'. *Comparative Politics* 30(2): 193–212.

Naim, M. (1994) 'Latin America: The Second Stage of Reform'. *Journal of Democracy* 5(4): 32–48.

Nebbia, G. and Vann, B. (2000) 'The Coup in Ecuador: A Grim Warning' (2 February). Available at World Socialist Website, wsws.org (last accessed 2 February 2000).

Needler, M. (1964) *Anatomy of a Coup d'Etat: Ecuador 1963*. Washington: Institute for the Comparative Study of Political Systems.

New York Times (2005) 'Hemispheric Summit Marred by Violent Anti-Bush Protests', available at www.nytimes.com/2005/11/05/international/americas/05prexy.html (last accessed 25 September 2009).

Newman, A. (2009) 'Summit of the Americas Ends in Uncertainty'. *New American*, 20 April 2009, available at www.thenewamerican.com (last accessed 28 September 2009).

Norden, D. (1996) *Military Rebellion in Argentina: Beween Coups and Consolidation*. Lincoln: University of Nebraska Press.

Norden, D. (1998) 'Democracy and Military Control in Venezuela; from subordination to insurrection'. *Latin American Research Review* 33(2): 143–65.

Norden, D. (2003) 'Democracy in Uniform; Chávez and the Venezuelan Armed Forces', in S. Ellner and D. Hellinger (eds), *Venezuelan Politics in the Chávez Era*. Boulder, CO: Lynne Rienner.

REFERENCES

Nueva Sociedad (2008) 'Los colores de la izquierda'. *Nueva Sociedad* (217).
Nun, J. (1976) 'The Middle Class Military Coup Revisited', in A. Lowenthal (ed.), *Arms and Politics in Latin America*. New York: Holmes and Meier.
O'Donnell, G. (1973) *Modernization and Bureaucratic Authoritarianism: Studies in South American Politics*. Berkeley: University of California, Institute of International Studies.
O'Donnell, G. (1994) 'Delegative Democracy'. *Journal of Democracy* 5(1): 55–69.
O'Donnell, G. (1995) 'Do Economists Know Best?' *Journal of Democracy* 6(1): 23–8.
O'Donnell, G. (1999) 'Horizontal Accountability in New Democracies', in L. Schedler, M. Diamond and M. Plattner (eds), *The Self-Restraining State; Power and Accountability in New Democracies*. Boulder, CO: Lynne Rienner.
O'Donnell, G., Schmitter, P. and Whitehead, L. (eds) (1986) *Transitions from Authoritarian Rule: Prospects for Democracy*. Baltimore: Johns Hopkins University Press.
Oelsner, A. (2005) *International Relations in Latin America: Peace and Security in the Southern Cone*. London: Routledge.
Pachano, S. (2008) 'El precio del poder: izquierda, democracia y clientelismo en Ecuador'. Ponencia presentada al Segundo Coloquio Internacional de Ciencia Política, 'Gobiernos de Izquierda en Iberoamérica en el Siglo XX, Xalapa, Veracruz, Mexico, 20, 21 and 22 de octubre de 2008.
Pallares, A. (2002) *From Peasant Struggles to Indian Resistance: The Ecuadorian Andes in the Late Twentieth Century*. Norman: University of Oklahoma Press.
Palmer, D. C. (2006) *US Relations with Latin America during the Clinton Years. Opportunities Lost or Opportunities Squandered?* Gainesville: University Press of Florida.
Panizza, F. (2000) 'Neopopulism and its Limits in Collor's Brazil'. *Bulletin of Latin American Research* 19(2): 177–92.
Panizza, F. (2005) 'Introduction', in F. Panizza (ed.), *Populism and the Mirror of Democracy*. London: Verso, pp. 1–31.
Panizza, F. (2008) 'Economic Constraints and Strategic Choices: The Case of the Frente Amplio of Uruguay's First Year in Office'. *Bulletin of Latin American Research* 27(2): 176–96.
Panizza, F. (2009) *Contemporary Latin America: Development and Democracy beyond the Washington Consensus*. London: Zed Press.
Panizza, F. and Miorelli, R. (2009) 'Populism and Democracy in Latin America'. *Ethics and International Affairs* 23(1): 39–46.
Paris, F. (2007) 'Institutional Failure in Venezuela: The Cases of Spending Oil Revenues and the Governance of PdVSA' . PhD thesis, London School of Economics.
Passini, M. and Ramanzini, H., Jr (2009) 'Uma análise das limitações estruturais do Mercosul a partir das posições da Política Externa Brasileira'.

Paper prepared for delivery at the 28th Congress of the Latin American Studies Association, Rio de Janeiro, Brazil, 11–14 June 2009.

Payne J. M., Zovatto, D. F., Carrillo, F. and Zavala, A. (2002) *Democracies in Development*. Washington: Inter-American Bank.

Pazmiño, C. (2005) 'Espectáculo y publicidad política. Análisis de las elecciones 2002 en Ecuador'. Tesis de grado. Universidad Central del Ecuador, Facultad de Comunicación Social, Quito.

Peceny, M. (1994) 'The Inter-American System as a Liberal "Pacific Union"?' (Review essay). *Latin American Research Review* 29(3): 188–201.

Penfold-Becerra, M. (2007) 'Clientelism and Social Funds: Evidence from Chávez's Misiones'. *Latin American Politics and Society* 49(4): 63–84.

Peña, F. (2009) 'La integración del espacio sudamericano. ¿La Unasur y el Mercosur pueden complementarse?' *Nueva Sociedad* 219 (Jan.–Feb.): 46–58.

Pérez Flórez, G. (2009) 'Unasur: la apuesta de Brasil'. *Política exterior* 23: 149–60.

Perreault, T. (2006) 'From the Guerra del Agua to the Guerra del Gas: Resource Governance, Neoliberalism and Popular Protest in Bolivia'. *Antipode* 38: 150–72.

Peruzzotti, E. (2008) 'Populismo y Representación Democrática', in C. de la Torre and E. Peruzzotti (eds), *El Retorno del Pueblo: Populismo y nuevas democracia en América Latina*. Quito: Flacso Ecuador/Ministerio de Cultura, pp. 97–124.

Petkoff, T. (2008) 'Elections and Political Power: Challenges for the Opposition'. *Harvard Review of Latin America* (Fall): 11–13.

Petras J. and Veltmeyer, H. (2005) *Social Movements and State Power: Argentina, Brazil, Bolivia and Ecuador*. London and Ann Arbor, MI: Pluto Press.

Philip, G. (1982) *Oil and Politics in Latin America: Nationalist Movements and State Companies*. Cambridge: Cambridge University Press.

Philip, G. (1985) 'Military Rule in South America: The Dilemmas of Authoritarianism', in C. Clapham and G. Philip (eds), *The Political Dilemmas of Military Regimes*, Worcester: Billing and Sons, pp. 128–50.

Philip, G. (1992) 'Venezuelan Democracy and the "Coup Attempt of February 1992"'. *Government and Opposition* 27(4): 470–85.

Philip, G. (2003) *Democracy in Latin America: Surviving Crisis and Conflict?* Cambridge: Polity.

Phillips, N. (2003) 'The Rise and Fall of Open Regionalism? Comparative Reflections on Regional Governance in the Southern Cone of Latin America'. *Third World Quarterly* 24(2): 217–34.

Phillips, N. (2008) 'The Politics of Trade and the Limits to US Power in the Americas', in D. Sánchez-Ancochea and K. C. Shadlen (eds), *The Political Economy of Hemispheric Integration: Responding to Globalization in the Americas*. New York: Palgrave Macmillan, pp. 147–69.

Pierri, R. (2009) 'Mercosur and the Andean Community sign free trade pact'. bilaterals.org, available at www.bilaterals.org/article.php3?id_article=860 (last accessed 4 December 2009).

Pion-Berlin, D. (2007) 'Military Responses to Civilian Praetorianism in Latin America'. Paper prepared for delivery at the XXVII Congress of the Latin American Studies Association, Montreal, Canada, 5–8 September.

Polanyi, K. (1957) *The Great Transformation*. Boston: Gower Beacon Press.

Portes, A. and Hoffman, K. (2003) 'Latin American Class Structures: Their Composition and Change during the Neoliberal Era'. *Latin American Research Review* 38(1): 41–82.

Prakash, S. and Selle, P. (eds) (2004) *Investigating Social Capital: Comparative Perspectives on Civil Society, Participation and Governance*. New Delhi: Sage Publications.

Przeworski, A. (1991) 'Transitions to Democracy', in A. Pzeworski, *Democracy and the Market: Political Reform in Eastern Europe and Latin America*. Cambridge: Cambridge University Press, pp. 51–99.

Putnam, R. D. (2000) *Bowling Alone: The Collapse and Revival of American Community*. New York: Simon and Schuster.

Ranis, P. (1995) *Class, Democracy, and Labor in Contemporary Argentina*. New Brunswick, NJ: Transaction.

Reid, M. (2002) 'Mercosur: A Critical Overview', Chatham House Mercosur Study Group, 18 January 2002 (manuscript).

Reid, M. (2007) *Forgotten Continent: The Battle for Latin America's Soul*. New Haven: Yale University Press.

Riggirozzi, P. (2009) 'After Neoliberalism in Argentina: Reasserting Nationalism in an Open Economy', in J. Grugel and P. Riggirozzi (eds), *Governance After Neoliberalism in Latin America*. New York: Palgrave Macmillan, pp. 89–111.

Riutort, M. (2007) 'La Economía Venezolana en el 2007 y Perspectivas para el 2008'. *Temas de Coyuntura* 56 (December): 115–26.

Rivarola Puntigliano, A. (2008) 'Critical Debates. Suspicious Minds: Recent Books on US–Latin American Relations'. *Latin American Politics and Society* 50(4): 155–72.

Roberts, K. (1995) 'Neoliberalism and the Transformation of Populism in Latin America: The Peruvian Case'. *World Politics* 48: 82–116.

Roberts, K. (1997) 'Beyond Romanticism: Social Movements and the Study of Political Change in Latin America'. *Latin American Research Review* 32(2): 137–51.

Roberts, K. (2002) 'Social Inequalities without Class Cleavages in Latin America's Neoliberal Era'. *Studies in Comparative International Development* 36(4) (Winter): 3–33.

Roberts, K. (2003) 'Social Correlates of Party System Demise and Populist Resurgence in Venezuela'. *Latin American Politics and Society* 45(3): 35–58.

Roberts, K. (2004) 'Social Polarisation and Populist Resurgence in Venezuela', in S. Ellner and D. Hellinger (eds), *Venezuelan Politics in the Chávez Era.* Boulder, CO: Lynne Rienner, pp. 55–72.

Roberts, K. (2007) 'Latin America's Populist Revival'. *SAIS Review* XXVII(1) (Winter–Spring): 3–15.

Rodríguez, M. (1991) 'Public Sector Behaviour in Venezuela', in F. Larrain and M. Selowsky (eds), *The Public Sector and the Latin American Crisis.* San Francisco: International Center for Economic Growth.

Rospigliosi, F. (2000) *Montesinos y las fuerzas armadas; como controlar durante una década las instituciones militares.* Lima: Instituto de Estudios Peruanos.

Rubin, J. W. (2004) 'Meaning and Mobilizations: A Cultural Approach to Social Movements and the State'. *Latin American Research Review* 39(3) (October): 106–42.

Romero, A. (1997) 'Rearranging the Decks on the Titanic: The Agony of Democracy in Venezuela'. *Latin American Research Review* 32(1): 7–30.

Salman, T. (2006) 'The Jammed Democracy: Bolivia's Troubled Political Learning Process'. *Bulletin of Latin American Research* 25(2): 163–82.

Salman, T. (2007) 'Bolivia and the Paradoxes of Democratic Consolidation'. *Latin American Perspectives* 34(6): 111–30.

Sanabria, H. (1999) 'Consolidating States, Restructuring Economies, and Confronting Workers and Peasants: The Antinomies of Bolivian Neoliberalism'. *Comparative Studies in Society and History* 41(3) (July 1999): 535–62.

Sanjinés C., J. (2004) 'Movimientos sociales y Cambio Político en Bolivia'. *Revista Venezolana de Economía y Ciencias Sociales* 10(1) (enero–abril): 203–18.

Santa Cruz, A. (2005) 'Monitoring Elections, Redefining Sovereignty: The 2000 Peruvian Electoral Process as an International Event'. *Journal of Latin American Studies* 37(4) (November): 739–67.

Schamis, H. (2008) 'Populism, Socialism and Democatic Institutions', in L. Diamond, M. Plattner and D. A. Brun (eds), *Latin America's Struggle for Democracy.* Baltimore: Johns Hopkins University Press, pp. 48–62.

Schmitt, C. (1988) *The Crisis of Parliamentary Democracy.* Cambridge, MA: The MIT Press.

Schmitt, C. (1996 [1927]) *The Concept of the Political*, 2nd edn, trans. George D. Schwab. Chicago: University of Chicago Press.

Schumpeter, J. A. (1950) *Capitalism, Socialism and Democracy*, 3rd edn. New York: Harper Torchbooks.

Second Summit of the Americas (1998) Santiago Declaration, Santiago de Chile April 18–19, 1998 available at: www.summitamericas.org/ii_summit/ ii_summit_dec_en.pdf (last accessed 4 December 2009).

SELA (2007) 'Venezuela ratifica la cláusula democrática del Mercosur', available at http://sela.org/sela/ImpNoticia.asp?id=9449 (last accessed 8 December 2009).

Seligson, M. (2008) 'The Rise of Populism and the Left', in L. Diamond, M. Plattner and D. A. Brun (eds), *Latin America's Struggle for Democracy*. Baltimore: Johns Hopkins University Press.

Serbin, A. (2006) 'Cuando la limosna es grande. El Caribe, Chávez y los límites de la diplomacia petrolera'. *Nueva Sociedad* 205 (septiembre–octubre): 75–91.

Serbin, A. (2009) 'América Latina en un mundo multipolar: ¿Es la Unasur una alternativa?' *Nueva Sociedad* 219 (Jan.–Feb.): 145–56.

Sheahan, P. (2006) 'The Andean Economies: Questions of Poverty, Growth and Equity', in P. Drake and E. Hershberg, *State and Society in Conflict: Comparative Perspectives on Andean Crises*. Pittsburgh: University of Pennsylvania Press, pp. 99–133.

Shifter, M. (2009) 'Managing Disarray: The Search for a New Consensus', in A. Cooper and J. Heine (eds), *Which Way Latin America? Hemispheric Politics Meets Globalization*. New York: United Nations University Press, pp. 50–63.

Shifter, M. and Jawahar, V. (2005) 'Latin America's Populist Turn'. *Current History* 104(679): 51–7.

Shifter, M. and Joyce, D. (2009) 'No Longer Washington's Backyard'. *Current History* (February): 51–7.

Silva, E. (2007) 'Challenging Neoliberalism in Latin America'. Paper prepared for delivery at the 2007 Congress of the Latin American Studies Association, Montreal, Canada, 5–8 September.

Smith, P. H. (1999) 'Trouble Ahead? Prospects for US Relations with Latin America', in A. Fishlow and J. Jones (eds), *The United States and Latin America: A Twenty-First Century View*. New York and London: W. W. Norton, pp. 174–96.

South American Union of Nations Constitutive Treaty (2009), available at www.comunidadandina.org/ingles/csn/treaty.htm (accessed 9 December 2009).

Spronk, S. and Webber, J. R. (2008) 'Struggles against Accumulation by Dispossession in Bolivia: The Political Economy of Natural Resource Contention', in R. Stahler-Sholk, H. E. Vanden and G. D. Kuecker (eds), *Latin American Social Movements in the Twenty-First Century: Resistance, Power and Democracy*. Lanham, MD: Rowman and Littlefield, pp. 77–91.

Stahler-Sholk, R., Vanden, H. E. and Kuecker, G. D. (2007) 'Globalizing Resistance: The New Politics of Social Movements in Latin America'. *Latin American Perspectives* 34: 5–16.

Starr, P. and Oxhorn, P. (1999) 'Introduction: The Ambiguous Link Between Economic and Political Reform', in P. Oxhorn and P. Starr (eds), *Markets and Democracy in Latin America: Conflict or Convergence?* Boulder, CO and London: Lynne Rienner, pp. 1–41.

Stefanoni, P. (2003) 'MAS-IPSP: la emergencia del nacionalismo plebeyo'. *OSAL* Año IV, 12 (September–December): 57–68.

Stiglitz, J. (2006) 'Is Populism Really so Bad for Latin America?' *New Political Quarterly* (Spring): 61–2.

Stepan, A. (1971) *The Military in Politics: Changing Patterns in Brazil*. Princeton: Princeton University Press.

Stokes, S. (2001) *Mandates and Democracy: Neoliberalism by Surprise in Latin America*. Chicago: University of Chicago Press.

Sweeney, J. (2005) 'Venezuela and Hugo Chávez: Reflections from the Mar del Plata Summit', available at http://crisis.com/index.php?content=lett ers/200511131325 (last accessed 25 September 2009).

Taggart, P. (2000) *Populism*. Buckingham: Open University Press.

Tamayo, E. (1996) *Movimientos Sociales: La Riqueza de la Diversidad*. Quito: ALAI.

Tanaka, M. (2005) 'Peru 1980–2000: Chronicle of a Death Foretold? Determinism, Political Decisions and Open Outcomes', in F. Hagopian and S. Mainwaring (eds), *The Third Wave of Democratisation in Latin America: Advances and Setbacks*. New York: Cambridge University Press.

Tapia Mealla, L. and Toranzo Roca, C. (2000*) Retos y dilemas de la representación política*. La Paz: PNUD/Edobol.

Templeton, A. (1995) 'The Evolution of Popular Opinion', in L. Goodman et al., *Lessons of the Venezuelan Experience*. Baltimore: Johns Hopkins University Press, pp. 79–114.

Third Summit of the Americas (2001) Declaration of Quebec City, Quebec City, Canada, April 20–22, 2001, available at www.summit-americas.org/iii_summit/iii_summit_dec_en.pdf (last accessed 6 December 2009).

Ticona, A. (2000) *Organización y Liderazgo Aymara, 1979–1996*. La Paz: Universidad de la Cordillera, AGRUCO.

Trein, F. and Cavalcanti, F. G. (2007) 'Uma análise crítica do acordo de associação estratégica entre a União Européia e a América Latina e o Caribe – a Cúpula de Viena'. *Revista Brasileira de Política Internacional* 50(1): 66–85.

Trinkunas, H. (2005) *Crafting Civilian Control of the Military in V enezuela: A Comparative Perspective*. Chapel Hill: University of North Carolina.

Valenzuela, A. (2008) 'Latin American Presidents Interrupted', in L. Diamond, M. Plattner and D. A. Brun (eds), *Latin America's Struggle for Democracy*. Baltimore: Johns Hopkins University Press, pp. 3–17.

Van Cott, D. (2003) 'Indigenous Struggle' (Review Essay). *Latin American Research Review* 38(2) (June): 220–33.

Van Cott, D. (2005) *From Movements to Parties in Latin America: The Evolution of Ethnic Politics*. Cambridge: Cambridge University Press.

Van Cott, D. (2008) 'Latin America's Indigenous Peoples', in S. Diamond, M. Plattner and D. A. Brun (eds), *Latin America's Struggle for Democracy*. Baltimore: Johns Hopkins University Press.

Vanden, H. E. (2008) 'Social Movements, Hegemony, and New Forms of Resistance', in R. Stahler-Sholk, H. E. Vanden and G. D. Kuecker (eds), *Latin American Social Movements in the Twenty-First Century: Resistance, Power and Democracy*. Lanham, MD: Rowman and Littlefield, pp. 39–55.

Velasquez-Donaldson, C. (2007) 'Analysis of the Hydrocarbon Sector in Bolivia: How are the Gas and Oil Revenues Distributed?' Brendeis: Institute for Advanced Development Studies.

Vilas, C. (1988) El Populismo Latinoamericano: Un enfoque estructural. *Desarrollo_Económico* 28(111) (Oct.–Dec.): 323–52.

Villanueva, V. (1972) *El CAEM y La Revolucion de las Fuerzas Armadas*. Lima: Instituto de Estudios Peruanos.

Weffort, F. (1998) 'El populismo en la política brasilena', in María M. Mackinnon and Mario A. Petrone (eds), *Populismo y Neopopulismo en América Latina. El problema de la cenicienta*. Buenos Aires: Eudeba, pp. 135–52.

Weyland, K. (2001) 'Clarifying a Contested Concept: Populism in the Study of Latin American Politics'. *Comparative Politics* 34(1): 1–22.

Weyland, K. (2002) 'Limitations of Rational Choice Institutionalism for the Study of Latin American Politics'. *Studies in Comparative International Development* 37(1): 57–29.

Weyland, K. (2003) 'Economic Voting Reconsidered: Crisis and Charisma in the Election of Hugo Chávez'. *Comparative Political Studies* 36(7): 822–48.

Weyland, K. (2004) 'Neoliberalism and Democracy in Latin America: A Mixed Record'. *Latin American Politics and Society* 46(1) (Spring): 135–57.

Weyland, K. (2007) 'Politics and Policies of Latin America's Two Lefts: The Role of Party Systems vs. Resource Bonanzas'. Paper prepared for the panel on Democracy and Governability in the Andes, XXVI International Congress of the Latin American Studies Association, Montreal, 5–8 September 2007.

Weyland, K., Madrid, R. L. and Hunter, W. (2010) *Leftist Governments in Latin America; Successes and Shortcomings*. New York: Cambridge University Press.

Whitehead, L. (1992) 'The Alternatives to "Liberal Democracy": A Latin American Perspective'. *Political Studies* XL (Special Issue): 146–59.

Whitehead, L. (2001) 'Bolivia and the Viability of Democracy'. *Journal of Democracy* 12(2): 6–16.

Whitehead, L. (2002) *Democratization: Theory and Experience*. Oxford: Oxford University Press.

Wiarda, H. J. (1995) 'After Miami: The Summit, the Peso Crisis, and the Future of US–Latin American Relations'. *Journal of Interamerican Studies and World Affairs* 37(1) (Spring): 43–69.

Williamson, J. (ed.) (1990) 'Latin American Economic Adjustment: How Much Has Happened?' Washington, DC: Institute for International Economics.

Wolff, J. (2007) '(De-)Mobilising the Marginalised: A Comparison of the Argentine Piqueteros and Ecuador's Indigenous Movement'. *Journal of Latin American Studies* 39: 1–29.

Wolff, J. (2009) 'De-idealizing the Democratic Civil Peace: On the Political Economy of Democratic Stabilization and Pacification in Argentina and Ecuador'. *Democratization* 167(5): 998–1026.

World Bank (2000) *World Development Report 2000/2001: Attacking Social Poverty*. Oxford and London: Oxford University Press.

World Bank (2006) *World Development Report 2006: Equity and Development*. Oxford and London: Oxford University Press.

Worsley, P. (1969) 'The Concept of Populism', in G. Ionescu and E. Gellner (eds), *Populism: Its Meaning and National Characteristics*. London: Macmillan, pp. 212–21.

Yashar, D. (2005) *Contesting Citizenship in Latin America: Indigenous Movements, the State and the Political Challenge in Latin America*. Cambridge: Cambridge University Press.

Yashar, D. (2006) 'Indigenous Politics in the Andes: Changing Patterns of Recognition, Reform and Representation', in S. Mainwaring, A. Bejarano and Pizarro Leongómez (eds), *The Crisis of Democratic Representation in the Andes*. Stanford: Stanford University Press.

Yergin, D. (1991) *The Prize: The Epic Quest for Oil, Money and Power*. New York: Simon and Schuster.

Zago, A. (1998) *La Rebelion de los Angeles: Reportaje, los Documentos del Movimiento*. Caracas: Warp.

Zakaria, F. (1997) 'The Rise of Illiberal Democracy'. *Foreign Affairs* 76(6): 22–43.

Zakaria, F. (2003) *The Future of Freedom: Illiberal Democracy at Home and Abroad*. New York: W. W. Norton.

Zamosc, L. (2007) 'The Indian Movement and Democracy in Ecuador'. *Latin American Politics and Society* 49(3): 1–34.

Zuazo, M. (2009) *Como nació el MAS. La ruralización de la política en Bolivia. Entrevistas a 85 parlamentarios del partido*. La Paz: Friedrich Ebert Stiftung.

Zuquete, J. P. (2008) 'The Missionary Politics of Hugo Chávez'. *Latin American Politics and Society* 50(1): 91–121.

INDEX

Alarcón, Fabián 32
ALBA 150, 151, 162–4, 165, 171, 172
Alfaro, Eloy 89
Alfonsín, Raúl 16, 48, 106, 155
Allende, Salvador 29, 147
Alvarado, Juan Velasco 179
Alvarez, Bernardo 131
Amorim, Celso 161
Andean Community of Nations 161
Antigua 162
Arditi, B. 73
Argentina 1, 3–4, 147, 181–2
  and Bolivian gas politics 142, 144, 145, 147
  mass protests 47–9
  and MERCOSUR 154, 155, 158, 159
  military intervention 15, 16, 18
  Peronism 4, 16, 48, 49, 124, 147, 180
  plebiscitary politics 113
  populism 69, 71, 72
  presidential re-election 118, 120
  presidential weakness 106, 107
  and South American integration 152–3, 161, 163
  and Venezuelan oil politics 132
Aristide, Jean-Bertrand 168
Arteaga, Rosalía 32

Bachelet, Michelle 161
Banzer, Hugo 14, 18, 36, 59, 77
Barbuda 162
Bielsa, Rafael 154
Bolivar, Simón 95, 103
Bolivia 2, 175, 176, 177–8
  Aymara movement 59, 60
  'Black September' 61–2
  civil disobedience campaign 13, 14
  COB 57, 58, 81
  coca economy 7, 36, 37, 58, 60, 80–1
  constitutional changes 64, 66, 83–4, 111–12, 116
  CPSC (Comité Pro Santa Cruz) 64
  democracy 76–7, 77–8
  gas politics 11, 37, 60, 62, 89, 116, 123, 124, 125, 126, 127, 132, 137, 140–7
  government collapse (2003 and 2005) 36–9
  high politics and socio-economic issues 5, 6, 7, 8
  indigenous people/movements 7, 8, 50, 51, 57–63
  inter-civil society conflicts 63–4
  MAS (Movimiento al Socialismo) 36–7, 39, 48, 56, 57, 60, 76, 78, 80–5, 87, 111

Bolivia (cont.)
and MERCOSUR 154, 155
military-political behaviour
13–14, 18, 35–9
MIP (Pachakuti Indigenous
Movement) 59–60, 78
MIR (Movement of the
Revolutionary Left) 77
MRTK (Movimiento
Revolucionario Tupac Katari)
60
New Economic Policy (NEP)
76–7
Nueva Fuerza Republicana party
38
opposition activity 105
Peasant–Military Pact 58
Plan Dignidad 59
plebiscitary politics 111–12,
115–16
PODEMOS (Poder Democratico
y Social) 111
political institutions 178
politics of mass protest 39, 42,
48, 57–64, 65–7, 178
populism 76–85, 86–7, 94,
98–9, 100, 101
presidential weakness 106, 107
recall votes 116, 117
regional divisions 112
regional economic development
79
and South American integration
162, 164
steel industry 146
strikes 36
trade unions 35, 36, 57–60, 62
and UNASUR 160
water wars 60, 61, 89
YPFB 146
see also Morales, Evo
Bowman, Glenn 71
Brady Plan 1
Brazil 3, 18, 44, 177
and Bolivian gas politics 142,
144–5

Lieutenants' Revolt 178
mass protests 46–7, 48, 49
and MERCOSUR 154, 155,
158, 159
oil politics 125
Partido dos Trabalhadores (PT)
177
Petrobras 164
populism 69, 71, 180
presidential weakness 106,
107
social movements 50, 56
and South American integration
150, 154, 155, 163, 164,
171–2
and UNASUR 160, 161–2
Brecht, B. 104
British Embassy in Venezuela
reports on coup attempts 24–5,
26
Bucaram, Abdalá 31–2, 33, 34, 42,
53
and populism 86, 87
and presidential weakness 107
Bush, George W. 153, 165–6, 167,
168, 173
Bush, George W. H. 151, 168
Buxton, Julia 94

Caldera, Rafael 23, 25, 135
Cammack, Paul 71
Canovan, Margaret 72–3
Cárdenas, Lázaro 69
Carmona, Pedro 28, 30, 105
Casas-Zamora, Kevin 169
Castro, Fidel 162
Castro, Luis 103
Catholic Church 61, 95
Chávez, Hugo 3, 4, 17, 176, 177,
179, 183
and Argentina 3, 4
constitutional reform 30, 94–5
coup attempt against (2002) 9,
27–30
coup attempt by (1992) 13,
23–6

election victories 2, 9, 13, 92–3, 108–9, 110
and ethnic issues 8
foreign policy 123–4
gas politics 140–1, 144–5, 147
high politics and socio-economic issues 4, 5, 6, 8
and MERCOSUR 157–8
and the Miami Consensus 150
and military-political behaviour 18, 40
and Obama 137, 169–70
oil politics 123, 124, 125–7, 127–40, 147, 147–8
and OPEC 127, 135–6
and PdVSA 126, 130–4, 135, 148
and personalist politics 102–3, 104, 105, 108–10
and plebiscitary politics 11, 110, 112, 116, 121, 122
political career 13
and the politics of mass protest 45
and populism 10, 68, 69, 72, 73, 87, 89, 92–8, 99, 100, 101, 179, 180–1
and presidential re-election 118, 119, 120, 121
and presidential weakness 106, 107
recall votes 117
and regional diplomacy 11–12
and South American integration 153, 154, 161, 162, 163–4, 164, 165, 166, 172
see also Venezuela
Chile 17, 18, 43, 44, 177
and Bolivian gas politics 141, 142, 143
overthrow of Allende government 29
plebiscitary politics 114–15
populism 69
presidential re-election 119–20

and UNASUR 161
and the USA 168
China 134, 166
civil disobedience 9, 40, 178
civil society 42–6, 49–50
inter-civil society conflicts 41–2, 63–4, 66–7
and the Miami Consensus 174–5, 178
Civil Society I and II 46, 55, 67, 69
civil society organizations (CSOs) 42, 43–4, 46, 65
Bolivia 63–4
civilians
and military-political behaviour 17, 18, 19–20, 23
Clinton, Bill 165
coca economy in Bolivia 7, 36, 37, 58, 60, 80–1
Cold War 1, 74, 171, 178
Collor de Mello, Fernando 46–7, 71, 88, 106, 107, 155
Colombia 107, 116, 120
and South American integration 154, 155, 161
Conaghan, C. 21
constitutional changes
Bolivia 64, 66, 83–4, 111–12, 116
Ecuador 111
and presidential weakness 108
Correa, Rafael 3, 4, 9, 177
election victories 2, 9, 35, 90–1, 111
gas politics 140–1
high politics and socio-economic issues 4, 5, 6, 8
and the indigenous movement 54–5
oil politics 124
and personalist politics 102–3, 104, 105
and plebiscitary politics 11, 110–11, 115, 122
political career 14

Correa, Rafael (cont.)
  and politics of mass protest 42
  and populism 10, 68, 69, 73, 85,
    86, 88–91, 98, 99, 100, 101,
    179, 180–1
  and presidential weakness 106,
    107
  and South American integration
    165, 166
  see also Ecuador
Cuba 1, 132, 162, 175
  and the USA 166, 168–9
culture and personalist politics
  103–4

De la Rúa, Fernando 47–8, 106,
    107
debt crisis 1, 2
democracy
  in Bolivia 76–7, 77–8
  and civil society 42, 44–5,
    49–50
  liberal democracy and the Miami
    Consensus 174–5
  and MERCOSUR 156
  and personalist politics 104–5
  and political
    deinstitutionalization 178–9
  and populism 68, 70, 72–3, 75,
    77, 94–5, 100–1
  and presidential re-election 121
  and recall votes 117–18
  and the Santiago Declaration
    151
  and South American integration
    150, 166–8
  'third wave' democratic politics
    15–16, 18, 20–2, 121–2
  in Venezuela 94–8, 121
  see also Schumpeterian
    democracy
democratic socialism 122
Diamond, Larry 65
dictatorships
  absence of military dictatorships
    178–9

and mass praetorianism 43, 45,
    178
  and military-political behaviour
    9, 19, 39, 178, 179
  and plebiscitary politics 114,
    122
Dominica 162
Duarte, Nicanor 119
Duhalde, Eduardo 48, 161

Echeverria, Luis 147
economic development 6–7
  ALBA project of regional
    integration 162–3
  ISI mode of 70, 74–5
  and oil prices 123–4
economic nationalism 1, 2, 5, 175,
    183–4
  and populism 70, 80, 99
  and Venezuelan oil politics 133
Ecuador 179
  anti-Gutiérrez movement 14
  CODENPE 54–5
  CONAIE 31, 33, 34, 52–4,
    55–6, 66, 91
  constitutional reform 111
  election of Correa 2
  Gutiérrez coup 14, 17, 18, 33–4
  high politics and socio-economic
    issues 5, 6, 7, 8
  indigenous people/movements 7,
    8, 31, 50, 51–6, 91
  military-political behaviour 14,
    19, 30–5
  oil production/politics 11, 124
  Pachakutik 53–4, 55, 87
  plebiscitary politics 110–11, 115
  political institutions 177
  politics of mass protest 48, 51–6,
    66, 178
  populism 69, 85–91, 98, 99, 101
  presidential weakness 106, 107
  and South American integration
    155, 161, 162
  and Venezuela 29
  see also Correa, Rafael

Edwards, Bob 45–6
Ellner, S. 100–1
Encarnación, Omar 45
ethnic issues 7–8
European Union
  and MERCOSUR 156
executive–legislature relations
  and presidential weakness 106,
    108

Fitch, J. 31
Foley, Michael 45–6
France 103, 134
free market economics
  and populism 68, 74–5,
    78–9
FTAA (Free Trade Area of the
    Americas) 11, 123, 149, 167,
    174, 176
  and MERCOSUR 156
  and the Summits of the Americas
    151, 152, 153, 154
Fujimori, Alberto 1, 6, 19, 20–2
  and personalist politics 102,
    120
  and plebiscitary politics 115,
    122, 176
  and populism 71
  and presidential weakness 107

Galeano, Eduardo
  Open Veins of Latin America
    137, 169–70
García, Alan 107, 147
gas politics in Bolivia 60, 62, 89,
    116, 123, 124, 125, 126, 127,
    132, 137, 140–7
Gaulle, Charles de 103
globalization 50, 58
Grenadines 4, 162
Grugel, J. 48
Guatemala 106
Guevara, Che 89
Gutiérrez, Lucio 14, 17, 18, 33–4,
    40, 179
  and mass protests 42, 56

and populism 86, 87–8
  and presidential weakness 107
Guyanas 160

Haiti 168
Hakim, Peter 165
Harten, Sven 80
Haya de la Torre, Victor 69
Hellinger, D. 129
hierarchism
  and military-political behaviour
    17
Hochstetler, Kathryn 41
Honduras 4, 102, 106, 120, 179,
    183
  military intervention 15–16,
    18
horizontal accountability
    institutions
  and personalist politics 103
Humala, Ollanta 4, 18
human rights
  and the Miami Consensus 168
  violations 22–3
Huntington, Samuel 41, 43, 45,
    178
Hurrell, Andrew 159

Ibañez, Carlos 69
Ibarra, José María Velasco 30–1,
    69, 176
  populist politics 69, 85–6, 99
Inácio de Silva, Luis 144
IMF (International Monetary Fund)
    75, 90, 158, 163
India 166
indigenous people/movements 7–8,
    50
  Bolivia 7, 8, 50, 51, 57–63, 82
  Ecuador 7, 8, 31, 50, 51–6
Inter-American Development Bank
    (IDB) 2
inter-civil society conflicts 41–2
  Bolivia 63–4
Iran 136, 146, 166
Iraq 136, 165, 168

ISI (Import Substituting Industrialization) 70, 74–5, 176
Islamic fundamentalism 166

Kazin, Michael 73
Kirchner, Cristina Fernández de 3–4, 118, 158, 181–2
Kirchner, Néstor 3–4, 48, 118, 120, 144, 153, 158, 181–2

La Torre, Carlos de 85–6
Laclau, E. 10, 69
Larrea, Ana María 86
Lechín, Juan 81
legal accountability
  for military or political figures 19
Linz, J. 104, 106
Locke, John 167
López Portillo, José 147
Lula da Silva, Luiz Inácio 3, 164, 167, 181

Madrid, Raúl 82
Mahuad, Jamil 33, 34, 42, 53, 56, 66
  and populism 86–7, 88
Mainwaring, S. 21, 66
Malamud, Carlos 170
Mar del Plata Declaration (2005) 153–5, 169, 182
Márquez, Gustavo 153
mass protests 9–10, 41–67
  Bolivia 39, 42, 48, 57–64, 65–7
  civil society and mass praetorianism 41, 42–6, 178
  in comparative perspective 46–50
  Ecuador 48, 51–6, 66
Medina, Pablo 24
Menem, Carlos 3, 16, 48
  and populism 71
  and presidential re-election 120
  and presidential weakness 107
  and South American integration 155, 161

MERCOSUR (South American Common Market) 150, 151, 154, 155–9, 162, 163, 164, 171
  and UNASUR 159, 160, 161
Mesa, Carlos 38–9, 42, 85, 87
  gas politics 143
  and plebiscitary politics 116
Mexico 69, 147
  export diversification 137
  and MERCOSUR 155
  and NAFTA 149
  oil politics 125, 127, 134–5, 135–6
  Revolution 119, 175
  and the USA 168
Miami Consensus 1, 2, 3, 11, 14, 149–50, 173, 182–3
  and Chávez 150, 172
  and civil society 174–5, 178
  and economic reforms 123
  and gas politics 126
  and human rights 168
  and MERCOSUR 155
  and populism 68, 76, 99
  and socialism 122
  and twenty-first century Latin America 176
  unravelling 151–4, 165, 166, 176
  see also FTAA (Free Trade Area of the Americas)
military-political behaviour 13–40
  Bolivia 13–14, 18, 35–9
  changed patterns of 16–18
  and civilians 17, 18, 19–20, 23
  constraints on 18–20
  and dictatorship 9, 19, 39, 178
  Ecuador 14, 19, 30–5
  military intervention in Latin America 15–16
  in Peru 20–2
Moncayo, General 32

Montesinos, Vladimiro 20, 21
Morales, Evo 3, 4, 9, 177
  electoral victory (2005) 1, 2, 9,
    38
  gas politics 126, 132, 141,
    143–5, 146–7, 164
  high politics and socio-economic
    issues 4, 5, 6, 8
  and the MAS 36–7, 39
  and personalist politics 102–3,
    104, 105
  and plebiscitary politics 11,
    111–12, 116, 122
  political career 13–14
  and politics of mass protest 42,
    62, 64
  and populism 68, 69, 73, 76,
    80–4, 85, 87, 91, 98, 99, 100,
    101, 179, 180–1
  and presidential re-election 118,
    119
  and presidential weakness 106,
    107
  and radical populism 10
  recall votes 117
  and South American integration
    153, 161, 165, 166
  see also Bolivia
Motta, Sara 69
Mujica, José Pepe 181

NAFTA (North American Free
  Trade Agreement) 149
Negroponte, John 168
neoliberalism
  in Bolivia 76–7
  and mass protests 49–50
  and MERCOSUR 157–8
  and populism 75–6, 90, 95
Nicaragua 4, 162, 166, 175
Noboa, Alvaro 34, 87
Noboa, Gustavo 53
non-governmental organizations
  (NCOs)
  and civil society 44
Noriega, Roger 168

OAS (Organization of American
  States) 34, 161, 168
Obama, Barack 137, 168–9,
  169–70, 173
Obrador, Lopez 4
O'Donnell, Guillermo 43, 104
Odría, Manuel A. 18
oil production/politics 6, 11,
  123–40, 182
  and economic development
    123–4
  Ecuador 11, 124
  and South American integration
    162, 163
  Venezuela 6, 11, 12, 27,
    123–4, 124–7, 127–40,
    147–8, 182
OPEC and Venezuela 124, 127,
  134–6, 138
Organization of American States
  (OAS) 34, 161, 168
Ortega, Daniel 166
Oviedo, Lino 156

Palacio, Alfredo 35, 88
Pallares, Amalia 51
Palmer, David Scott 165
Paraguay 4, 15, 107, 160
  and MERCOSUR 154, 155,
    156, 158, 159
  presidential re-election
    119
Passini, M. 207
Patriótico, Polo 109
Paz Estenssoro, Victor 35–6, 58,
  76–7, 81
PdVSA (Petróleos de Venezuela
  S.A.) 126, 127–34, 135, 138,
  140, 148, 164
Peceny, Mark 149
Pérez, Carlos Andrés 13, 22, 23,
  25, 26, 130
Pérez Jiménez, Marcos 114
Perón, Isabel 118
Perón, Juan 18, 69, 72, 99, 118,
  147, 176

personalist politics 102–6, 176,
177
Venezuela 103, 108–10
Peru 1, 4, 147, 179
economic decline 5–6
indigenous people 7
and MERCOSUR 155
military-political behaviour 15,
18, 19, 20–2, 24
plebiscitary politics 114, 115
populism 69, 71
presidential weakness 106, 107
Petrocaribe 163
PETROSUR 163
Pinochet, Augusto 18, 19, 30,
102
and plebiscitary politics 114–15,
121, 122, 176
and presidential re-election
119–20
Pion-Berlin, David 62
plebiscitary politics 2, 10–11, 102,
104, 105, 121, 122, 176
Bolivia 11, 111–12, 115–16
defining plebiscites 112–13
Ecuador 110–11, 115
recall votes 116–18
regional context of 112–16
Venezuela 11, 110
Polanyi, Karl 49
political change 176–7
political polarization 175, 178,
183
populism 10, 11, 68–101, 177,
178, 179–81
Bolivia 76–85, 86–7, 94, 98–9,
100, 101
and democracy 68, 70, 72–3, 75,
77, 94–5, 100–1
Ecuador 69, 85–91, 98, 99, 101
meaning of in Latin American
history 68–73
and South American integration
150
Venezuela 10, 69, 72, 92–8, 99,
101

presidential re-election 102,
118–21
presidential weakness 106–8
protest movements see mass
protests
public opinion
and military-political behaviour
19, 22, 25, 37–8
and protest politics 10
Putin, Vladimir 104
Putnam, Robert 46

Quebec Declaration (2001) 152,
166
Quispe Huanca, Felipe 59–60, 62,
79

racial discrimination
in Bolivia 82
in Ecuador 52
radical populism see populism
Ramanzini, Jr, H. 171
Ramírez, Rafael 131–2
recall votes 116–18
referendums 113–14, 115
recall votes 116–18
regional economic diplomacy 5,
11–12
regional integration 149–73
ALBA 150, 162–4, 165, 171,
172
coordination problems 171–2
and the Mar del Plata
Declaration (2005) 153–5
MERCOSUR 150, 151, 154,
155–9, 162, 163, 164, 171
PETROSUR 163
Summits of the Americas 151–5,
168–70
UNASUR 150, 159–62, 164,
165, 171, 172
and the USA 149, 150, 151,
161, 164, 165–70, 173
Reich, Otto 168
revolutions in Latin America 175
Riggirozzi, P. 48

Roberts, K. 84, 92
Rodríguez, Ali 131–2, 135
Rodríguez, Eduardo 38
Rodríguez, Miguel 130
Roldós, Jaime 52
Roosevelt, Franklin 118
Russia 104, 146, 166
  oil politics 134–5

Saa, Rodríguez 106
Saint Vincent 162
Salman, T. 65–6
Samper, president of Colombia 107
Sánchez Barzain, José Carlos 37
Sánchez de Lozada, Gonzalo 36,
    37, 42
  gas politics 143
  and mass protests 61, 62, 63
  and plebiscitary politics 116
  and populism 77–8, 85, 87
  and presidential weakness 107
Santiago Declaration (1998) 151,
    153
Sarney, José 155
Saudi Arabia
  and Venezuelan oil politics
    135–6
Schmitt, Carl 179
Schumpeterian democracy
  and military-political behaviour
    14–15, 40
Serrano, Jorge 106
Shifter, Michael 150
Siles Zuazo, Hernán 35, 57–8, 77,
    81
Silva, Eduardo 49
Smith, Peter 170
social mobilization
  and military intervention 17
social movements
  and indigenous people 7–8, 52–6
  and mass protests 50, 52–6,
    57–64, 65–6
  and populism 86–7
social polarization 175
socialism

democratic 122
  and economic policies 147–8
  and MERCOSUR 159
  and South American integration
    167
  twenty-first century 1–3, 42,
    122, 175, 183
socialist plebiscitarianism 102
socio-economic issues 4–8
Solares, Jaime 62
Soviet Union 1, 166
Spronk, S. 60–1
Stalin, Josef 147
Stepan, A. 104
Switzerland 113

Tanaka, M. 21
terrorism 165, 166
'third wave' democratic politics
  military intervention in 15–16,
    18, 20–2
Tibán, Lourdes 54
Tocqueville, Alexis de
  Democracy in America 45
trade unions
  Bolivia 35, 36, 57–60, 62
  and populism 75
Trinidad and Tobago Summit
    (2009) 168–9

UNASUR (Unión de Naciones
    Suramericanas) 150, 159–62,
    164, 165, 171, 172
United Nations 154
United States 2, 178
  and Bolivia 37, 82–3, 144
  direct voting 113
  and military-political behaviour
    in Latin America 19, 26, 30,
    33–4
  Monroe Doctrine 153, 165,
    168
  and NAFTA 149
  and populism in Ecuador 87
  and presidential re-election 118
  presidential removal 107

United States (cont.)
  and South American integration
    149, 150, 151, 161, 164,
    165–70, 173
  see also Miami Consensus
Uribe, Alvaro 120
Uruguay 44, 119, 177, 181
  plebiscitary politics 114, 115
  and South American integration
    154, 155, 158, 159, 163

Valle, Italo del 22–3
Vargas, Antonio 53
Vargas, Getúlio 18, 69
Vázquez, Tabaré 167
Velasco, President of Peru 24
Velásquez, Ramón J. 26
Venezuela
  AD (Acción Democratica) 109,
    130
  and Argentina 3
  Caracazo 49
  Carmona coup attempt (2002)
    17–18, 19, 27–30, 105, 117,
    168, 179
  Co-ordinadora Democratica 27
  COPEI 109
  coup attempt (1992) 13, 23–6
  coup attempt (1993) 18, 26
  economic development 6–7,
    123–4, 125, 133
  election boycotts 105
  ethnic issues 8
  FEDCÁMERAS 95
  high politics and socio-economic
    issues 5, 6–7, 8
  and Iran 166
  and MERCOSUR 157–8, 159
  military-political behaviour 13,
    17–18, 19, 22–30
  Misiones 132
  oil production/politics 6, 11, 12,
    27, 123–4, 124–7, 127–40,
    147–8, 162, 163, 182

  and OPEC 124, 127, 134–6, 138
  opposition activity 105
  PdVSA (Petróleos de Venezuela
    S.A.) 126, 127–34, 135, 138,
    140, 148, 164
  personalist politics 103, 108–9
  plebiscitary politics 110, 114
  political institutions 177
  politics of mass protest 49
  populism 10, 69, 72, 92–8, 99,
    101
  presidential weakness 106, 107
  recall votes 116–18
  regional diplomacy 11–12
  and Russia 166
  and South American integration
    150, 152, 161, 162, 163–4,
    167, 171, 172
  strikes 28, 105, 117
  'third wave' democratization
    121–2
  urban riots (1989) 22–3
  see also Chávez, Hugo

Washington Consensus 1, 169,
  174, 175
  and economic reforms 123
  and MERCOSUR 155, 157
  see also Miami Consensus
Wasmosy, Juan Carlos 156
Webber, J. R. 60–1
Whitehead, Laurence 57, 58, 61,
  74
Wiarda, Howard 167
Williamson, J. 1
Wolff, Jonas 52
World Bank 90
World Trade Organization (WTO)
  158

Yashar, Deborah 55

Zakaria, Fareed 45, 104
Zelaya, Manuel 15–16, 102, 106